International Human Rights Norms in the Nordic and Baltic Countries

International Human Rights Norms in the Nordic and Baltic Countries

edited by

Martin Scheinin

NORDIC HUMAN RIGHTS PUBLICATIONS

MARTINUS NIJHOFF PUBLISHERS

THE HAGUE / LONDON / BOSTON

A C.I.P. Catalogue record for this book is available from the Library of Congress

ISBN 90-411-0153-5 (HB)

Published by Kluwer Law International,
P.O. Box 85889, 2508 CN The Hague, The Netherlands.

Sold and distributed in the U.S.A. and Canada
by Kluwer Law International,
675 Massachusetts Avenue, Cambridge, MA 02139, U.S.A.

In all other countries, sold and distributed
by Kluwer Law International,
P.O. Box 85889, 2508 CN The Hague, The Netherlands.

Nordic Human Rights Publications is a joint-venture cooperation between the Nordic human rights centres and institutes in Norway, Sweden, Finland, Iceland and Denmark.

Printed on acid-free paper

Kluwer Law International incorporates the publishing programmes of
Graham & Trotman Ltd, Kluwer Law and Taxation Publishers,
and Martinus Nijhoff Publishers.

Printed in the Netherlands

CONTENTS

The Authors

Ole Espersen, Commissioner of the Council of the Baltic Sea States on Democratic Institutions and Human Rights, including the Rights of Persons belonging to Minorities

Ragnar Aðalsteinsson, Advocate to the Icelandic Supreme Court

Kyrre Eggen, Research Fellow at the University of Oslo, Institute for Computers and Law

Göran Melander, Director of the Raoul Wallenberg Institute of Human Rights and Humanitarian Law, University of Lund

Aap Neljas, Member of Parliament, Estonia

Birgitte Kofod Olsen, Legal Researcher at the Danish Centre for Human Rights

Martin Scheinin, Associate Professor of Constitutional Law at the University of Helsinki, Department of Public Law

Stefán M. Stefánsson, Professor of Law, University of Iceland

Vilenas Vadapalas, Chairman of the Department of International and Comparative Law of Vilnius University

Ineta Ziemele, Lecturer in International Law at the University of Latvia, Adviser to the Prime Minister

FOREWORD

by Ole Espersen,
Commissioner of the Council of the Baltic Sea States on Democratic Institutions and Human Rights, including the Rights of Persons belonging to Minorities

It gives me professional and even personal pleasure to welcome the publication of a comparative study on the implementation of international human rights norms in all the Nordic and the three Baltic countries. I have tried to follow the Nordic debate on the incorporation and implementation of human rights treaties since writing my own doctoral dissertation in a closely related theme in 1970.

In today's world we are witnessing a unique historic development. A number of our neighbouring countries are in a transitional period moving towards democratic constitutions, free and general elections and undertaking obligations within the field of human rights etc.

We are all aware of the historical background. We also understand and support the genuine desire of these countries to achieve the status of true democracies. What we cannot be sure of yet is the time and effort needed in order to achieve this goal. However, the speed has until now been quite impressive. Furthermore, the close cooperation with neighbouring countries - official authorities, NGOs and international organisations has been impressive. I dare say that never before have nations or international organisations to such a degree shown an interest in and a willingness to assist with human and financial resources to the benefit of the process which we all so fervently wish success.

Simultaneously, with this transitional period in the new or restored democracies including the Baltic States, another important transition is taking place in the Nordic countries: incorporation of international human rights norms in order to achieve a more direct application. In several Nordic countries, human rights conventions have been incorporated and are now applicable in our courts as domestic norms. Maybe partly due to this recent development in the neighbouring countries some of the new or restored democracies find themselves in a situation where the status of international law is somewhat unclear - as indicated by this book.

The present book illustrates extremely well both kinds of transition and their interconnections. I agree with the editor that in a few years probably all Nordic and Baltic states will have formally integrated at least some human rights conventions as part of their domestic law.

The main purpose of this book is not to deal with the substance of human rights in the various countries. It deals with the way in which those human rights, which the country in question has decided to adhere to, should be implemented by courts and other national institutions. In this respect, it reveals problems and suggests solutions. At the same time, it demonstrates the complexity in moving towards an open and free democracy which respects fundamental human rights. In doing so, it bears witness to an unprecedented historical development while at the same time serving as a tool for those who are responsible for furthering this development, be they politicians, legal experts, advisors or interested human beings in general.

It is my hope that within the next couple of years, a second volume will be written: a book on the substance of basic human rights in our countries. This would analyse the outcome of the transition. But I advise the publishers to wait a year or two before finalizing this next volume. Many rights or standards are emerging in our countries right now, and they should be included to depict a region which will, I am sure, consist of citizens enjoying rights which every human being should be accorded in the future.

Copenhagen, August 1995

Ole Espersen

1. General Introduction

by Martin Scheinin,
University of Helsinki

1. A JOINT NORDIC AND BALTIC EXERCISE

The domestic status of international human rights norms within various jurisdictions and constitutional settings is an old but continuous discourse. Comparative studies, such as the already classic book by Andrew Drzemczewski[1] or Søren Stenderup Jensen's relatively recent dissertation[2] on the situation in the three Scandinavian countries dwell deep into the subject. A third study belonging to the same group of high-quality comparative works is the two-part article by Jörg Polakiewicz and Valérie Jacob-Foltzer[3]. All three have certain common characteristics that may be mentioned here, because they provide at least part of the explanation for why this book has been considered necessary. First, the above-mentioned studies all relate only to the group of states that, at the time of research, were parties to the European Convention on Human Rights. And secondly, the studies deal with the domestic status of one specific human rights treaty, namely the European Convention on Human Rights.

In both respects this book is different. We are making a comparative study within a certain geographical region, namely all five Nordic countries and the three Baltic countries. All the Nordic countries are parties to the European Convention on Human Rights, though Finland only acceded in 1990. The situation in the Baltic

[1] A. Drzemczewski, *European Human Rights Convention in Domestic Law*, 1983.

[2] S.S. Jensen, *The European Convention on Human Rights in Scandinavian Law*, 1992.

[3] J. Polakiewicz and V. Jacob-Foltzer, "The European Human Rights Convention in Domestic Law", *Human Rights Law Journal*, vol. 12 (1991) pp. 65-84 and 125-142.

M. Scheinin (ed.), International Human Rights Norms in the Nordic and Baltic Countries, 11–26.

countries is different as Lithuania has just ratified the Convention and Estonia and Latvia have so far only signed it. This situation has been one of the many reasons why our comparison does not relate solely to the European Convention but tries to cover the full normative framework of international human rights. Issues like the domestic status of economic, social and cultural rights, of the two United Nations Covenants of 1966, and of international human rights instruments other than treaties are discussed throughout the book.

An additional reason behind the production of a new book in this field is the fact that in the 1990s we are witnessing an amazingly fast process of change in the domestic status of international human rights norms, not only in the Baltic countries but also in the Nordic countries. Just within a couple of years, all the Nordic countries have taken or will take the step of making the European Convention part of their domestic law through incorporation. In addition, Finland has traditionally extended, and most likely Norway will extend incorporation to other human rights treaties as well.

Because of the three above-mentioned factors, it was felt in the preparations for the 10th Nordic Symposium on Human Rights that the discussion needed fresh inputs and new angles. One day of the Symposium, held in November 1994 in Copenhagen was allocated to Nordic and Baltic experiences in the field of the domestic status of international human rights treaties. On the basis of country reports prepared for the Symposium and the one-day discussions in Copenhagen the authors have continued their cooperation in order to produce a comprehensive and up-to-date comparative study on the domestic status of international human rights norms in all the Nordic and Baltic countries.

2. DOMESTIC STATUS OF INTERNATIONAL HUMAN RIGHTS NORMS

2.1 Dualism and Monism Revisited. There are various methods through which states implement international treaties into their domestic law. Traditionally, these methods have been classified by using a rough dichotomy to "dualistic" and "monistic" countries. In the former, domestic law and international law are understood as two separate legal systems. In the latter group of countries, international law and domestic law together form a unified legal system, often characterised by the primacy of international norms.

Nowadays, the classifications dualism and monism are largely outdated. The wide use of "compromise" implementation methods like incorporation, the processes towards constitutional regulation of the legal effect of international norms, the possibility for the judiciary to apply open sources of law doctrines that allow wide use of international norms even without their formal status as norms of domestic law, and the growing heterogeneity of "international norms" all contribute towards the traditional distinction between "dualism" and "monism" having less and less relevance in assessing the concrete operation of various international norms in the constitutional and legal framework of a given country.

2.2 Various Methods of Treaty Implementation. There is no generally accepted classification for the rich variety of existing domestic methods for the implementation of international treaties. The starting-point given to the authors of this book, is the following classification in five different methods.[4]

Adoption: International treaties are part of domestic law as a consequence of international ratification and (usually) domestic publication only; no separate legislative measure is needed.

Incorporation: In order to implement an international treaty, a separate domestic enactment is approved, for the purpose of giving all or part of the treaty provisions domestic legal validity, without repeating the material contents of the provisions in the text of the enactment.

Transformation: The treaty provisions themselves do not receive formal status within domestic law (through adoption or incorporation), but relevant domestic laws are amended for the purpose of bringing their substance into harmony with the treaty provisions in question.

Passive transformation: A special case of transformation is the situation when no amendments to existing domestic laws are needed in order to achieve harmony with the treaty provisions.

---

[4] The definitions were given in the questionnaire sent to the authors prior to the 10th Nordic Symposium on Human Rights, held in Copenhagen in November 1994. The questionnaire was drawn up by professor Allan Rosas and the editor.

Reference: A domestic enactment includes a clause on the applicability or even priority of international treaties (or a specific treaty) in matters covered by the law in question; this method is also called as "sector-monism".

The reader will note that none of the eight countries covered in the book uses only one of these methods. Transformation, incorporation and reference, for example, can be applied side by side, and the degree of dualism or monism is determined by which of the methods is used most frequently. Even the ultimate dividing line between pure monism (adoption) and various shades of dualism is flexible, since what actually becomes decisive is the juridical-technical form of the decision through which Parliament gives its consent to the international ratification of a treaty. In Finland Parliament makes, in one and the same session, *two* decisions by which it (a) gives its consent to ratification and (b) enacts a domestic Act of Parliament through which the provisions of the treaty are given the force of domestic law. Such a formal procedure can easily be described as corresponding to the dualistic theory. In Estonia and in Lithuania, Parliament makes, in a similar situation, only *one* decision, and the observer will have to decide on the "monistic" or "dualistic" nature of the legal system by finding out whether this decision takes the form of enacting a domestic Act of Parliament or of giving Parliamentary approval to international ratification in some other technical form.

Compared to the traditional *theoretical* adherence to dualism by the Nordic countries, the Baltic countries are somewhat more "monistic". In the Lithuanian Constitution there is a strong emphasis on the monistic elements, albeit this approach is partly compromised by an understanding according to which the only treaties to automatically become part of applicable domestic law are those ratified by Parliament. In Estonia, we find a monistic approach to general principles of international law but a "dualistic" understanding of treaties requiring incorporation before their domestic applicability. The classification of Latvia as a dualistic or monistic country remains unresolved.

Moreover, the relevance of a distinction between dualism and monism is questioned by the fact that the judiciary is, in most countries, equipped with such tools for legal reasoning that enable it to take into account international norms, human rights norms in particular. This is true even for countries of traditional dualism where international treaties, formally speaking, do not have the status of domestic legal norms. For a considerable time, the judicial practice of the Supreme Court of Norway was clearly more open to the application of international human rights treaties than the case law of the Finnish courts, despite the fact that Norway adheres to "traditional dualism" (transformation as the prevailing method for implementing international treaties), whereas in Finland one could, at least on the abstract level, speak of *de facto* monism due to the fact that the incorporation of international treaties had become a standard practice.

One additional conceptual comment must be made on the term incorporation. Above, the word was used as a technical term, referring to one specific method for the domestic implementation of international treaties. It must be kept in mind, however, that in the international discussion the term is often used also in a more general sense, as referring to all technical solutions through which international treaty provisions become applicable as domestic legal norms. In this wider sense, the term incorporation covers the technical implementation methods of adoption and incorporation. The reader of our book is instructed to keep these problems of terminology and classification in mind when going through the various country studies. The terminological starting-point for our authors is the same, but due to differences in the constitutional settings and legal traditions of each country, variation of nuances still occurs.

3. GOING BEYOND TRADITIONAL ISSUES OF STATUS

Professor Benedetto Conforti expresses the view of many contemporary scholars of international and constitutional law when he writes:

> "I find little interest in the traditional approach to the question, based on the age-old dispute between monists and dualists, between those for 'adoption' and those for 'incorporation' or 'transformation' of international law into municipal law. Instead, I shall address from a practical rather than theoretical perspective the question of how to achieve the critical objective of consideration of international law as law within the State, complete with all legal safeguards including those related to adjudication."[5]

---

[5] B. Conforti, *International Law and the Role of Domestic Legal Systems*, 1993 p. 13-14.

As it seems that *all* Nordic and *all* Baltic states will in the very near future have made at least some human rights treaties formally part of domestic law, the old discussion on whether "to incorporate or not to incorporate", is largely outdated. This does not mean, however, that the need to analyse elements of and obstacles to the effective domestic implementation of international human rights norms would have lost its significance. On the contrary, attention is shifting to problems that are more concrete than the traditional discussion of formal issues of status.

3.1 The Role of Domestic Courts as the Key. According to Conforti[6], the application of international law by municipal courts and other domestic legal operators is simply the "keystone" of international law itself. Similarly to Pieter van Dijk, he emphasises the role and attitudes[7] of the judiciary in determining the domestic effect of international law. To Conforti, more important than the characterisation of a legal system as "dualistic" or "monistic" is whether the judges are "liberal" or "conservative".[8]

The country studies in this book provide evidence that the domestic role and effect of international human rights norms cannot be assessed abstractly, on the basis of a study of the written Constitution of a given country. What eventually counts is whether the courts apply human rights norms in their concrete decisions. In this respect, the situation today is that case law on international human rights treaties in all five Nordic countries is considerably rich and growing rapidly, whereas in the Baltic countries, the Lithuanian Constitutional Court seems to be the only judicial authority that has so far managed to develop some jurisprudence in the field. Some of the Nordic countries, e.g. Sweden and Finland, provide strong support for the contention that when the first steps have been taken by domestic courts to build a human rights jurisprudence, the growth of case law may be amazingly rapid.

Some of the many court cases reported in this book show how the role of international human rights norms may in a concrete case be

---

[6] *Op.cit.*, p. 9.

[7] P. van Dijk, "Domestic Status of Human Rights Treaties and the Attitude of the Judiciary", in M. Nowak - D. Steurer - H.Tretter (eds.), *Progress in the Spirit of Human Rights*, 1988 pp. 631-649.

[8] Conforti, *op.cit.*, p. 26.

very strong even in countries where the "dualistic" nature of the constitutional setting seems, *prima facie*, to form barriers to the effective implementation of international law. Even prior to formal incorporation, the Norwegian and Icelandic Supreme Courts have shown their capability and willingness to allow human rights treaty provisions factual priority in relation to domestic law.[9] In relation to the principle of legality, such far-reaching interpretations become legitimate because of the incontested *axiological* weight of human rights and through the courts' careful and juridically correct reasoning.

The existence of the system of individual complaints and an international court have greatly contributed to the success of the European Convention on Human Rights. When domestic judges in the contracting states have seen that the European Commission and Court of Human Rights function and that the Court ultimately hands down judicial rulings, they have gradually become convinced of the fact that human rights law is really *law*, by all international and domestic standards. A somewhat worrying side-effect of the success of the European Convention is the fact that many domestic judges nowadays feel tempted to adapt themselves to a position of *unindependent or passive interpretation* of the Convention. For them, it is sufficient to analyse existing case law by the European Court of Human Rights. If no precedent can be found, those following a "minimalist" approach see no need to apply the Convention. Our Chapter on Denmark deserves attention on this point, since the Danish Supreme Court seems to restrict itself to quite an unindependent application of the European Convention. Similar trends may be identified in certain pronouncements by Norwegian and Swedish courts, and also the case 1995:7 by the Finnish Supreme Court might indicate a move towards a more passive position. In the last-mentioned case, a defendant was denied free legal assistance as the majority of the Supreme Court, after having analysed existing case law of the European Court of Human Rights, came to the conclusion that free legal assistance was not guaranteed by Article 6 of the ECHR under the circumstances of the present case.

---

[9] See, below, the discussion on the Norwegian cases Rt. 1984 p. 1174 and 1994 p. 610, and on the Islandic Supreme Court ruling 1992.174.

The alternative to an unindependent interpretation is a more "activist" or more "liberal" orientation by domestic judges, according to which the national judge must also *develop* international human rights law by giving new answers to new questions. For such a creative approach it is clearly an advantage that international human rights law is *pluralist* in character: there is not only one human rights convention but a complex network of treaties drawn up within different international organisations and covering many situations that would fall outside the protection of any single convention taken alone.

3.2 The Relevance of Various Drawback Doctrines. The "minimalist" approach of domestic judges is not the only barrier for the effective realisation of international human rights norms through the operation of domestic courts. From the context of the constitutional law of the United States, we are familiar with certain "drawback doctrines" that have the effect of barring access to the courts or the applicability of international norms in certain cases. In the Nordic and Baltic countries, the act of state doctrine or the political question doctrine[10] do not appear to find support.

Two other theoretical constructions are, however, of relevance in the context of the Nordic and Baltic countries and they seem to constitute at least potential threats to the effective implementation of human rights, namely the rule of *lex posterior derogat legi priori* and the doctrine of self-executing treaties.

Although Norway is expected to be a partial exception, so far the incorporation of the European Convention on Human Rights has, in the basically dualistic Nordic countries, taken place through an ordinary Act of Parliament. Albeit some constitutional provisions exist which modify the picture in some of these countries, the starting point for courts and authorities is that international treaties incorporated through an Act of Parliament have the *same* hierarchical status as (other) ordinary laws. Also in Lithuania, the hierarchical status of

---

[10] On these two doctrines, see R. Lillich, "The Role of domestic Courts in Promoting International Human Rights Norms "*New York Law Review*, vol. 24 (1978) pp. 153-177, J.E. Smith, *The Constitution and American Foreign Policy*, 1989 p. 3, 75 and 134-137, and Conforti, *op.cit.*, p. 14-24. In short, the act of state doctrine denies access to court in issues that relate to the foreign policy of *the country in question*, because it is not the judiciary's task to decide on foreign policy. The political question doctrine, in turn, limits the power of courts to deal with cases that relate to measures undertaken by *another* sovereign state.

international treaties is, at least *prima facie* the same as that of ordinary Acts of Parliament. Therefore, new pieces of legislation form a potential threat to the applicability of human rights treaties. According to the *last in time* or *lex posterior* rule new Acts of Parliament would seem to supersede the provisions in such treaties.

As explained by our authors, this does not have to be the case even in countries where there is no explicit constitutional clause on the supremacy of international law. The *lex posterior* rule can be interpreted to include as a precondition the intention by the domestic legislator to supersede an earlier treaty-based norm before judicial authorities are allowed to apply the rule to the detriment of the country's international commitments. A domestic Act of Parliament drawn up at a later point is to be given priority in relation to an incorporated human rights treaty only if Parliament stated, when enacting the law in question, that it had the intention of deviating from the treaty. Through such a construction the constitutional setting based on the sovereignty of Parliament can be maintained simultaneously as it is made highly improbable that courts would ever set aside a human rights treaty because of the *lex posterior* rule.[11]

In our chapters on Estonia and Norway, it is presented as at least a potential precondition for the direct applicability of human rights treaties that the treaty provision is sufficiently clear and unambiguous. In the Norwegian Supreme Court case Rt. 1994 p. 610, this requirement was presented by the Court, not as a condition for applicability in general but for setting aside Norwegian rules. This line of argumentation may be understood as referring to the doctrine of self-executing treaties.[12] In its extreme forms, this doctrine can seriously weaken the domestic role of international human rights norms, since it simplifies the rich variety of legal issues to be met when applying international law to one all-or-nothing question: does the international provision have *full* direct applicability or is it simply *irrelevant* for the judge? The understanding of legal norms being applicable in several ways and degrees, including their effect on the interpretation of other

[11] A similar position is presented by B. Conforti, *op.cit.*, p. 47.

[12] For the doctrine of self-executing treaties, see Y. Iwasawa, "The Doctrine of Self-Executing Treaties in the United States: A Critical Analysis", *Virginia Journal of International Law*, vol. 26 (1986) pp. 627-692 and Th. Buergenthal, "Self-Executing and Non-Self-Executing Treaties in National and International Law", *Requeil des Cours*, vol. 235 (1992-IV) pp. 303-400.

norms, makes relative the notion of direct applicability and shows that a categorical distinction between "self-executing" and "non-self-executing" treaty provisions is impossible.[13] On the basis of existing case law, it seems that extreme versions of the doctrine are not likely to find support in the Nordic (or Baltic) countries. It is another matter that the formulation of a treaty provision might affect the *way* in which it is applied.

3.3 Broadening the Scope of Applicable Rights: Social Rights, "Soft Law" etc. Extreme versions of the doctrine of self-executing treaties tend to limit the domestic applicability of international human rights to a traditional core of rights which bear a long conceptual and judicial tradition in domestic jurisdictions. For many, "freedom of expression" would be clear and precise legal language whereas "the right to social assistance" would be somewhat less self-evident.

The Nordic and Baltic countries are no exceptions to the general rule that traditional civil and political rights tend to be applied more often by courts and other authorities than economic, social and cultural rights. Still, this book provides evidence that there are neither logical nor legal obstacles that would stop economic, social and cultural rights from becoming applicable on a domestic level.

On the basis of the country studies included in this book, one may go one step further and state that even so-called "soft law" is of legal relevance. In Norway international human rights treaties have so far had no *formal* status in the domestic legal system. However, they have had considerable influence on the application of domestic laws. From Finland and some other countries, we find decisions by the Ombudsman and other authorities, occasionally even by courts, where, e.g. the human rights principles of certain documents of the Organisation for Security and Cooperation in Europe have been cited as affecting the outcome of *legal* reasoning. Such situations may be conceptualised by speaking of non-legal human rights instruments as *standards* or *yardsticks* that, formally speaking, are outside the realm of "law" but which still have an influence on the argumentation,

---

[13] For further elaboration of the argument, see M.Scheinin, "Direct Applicability of Economic, Social and Cultural Rights: A Critique of the Doctrine of Self-Executing Treaties", in Krz. Drzewicki - C. Krause - A. Rosas (eds.), *Social Rights as Human Rights: a European Challenge*, 1994.

interpretation and decision-making inside that sphere. It is interesting to note that right from the beginning the Lithuanian Constitutional Court has also shown its willingness to use in its reasoning international sources other than treaties.

3.4 Constitutional Protection of International Human Rights. The relatively recent Estonian and Lithuanian Constitutions and the separate Latvian Constitutional Law on Fundamental Rights all represent *transformation on the constitutional level* in relation to existing international human rights treaties. The same applies to the new (1995) Finnish and Icelandic Constitutional Chapters on Fundamental Rights, and also to the somewhat older Chapter Two of the Swedish Constitution Act. Such a line of development contributes to the harmonisation of the international and constitutional protection of fundamental rights. One dimension of such harmonisation is the growing role of international human rights norms in the interpretation of domestic constitutional provisions.

In addition, constitution-makers attach growing attention to the need to secure the observance of international human rights through special clauses in the domestic Constitution. Such clauses have recently been written into the Swedish (Chapter 2, Section 23), Norwegian (Section 110 C) and Finnish (Section 16a) Constitution. In Estonia (Articles 3 and 123) and in Lithuania (Article 138), the constitutional guarantees for international human rights are achieved through general clauses on domestic applicability and even supremacy of international treaties. Latvia, in turn, has affirmed its commitment to international human rights instruments through a separate Declaration.

3.5 The Principle of Legality. The rule of law, or the principle of legality, has many facets. Many of these are of immediate relevance in the context of the domestic application of international human rights. In the chapter on Denmark the so-called *rule of instruction* is presented, indicating that where domestic law leaves or seems to leave discretion to administrative authorities, international norms must be understood as limiting and guiding such discretion.

A traditional element in the legality principle, maybe particularly strong in Norway, is that obligations or other burdens may be put on the individual through a decision by Parliament only. Hence, a domestic Act of Parliament is always required when duties of private parties are established. A consequence of this element of the principle of legality is that there is a certain *asymmetry* in the law. Individuals are allowed to invoke a wider set of sources of law in relation to public authorities than the State is allowed to rely on against private parties.

As the origin of human rights lies in the protection of the individual against infringements by public authorities, the protection of human rights and the principle of legality very much support each other. Still, the principle of legality affects and even limits the applicability of human rights norms. Primarily, such considerations become relevant in relation to *Drittwirkung*, or the horizontal effect of human rights norms. Because the principle of legality requires that an Act of Parliament is enacted for the purpose of attaching legal consequences between private parties to a human rights provision, Drittwirkung in human rights law mostly takes the form of an *indirect* horizontal effect.

Against this background, it is quite obvious that a certain *contextuality* is needed when applying human rights norms. One and the same treaty provision might be directly applicable for the benefit of an individual against the State but will require support of other domestic provisions before being capable of solving a dispute between two private parties.

In some issues, like racial discrimination or torture, existing human rights treaties explicitly require their states parties to penalise certain acts. But within a much broader area the duty of states to respect and ensure human rights entails the need to enact legislation forbidding the violation of human rights by private parties. Hence, the domestic implementation of international human rights norms is never a matter for the judiciary only. The legislature, the administration and all branches of government contribute to this implementation.

4. SUBSTANTIAL HUMAN RIGHTS ISSUES IN THE NORDIC AND BALTIC COUNTRIES

The general framework of this book might seem formalistic to some readers. The core issue in the eight different country studies is the *status* or *role* of international human rights norms in the legal systems of the respective countries. Our book is, certainly, not an account of the substantial *human rights record* of the eight countries. The intention is more limited, but equally challenging. We are trying to provide reliable and precise information of the way in which international human rights norms operate in the legal context of the eight countries. Such an analysis can only be made through a combination of international human rights law and a good insight in the constitutional law of each country. The approach provides the necessary analytical framework for future evaluation and comparison of the actual human rights situation in the Nordic and the Baltic countries.

By comparative standards, the Nordic countries are known for their conscientious ratification practice of international human rights treaties. After reinstituting their independence, the Baltic Republics have taken rapid steps to follow the same path.[14] Maybe the most notable exception is formed by the Convention and the Protocol on the Status of Refugees, both ratified by more than 120 states but none of the Baltic states.

Among substantial human rights issues of concern in the Baltic states to, e.g., international non-governmental organisations are capital punishment, prison conditions and the rights of non-citizens. At least the last-mentioned problem area also relates, although in a different form, to the Nordic countries. The rights and treatment of refugees, asylum-seekers and immigrants is a source for constant criticism and action by domestic and international NGOs.

Another common area of concern can be identified in relation to the protection of social and economic rights, as asserted in international and regional human rights treaties. In all three Baltic countries, social and economic rights have a firm place in the domestic constitutional documents enacted after the reinstitution of independence. Still, it seems that the practical realisation of these constitutional promises has been compromised because of the rapid adaptation to market economy.

The Nordic countries, in turn, have a reputation of being able to *combine* an elaborated system for the protection of individual rights and a far-reaching social welfare policy within the so-called *Nordic model*. In our times of economic instability and European integration such a model seems less self-evident than in the past decades. There is

---

[14] To make just one comparison, based on uniform criteria, the United Nations publication *Chart of Ratifications as at 31 December 1994* gives the followind data on the ratification of 25 universal human rights treaties: Denmark 20, Estonia 11, Finland 20, Iceland 14, Norway 21, Latvia 16, Lithuania 5, and Sweden 20.

an ongoing discussion in at least some of the Nordic countries about which of the social and economic rights are to be secured in the form of genuine individual ("subjective") rights and which must be left to the discretion of the legislators as for concrete realisation. The current Icelandic and Finnish constitutional reforms to include social and economic rights in the catalogue of constitutionally secured fundamental rights represent attempts to solve the issue on the constitutional level.

5. THIS BOOK IS INTERACTIVE

In recent years, communication technology has taken great leaps. The Internet and its new user-friendly applications enable the use of world-wide electronic networks to many persons that are not specialists in computer technology. These developments are certainly a *challenge* to the traditional format of a printed book. Still, it is highly unlikely that the World Wide Web (WWW) or the tools designed for its use could actually *replace* the printed book.

This book represents one effort to take the challenge. The book is *interactive* through the Internet. Readers will be able to receive *updated information* on the separate chapters of our book and to give their *comments* through electronic mail. We will also try to provide links to *related* material available on the Internet, for instance the latest available texts of the Constitutions of the Nordic and Baltic countries. These links are based on *hypertext* which means that the reader can access new materials simply by pointing the appropriate reference to it when using a "browser" program inside the WWW.

In order to make use of these possibilities, the reader is advised to contact the following WWW site (through Netscape, Mosaic or similar browsers):

http://www.abo.fi/instut/imr/

This is the so-called *home page* of the Åbo Akademi University Institute for Human Rights (Finland). On this home page, you will find a link to a *sales publication list*, and in this list, to the book in your hands. By selecting this title, you will first be given some general information on the book and then two options: *updated information and links to related material,* and *comments*. By pointing at these titles you will be able to proceed.

Examples of updated information that will be made accessible through the above-mentioned Internet address are the official English translations of the Finnish and Icelandic new Constitutional Chapters on Fundamental Rights, the Norwegian Bill and, in due time, the Act of Parliament on the incorporation of human rights treaties, forthcoming constitutional amendments in the Baltic Republics, etc. The authors and the editor have done their best to provide as much up-to-date information as possible in the format of a book. The manuscripts of the various chapters were finalised between April and July 1995. Developments in August 1995 and onwards will be reported through the Internet for our readers.

In addition to using the *comments* option indicated above, you are always welcome to send your comments on this book to the editor via more conventional methods. The mailing address is:

Martin Scheinin
Department of Public Law
P.O.Box 4
FIN-00014 University of Helsinki
(or e-mail martin.scheinin@helsinki.fi)

6. ACKNOWLEDGEMENTS

Many people have contributed to the production of this book. Of them the gratitude of the authors and the editor is particularly great in relation to four persons. Professor *Allan Rosas* of the Åbo Akademi University Institute for Human Rights helped the editor in drawing up the questionnaire that was sent to the authors and served as the starting-point for the common exercise. Ms *Lone Tjustrup*, Ms *Helle Borgstrøm* and Ms *Marianne Garre* of the Danish Centre for Human Rights greatly contributed to the project, respectively, in the organising of the Copenhagen Symposium, in the tedious technical editing of the material to camera-ready printouts and in checking the English of our heterogeneous group of authors.

The publication of our book gives an opportunity to thank also all the institutions that through their financial support made the

Copenhagen Symposium possible. They include the Norwegian Ministry of Foreign Affairs; the Letterstedtska Foundation, Sweden; the Lannung Foundation, Denmark; the Icelandic Embassy in Denmark; Amnesty International, Denmark; and the Democracy Foundation, Denmark.

REFERENCES

Buergenthal, Thomas, "Self-Executing and Non-Self-Executing Treaties in National and International Law", *Requeil des Cours*, vol. 235 (1992-IV) pp. 303-400.

Chart of Ratifications as at 31 December 1994: Human Rights, International Instruments. New York and Geneva 1995: United Nations.

Conforti, Benedetto, *International Law and the Role of Domestic Legal Systems*. Dordrecht - Boston - London 1993: Martinus Nijhoff.

van Dijk, Pieter, "Domestic Status of Human Rights Treaties and the Attitude of the Judiciary", in Manfred Nowak - Dorothea Steurer - Hannes Tretter (eds.), *Progress in the Spirit of Human Rights; Festschrift Felix Ermacora*. Kehl am Rhein 1988: N. P. Engel.

Drzemczewski, Andrew Z., *European Human Rights Convention in Domestic Law; A Comparative Study*. Oxford 1983: Oxford University Press.

Iwasawa, Yuji, "The Doctrine of Self-Executing Treaties in the United States: A Critical Analysis", *Virginia Journal of International Law*, vol. 26 (1986) pp. 627-692.

Jensen, Søren Stenderup, *The European Convention on Human Rights in Scandinavian Law; A Case Law Study*. Gylling 1992: Jurist- og Økonomforbundets Forlag.

Lillich, Richard, "The Role of domestic Courts in Promoting International Human Rights Norms", *New York Law Review*, vol. 24 (1978) pp. 153-177.

Polakiewicz, Jörg and Valérie Jacob-Foltzer, "The European Human Rights Convention in Domestic Law", *Human Rights Law Journal*, vol. 12 (1991) pp. 65-84 and 125-142.

Scheinin, Martin, "Direct Applicability of Economic, Social and Cultural Rights: A Critique of the Doctrine of Self-Executing Treaties", in Krzysztof Drzewicki - Catarina Krause - Allan Rosas (eds.), *Social Rights as Human Rights: a European Challenge*. Turku/Åbo 1994: Åbo Akademi University Institute for Human Rights.

Smith, Jean Edward (- Sharryn Aiken - Katherine Koerner), *The Constitution and American Foreign Policy*. St. Paul, Minnesota 1989.

2. INCORPORATION AND IMPLEMENTATION OF HUMAN RIGHTS IN ESTONIA

by Aap Neljas
M.P., Estonia

1. INTRODUCTION

The independence of the Republic of Estonia was restored on 20 August 1991 and 16 September 1991. Estonia ratified basic United Nations human rights instruments. On 28 June 1992, the Estonian people adopted a new Constitution by referendum, thus replacing the Constitution of 1938.

The Constitution of 1992 guarantees basic human rights to all inhabitants in Estonia. "The Human Rights Bill" (Chapter II - Fundamental Rights, Liberties and Freedoms) in the Constitution is modelled on the UN Covenant on Civil and Political Rights and the UN Covenant on Economic, Social and Cultural Rights, as well as on the European Convention on Human Rights. The text of the 1992 Constitution is annexed and marked *Annex 1*.

The Constitution establishes human rights and liberties for everybody, political rights for all citizens and obliges the courts to uphold the rights and freedoms guaranteed in the Constitution. On the basis of the 1992 Constitution, Estonia founded a democratic political system and has succeeded in guaranteeing basic human rights for everyone. This has also been recognised by international organisations such as the United Nations, the Organisation for Security and Cooperation in Europe (the former CSCE) and the Council of Europe.

After 1990, Estonia has started to replace old Soviet legislation with its own national legislation based on democratic principles and modelled on international standards. The process has been successful - for example with regard to constitutional legislation establishing a democratic political system in Estonia and in the detailed constitutional

M. Scheinin (ed.), International Human Rights Norms in the Nordic and Baltic Countries, 27–72.

provisions on human rights. Acts on elections both at local and national levels, on local self-government, on political parties, on non-profit associations and on cultural autonomy for national minorities have been implemented just to give a few examples.

Unfortunately, due to the overload of work for the *Riigikogu* (The Estonian Parliament) some old Soviet acts are still in force in Estonia although they are constantly modified. The Criminal Code, for example, is a modified version of the old Soviet Criminal Code. Therefore, some years will pass before we are able to say that all basic Estonian acts correspond to modern European standards.

Estonia has signed the European Convention for the Protection of Human Rights and Fundamental Freedoms (on 14 May 1993). However, the Convention has not yet been ratified by the Riigikogu. Ratification will probably take place during 1995, although much work has to be done with regard to harmonising Estonian legislation to Convention standards and to deciding which, if any, reservations Estonia should make.

A lot of practical problems also hinder Estonia's progress in the human rights field - notably, the improvement of the conditions in Estonian prisons will depend on the financial resources which the state will be able to allocate for this purpose. Likewise, training and education of judges, lawyers and law enforcement officials will take some years.

2. STATUS OF HUMAN RIGHTS TREATIES

The Constitution of 1992 includes three basic articles that deal with international law and foreign treaties - namely Articles 3, 121 and 123. These provisions regulate the position of international law norms in the Estonian legal system and the way they are implemented:

> Art. 3. (...)Universally recognized principles and norms of international law shall be an inseparable part of the Estonian legal system.
> (...)
> Art. 121. The Riigikogu shall ratify and denounce treaties of the Republic of Estonia:
> (...)
> 2) the implementation of which requires the adoption, amendment or annulment of Estonian laws;
> (...)
> 5) where ratification is prescribed.

> Art. 123. The Republic of Estonia shall not conclude foreign treaties which which are in conflict with the Constitution.
> If Estonian laws or other acts are in conflict with foreign treaties ratified by the Riigikogu, the articles of the foreign treaty shall be applied.

As there have been no court cases yet in Estonia involving international human rights instruments, one can only make theoretical conclusions based on the Constitution and the 1993 Act on Foreign Relations.

On the basis of the Constitution and the Act on Foreign Relations, one could make the following conclusions about the validity and applicability of international human rights instruments in Estonia:

- On the one hand, all Estonian legislation shall be based on "universally recognised principles and norms of international law" (Art. 3 of the Constitution) and, consequently, the Government and the courts should interpret Estonian laws in a "human-rights-friendly" way;

- On the other hand, it is clear that in order to give foreign treaty provisions binding force within the Estonian legal system and to make their implementation possible, the foreign treaty in question has to be ratified by the Riigikogu (Art. 121 of the Constitution), or the consent of the Republic should be expressed by a separate legal measure: The Act on Foreign Relations (Art. 22) states, that "The Republic of Estonia's acceptance of the binding nature of an international agreement shall be considered to be expressed by the signature, exchange, ratification, acceptance, confirmation, accession to, and other procedures as set forth in the agreement in question".

The question whether Estonia adheres to a monistic or a dualistic approach to international law, is difficult to answer. Presently, some constitutional provisions suggest monism and others suggest dualism.

On the basis of Article 3 of the Constitution, one could say that customary international law ("universally recognised principles") becomes part of the Estonian legal system through adoption. This includes unwritten international law and probably also the Universal Declaration of Human Rights. However, it does not include international human rights treaties, irrespective of how many states have ratified them - if Estonia is not a ratifying state.

Consequently, the norms of international law (human rights treaty provisions) should be accepted by the state in order to become part of the Estonian legal system. In order to implement an international human rights treaty in Estonia, a separate domestic act must be approved with the purpose of giving all or some of the treaty provisions domestic legal validity without necessarily repeating the material contents of the treaty provisions in a domestic act.

This is done in connection with the ratification by the Riigikogu. The Riigikogu adopts a separate act, usually after two readings. In this way the norms of the international treaty in question will become part of the Estonian legal system through the method of incorporation. So far the Riigikogu has made no reservations to any human rights treaties that have been ratified by Estonia. Most human rights treaties ratified by Estonia were ratified by the Supreme Soviet in 1991, i.e., before the present Constitution was adopted.

The Act on Foreign Relations only contains a general statement about what will happen after the ratification of a treaty. The Act (Art. 26) states that "Fulfilment of the foreign agreement shall be ensured by the Government of the Republic," a definition which leaves room for court interpretation as to whether transformation of Estonian acts is necessary.

Because of the above-mentioned problem, there has also been discussion about the methods of domestic implementation of international treaties — the question is whether incorporation as a by-product of parliamentary ratification is sufficient to secure domestic validity of treaty provisions or whether it is necessary to actually transform them into Estonian laws. At present, there is consensus about incorporating international treaties *and* ideally transforming them into domestic acts in the future — but this is not a necessary condition for their validity.

The hierarchical status of ratified international treaties in the Estonian legal system is strictly regulated by the Constitution. Foreign treaties have an intermediate position between the Constitution and ordinary Acts of Parliament. The Constitution is considered a superior source of law because it was adopted by a direct act of *volonté générale*: a referendum (Articles 1, 105, 123 and 162 of the Constitution). This conclusion is based on the first sentence of Article 123: "The Republic of Estonia shall not conclude foreign treaties which are in conflict with the Constitution". According to this article, the Constitution clearly prevails in possible conflicts between its norms and an international treaty — a conflict unlikely to occur as the Constitution itself is modelled on human rights instruments. In the case of a conflict between an Act of Parliament (or a lower domestic enactment) and a ratified international treaty "the articles of the foreign treaty shall be applied" (Art. 123).

The procedure for solving such conflicts is established in the Act on Constitutional Review Court Procedure (*Annex 2*), Article 6 on "Who Has the Right to Directly Petition the National Court for Constitutional Review":

> "(1) The following shall have the right to directly petition the National Court for the court to determine whether a law, other legal act or foreign treaty is in accordance with the Constitution or the law:
> 1) the President of the Republic, in the cases stipulated in Article 107 of the Constitution;
> 2) the Legal Chancellor, in the cases stipulated in Article 142 of the Constitution and to determine whether a foreign treaty is in accordance with the Constitution;
> 3) any court, in the cases stipulated in Article 5 para. 2 of this Law."

3. DIRECT APPLICABILITY OF HUMAN RIGHTS TREATIES AND OTHER SOURCES OF INTERNATIONAL LAW BY ESTONIAN COURTS AND ADMINISTRATIVE AUTHORITIES

Estonian courts have not so far applied human rights treaties directly. There have, however, been constitutional disputes between the President and the Riigikogu, where the President has used the inconsistency with international human rights standards as a reason for rejecting an original bill and after that, the Riigikogu has amended the bill. Article 107 of the Constitution states that if Riigikogu re-adopts an Act which has been vetoed by the President, without any amendments, "the President may propose to the National Court to declare such an act unconstitutional."

If an Act adopted by the Riigikogu is not in accordance with the Constitution (or presumably with the ratified foreign treaty) or the ratified foreign treaty with the Constitution as the higher norm, then the Legal Chancellor should take action. Article 142 of the Constitution states:

> "If the Legal Chancellor considers that a legal act issued by the state legislature or executive or by a local government is in conflict with the Constitution or an Act of Parliament, he or she shall propose to the body which has adopted that act to bring it into accordance with the Constitution or the law within twenty days.
> If the act is not brought into accordance with the Constitution or the law within twenty days, the Legal Chancellor shall apply to the National Court to declare the act null and void."

As it was stated earlier, on the basis of Article 3 of the Constitution, the Government and the courts should interpret Estonian domestic law in a "human-rights-friendly" way. It is also possible for Estonian courts to use general human rights principles as a subsidiary source of law in their reasoning and as a normative basis of their decisions, especially as our Constitution's "human rights chapter" is modelled on international instruments. No court has actually done this so far.

Courts could theoretically also use ratified human rights treaties directly in motivating their decisions. In practice, the application of treaty provisions in a concrete case depends on how clearly formulated and concrete the treaty provisions are. Whether a concrete norm of international law is clear enough or not is up to the court in question to decide.

The right of all inhabitants in Estonia to protect their human rights and liberties in all courts is clearly established in Article 15 of the Constitution which states that:

> "Every person shall have the right to bring a case before the courts if his or her rights or liberties have been violated. Everyone whose case is being tested by a court of law shall be entitled to demand any pertinent law, other legal act or procedure to be declared unconstitutional.
>
> The courts shall observe the Constitution and shall declare as unconstitutional any law, other legal act or procedure which violates the rights and liberties laid down in the Constitution or which is otherwise in conflict with the Constitution."

One could conclude that it is possible that in the future, courts will deal with the rights established in ratified international treaties similarly to the ones established in the Constitution.

One could also conclude that if anyone made a claim in an Estonian court concerning a human rights violation on the basis of international human rights treaty provisions, she or he would probably have to go through proceedings related to the corresponding domestic legal norms. If she or he would try to use human rights treaty provisions as the primary argument in the court proceedings, it would probably be acceptable to the court, if the Estonian act in question contradicted any treaty provisions or if Estonian acts do not regulate the issue at all.

In any case, such a case would probably end in the National Court, at least one could conclude so on the basis of an analogy with the procedure of constitutional review. The procedure is established in

Article 5, "Constitutional Review in the Trial of Court Cases", of the Act on Constitutional Review Court Procedure:

> (1) If in the trial of a case, a court concludes that the applicable law or another legal act contradicts the Constitution, the court shall declare it to be in contradiction with the Constitution and shall not apply it.
>
> (2) If a court with its decision has declared a law or other legal act to be in contradiction with the Constitution and has refused to apply it, the court shall so inform the National Court and the Legal Chancellor, by which constitutional review proceedings in the National Court shall be initiated.

In the recent first case (30 September 1994), the National Court declared part of the new property act unconstitutional on the basis of a private law suit and a petition by the Tallinn Administrative Court. This indicates that it is possible to follow this line in the future also in cases where the act contradicts a ratified international human rights treaty.

In their everyday work, the Estonian Government and the administrative authorities closely follow existing international human rights instruments, also the ones not yet ratified by Estonia (like the ECHR) or those not legally binding (like CSCE documents). The Estonian authorities have actively sought advice from the Council of Europe and the CSCE/OSCE in the human rights field, especially for the preparation of new legislation (for example during drafting the Aliens Act, the Act on Cultural Autonomy and, most recently, the new Language Act). The permanent OSCE Mission in Estonia advises authorities on the planning of integration strategies for national minorities and Estonia's large alien population. The representatives of the OSCE participate actively in the work of the presidential Round Table, a consultative body to the Government in which minorities, aliens and Estonian political parties are represented. The Estonian Human Rights Institute is an independent body set up to monitor the human rights situation in Estonia.

4. ASSESSMENT OF LAW AND PRACTICE

As it was stated earlier, the Estonian legal system is generally in accordance with existing international standards of human rights. But there are still some serious gaps in the legislation. For example, Estonia has modified parts of the Criminal Code dating back to the Soviet period (minus "political crimes," homosexuality etc.) as well as most of the Criminal Court Procedure Code, which is to be replaced by new acts in the near future (the draft bills already exist). Estonia does not yet have specific legislation which deals with the specific problems relating to the expulsion of aliens and the status of refugees.

However, Estonia encounters the most serious problems in implementing acts in force. The Estonian police, the prison administration and even the courts lag behind customary European standards. This is partly a legacy from the Soviet period when those institutions were part of the repression apparatus of the totalitarian empire, and partly a result of Estonia's general economic situation only allowing limited financial resources to be allocated to this purpose. With regard to the building up of a police force and the changes in the prison administration system, Estonia has experienced problems of training and moreover, it will take considerable time to change the composition of the personnel. For example, in the Soviet system the prison guards were mostly conscripted servicemen who have had to be replaced by paid personnel.

Therefore, one could say that Estonia faces some serious problems in the implementation of international human rights treaties relating to prison administration and the treatment of prisoners and detainees. The prisons are in a bad condition and they do not have enough places (for example, there are problems with separating different groups of criminals on the basis of age, sex and the seriousness of crime). Most of the personnel was trained during the Soviet period and is often unable to ensure sufficient order in the prisons. Some of the guards treat the prisoners brutally. As a specific refugee centre does not yet exist (there is a plan to build one), refugees are often accommodated in prisons as aliens, who have illegally entered the country.

Most of these problems are basically of a financial nature and it is very difficult to see, how they may be solved in the near future without serious financial and technical help from other countries and international organisations.

5. RECENT DEVELOPMENT AND REFORM PLANS

Most reform plans to protect human rights have not yet been mentioned but they are linked to the harmonization of Estonian legislation with ECHR standards. The Government has established a special working group to prepare the ratification of the ECHR and to analyze Estonian legislation and prepare the necessary amendments. This working group started its work in October 1994, and it is now possible to get a picture of Estonia's problems in this connection.

First of all, there are practical problems, the solution to which does not only depend on the willingness of the Estonian authorities:

- Estonia has economic difficulties which make the strict observance of Article 3 of the ECHR extremely difficult in the near future, if not impossible, as it was described in the preceeding section.

- The border dispute between Estonia and Russia creates problems in the practical realization of the right to liberty of movement and freedom to choose a place of residence within Estonian territory (Prot. 4 Art. 2 of the ECHR), as Estonian citizens live in some parts of constitutionally defined Estonian territory which are in reality under Russian control (Setumaa).

Secondly, some problems require that new acts are adopted or existing acts changed. Some of those new acts already exist as drafts. One could mention the following acts, which are all not yet in force:

1. The Act on Compensation to Victims of Illegal Arrests, Detention and Conviction (Art. 5(5) of the ECHR; also Art. 13 and Prot. no. 7, Art. 3).
2. The Act on Public Gatherings, Meetings and Demonstrations (Art. 11 of the ECHR).
3. The Act on Special Situation, State of Emergency and State of War (Art. 15 of the ECHR; the relevant provisions of the Constitution). Particularly important and even unavoidable is the enactment of an Act on the State of Emergency because it is connected with our internal situation and possible derogations from the treaty-based and constitutional rights and liberties.
4. The Act on Extradition and Deportation (Art. 3; Prot. No. 4; Art. 1, Prot. No. 7 of the ECHR).
5. The Act on Exercising Freedom of Speech (Art. 10 (2) of the ECHR).
6. The Act on Entry and Collection of Data Concerning Inhabitants (Art. 8 of the ECHR).

7. The Act on Expropriation (Art. 1, Prot. No. 1 of the ECHR).
8. The Act on Psychiatry (Art. 5 of the ECHR).

In addition, death penalty is formally in force in Estonia and it has large popular support. Therefore, the ratification of Protocol No. 6 of the ECHR by Estonia is not evident.

The problems mentioned above are, of course, not the only ones that Estonia will face in the future. Especially the level for the realization of social and economic rights in reality depends on the Estonian economic situation in general and on political choices concerning the development in the social sphere versus the creating of favourable conditions for economic growth. The growth of social security to an average Western European level will depend on the progress of the Estonian economy in general.

The Republic of Estonia is currently going through a difficult process of change. Although Estonia has succeeded in establishing a democratic system and in guaranteeing basic human rights, a lot remains to be done. Estonia will continue to ratify basic human rights treaties in the future, but probably not so intensively as previously, until the difficulties with the implementation of the treaties already signed or ratified have been solved.

6. DISSEMINATION OF INFORMATION ABOUT INTERNATIONAL HUMAN RIGHTS INSTRUMENTS

The basic human rights treaties are published in Estonia and information about basic human rights instruments is available in Estonia. The publication of the Universal Declaration on Human Rights and of the two UN Covenants on Civil and Political Rights and on Economic, Social and Cultural Rights, as well as the CSCE final documents started, both in Estonian and in Russian, already during the late Soviet period, unfortunately not in large numbers. During the independence period the ECHR and basic UN conventions have been published in Estonian.

Human rights treaties are usually published as annexes to books or in special law magazines, less often as separate publications. Ratified foreign treaties are regularly published together with their Estonian translations in separate issues of the Government Gazette. The Estonian

National Library and other main libraries have a wide collection of international human rights treaties both in Estonian and in other languages. Through libraries it is also possible to access international databases. Modern Estonia is a market economy and it means that in order to translate and publish human rights conventions, the publisher needs a donation from either domestic of foreign sponsors. This has somewhat slowed down the publication of international human rights treaties.

ANNEXES

1. Constitution of the Republic of Estonia.
2. Law on Constitutional Review Court Procedure.
3. Law on the Application of the Constitution of the Republic of Estonia.

ANNEX 1

REPUBLIC OF ESTONIA
CONSTITUTION

(Unofficial translation)

Unwavering in their faith and with an unswerving will to safeguard and develop a state

which is established on the inextinguishable right of the Estonian people to national self-determination and which was proclaimed on February 24, 1918,

which is founded on liberty, justice and law,

which shall serve to protect internal and external peace and provide security for the social progress and general benefit of present and future generations,

which shall guarantee the preservation of the Estonian nation and its culture throughout the ages -

the Estonian people adopted, on the basis of Article 1 of the Constitution which entered into force in 1938, by Referendum held on June 28, 1992 the following Constitution:

CHAPTER I
General Provisions

Art. 1. Estonia is an independent and sovereign democratic republic wherein the supreme power of the state is held by the people. Estonian independence and sovereignty is interminable and inalienable.

Art. 2. The land area, territorial waters and airspace of Estonia are an inseparable and indivisible whole. Estonia is politically a unitary state wherein the division of its territory into administrative units shall be determined by law.

Art. 3. Governmental power shall be exercised solely on the basis of this Constitution and such laws which are in accordance with the Constitution. Universally recognized principles and norms of international law shall be an inseparable part of the Estonian legal system. Laws shall be published in the prescribed manner. Only laws which have been published shall have obligatory force.

Art. 4. The work of the Riigikogu, the President of the Republic, the Government of the Republic and the courts shall be organized on the principle of separate and balanced powers.

Art. 5. The natural wealth and resources of Estonia are national assets, which shall be used sparingly.

Art. 6. The official language of Estonia is Estonian.

Art. 7. The national colors of Estonia are blue, black and white. The dimensions of the national flag and the national coat-of-arms shall be determined by law.

CHAPTER II
Fundamental Rights, Liberties and Duties

Art. 8. Every child with one parent who is an Estonian citizen shall have the right, by birth, to Estonian citizenship.

Everyone who as a minor lost his or her Estonian citizenship shall have the right to have his or her citizenship restored.

No person who has acquired Estonian citizenship by birth may be deprived of it.No person may be deprived of Estonian citizenship because of his or her persuasion. Conditions and procedures for the acquisition, loss and restoration of Estonian citizenship shall be determined by the Law on Citizenship.

Art. 9. The rights, liberties and duties of everyone and all persons, as listed in the Constitution, shall be equal for Estonian citizens as well as for citizens of foreign states and stateless persons who are present in Estonia.

The rights, liberties and duties listed in the Constitution shall be extended to legal entities, to the extent that this is in accordance with the general aims of the legal entities, and with the nature of such rights, liberties and duties.

Art. 10. The rights, liberties and duties enumerated in the present Chapter shall not preclude other rights, liberties or duties which ensue from the spirit of the Constitution or are in accordance therewith and are compatible with human dignity and the principles of a society based on social justice, democracy and the rule of law.

Art. 11. Rights and liberties may be restricted only in accordance with the Constitution. Restrictions may be implemented only insofar as they are necessary in a democratic society, and their imposition may not distort the nature of rights and liberties.

Art. 12. All persons shall be equal before the law. No one may be discriminated against on the basis of nationality, race, color, sex, language, origin, creed, political or other persuasions, financial or social status, or other reasons. The propagation of national, racial, religious or political hatred, violence or discrimination is prohibited and punishable by law.

The propagation of hatred, violence or discrimination between social strata is equally prohibited and punishable by law.

Art. 13. Everyone shall have the right to the protection of the state and the law. The Estonian state shall extend to foreign countries its protection of its citizens.

The law shall protect everyone against arbitrary treatment by state authorities.

Art. 14. Guaranteeing rights and liberties shall be the responsibility of the legislative, executive and judicial powers, as well as of local government.

Art. 15. Everyone has the right to appeal to a court of law if his or her rights or liberties have been violated. Everyone whose case is being tested by a court of law shall be entitled to demand any pertinent law, other legal act or procedure to be declared unconstitutional.

The courts shall observe the Constitution and shall declare as unconstitutional any law, other legal act or procedure which violates the rights and liberties laid down in the Constitution or which is otherwise in conflict with the Constitution.

Art. 16. Everyone has the right to life. This right is protected by law. No one shall be arbitrarily deprived of his or her life.

Art. 17. No one's honour or reputation may be defamed.

Art. 18. No one may be subjected to torture or to cruel or degrading treatment or punishment.

No one may be subjected to medical or scientific experiments without his or her freely given consent.

Art. 19. Everyone shall have the right to free self- realization. In exercising their rights and liberties and fulfilling their duties, everyone must respect and consider the rights and liberties of other persons and observe the law.

Art. 20. Everyone shall have the right to liberty and security of person. No one shall be deprived of his or her liberty, except in such cases and procedures as determined by law:

1) to execute a sentence or an arrest warrant issued by a court of law;

2) in cases of disregard for an instruction by a court of law or in order to ensure the fulfillment of obligations determined by law;

3) to prevent a criminal act or the infringement of a civil law, or to bring a person who is justifiably suspect before a competent public authority, or to forestall his or her escape;

4) to arrange for a juvenile to be placed under supervision or to bring him or her before a competent public authority to determine whether supervision is required;

5) to place a person suffering from an infectious disease, mental illness, alcoholism or drug abuse in custody, if he or she is a danger to themselves or others;

6) to bar illegal settlement in Estonia and to enable expulsion from Estonia or extradition to a foreign state. No one shall be deprived of his or her liberty merely on the grounds of inability to fulfil a contractual obligation.

Art. 21. Anyone deprived of his or her liberty shall be informed promptly, and in such a language and manner which he or she understands, of the reason for the arrest, and his or her rights, and shall be given the opportunity to notify his or her family about the arrest. A suspected offender shall also be promptly given the opportunity to choose a legal adviser and to confer with him or her. The right of a suspected offender to notify his or her family of the arrest may only be restricted in such cases and procedures as determined by law, for the purpose of preventing a criminal act or in the interest of establishing facts in a criminal investigation.

No one may be held in custody for more than forty- eight hours without specific permission by a court. Such a decision shall be promptly made known to the person in custody, in such a language and manner which he or she understands.

Art. 22. No one may be held guilty of a criminal offence before a guilty verdict by a court has been delivered against that person.

No one shall be required during a criminal investigation to prove his or her innocence.

No one may be compelled to give testimony against themselves, or against close family.

Art. 23. No one may be pronounced guilty of an act, if that act did not constitute a crime under a law which was in effect at the time the act was committed.

No one may be given a more severe sentence than the one which was applicable at the time the offence was committed. If, subsequent to the offence being committed, a lighter sentence is determined by law, this lighter sentence shall be applied.

No one may be tried or sentenced for a second time for an offence for which he or she has already been finally convicted or acquitted in accordance with the law.

Art. 24. No one may be transferred against his or her will from the jurisdiction of a court, which has been determined by law, to the jurisdiction of another court.

Everyone shall have the right to be present during his or her trial.

Court hearings shall be public. The court may, in such cases and procedures as determined by law, decide to hold its hearings, wholly or in part, in closed session, for the protection of state or business secrets, public morals or the family life or privacy of persons, or where the interests of juveniles, the victim or justice so require.

Court judgements shall be made public, unless the interests of a juvenile, a matrimonial partner or a victim require otherwise.

Everyone shall have the right to appeal to a higher court against a judgement by a court in his or her case, in accordance with procedures determined by law.

Art. 25. Everyone shall have the right to compensation for moral and material injuries caused by anyone's unlawful action.

Art. 26. Everyone shall have the right to inviolability of family life and privacy. State and local government authorities and their officials may not interfere with any person's family life or privacy, except in such cases and procedures as determined by law for the protection of health or public morals, public order, the rights and liberties of other persons, the prevention of a crime or the apprehension of a criminal.

Art. 27. The family being fundamental for the preservation and growth of the nation, and as the basis for society, shall be protected by the state.

Spouses shall have equal rights.

Parents shall have the right and the responsibility for the raising and care of their children.

The protection of parents and children shall be determined by law.

The family shall be responsible for the care of dependent members.

Art. 28. Everyone shall have the right to health care. Estonian citizens shall be entitled to state assistance in the case of old age, inability to work, loss of provider, and need. The categories, the extent, and the conditions and procedures for assistance shall be determined by law. Unless otherwise determined by law, this right shall exist equally for Estonian citizens and citizens of foreign states and stateless persons who are present in Estonia.

The state shall encourage voluntary and local government social care.

Families with many children and the disabled shall be entitled to special care by state and local authorities.

Art. 29. Estonian citizens shall have the right to freely choose his or her field of activity, profession and place of work. The conditions and procedures for exercising this right may be determined by law. Unless otherwise determined by law, this right shall exist equally for Estonian citizens and citizens of foreign states and stateless persons who are present in Estonia.

No one may be compelled against his or her free will to perform work or service, except military or alternative service, or work required to prevent the spread of infectious diseases, or in cases of natural disasters or catastrophes, or work which by law is required of a person convicted of a crime.

The state shall organize vocational education and assist in finding work for persons seeking employment.

Working conditions shall be under state supervision.

Employers and employees may freely join unions and associations. Unions and associations of employees and employers may for the protection of their rights and legal interests use any means not prohibited by law. The conditions and procedures for exercising the right to strike shall be determined by law.

Procedures for settling labor disputes shall be determined by law.

Art. 30. Positions in state and local government shall be filled by Estonian citizens, in accordance with procedures determined by law. In accordance with the law, such positions may in exceptional cases be filled by foreign citizens or stateless persons.

The law may restrict the right of some categories of civil servants to engage in commercial activities and to form profit-making associations (Art. 31), as well as the right to join political parties and some other non-profit associations (Art. 48).

Art. 31. Estonian citizens shall have the right to engage in commercial activities and to form profit-making associations and leagues. The law may determine conditions and procedures for the exercise of this right. Unless otherwise determined by law, this right shall exist equally for Estonian citizens and citizens of foreign states and stateless persons who are present in Estonia.

Art. 32. The property rights of everyone are inviolable and enjoy equal protection. No property shall be expropriated without the consent of the owner except in cases of public interest, in accordance with procedures determined by law, and in exchange for equitable and appropriate compensation. Anyone whose property has been expropriated without his or her consent shall have the right to appeal to a court and to contest the expropriation, and the nature and amount of compensation.

Everyone shall have the right to freely manage, use and command his or her property. Restrictions shall be determined by law. Property may not be used against the public interest.

The law may establish, in the public interest, categories of property in Estonia which are reserved for ownership by Estonian citizens, certain categories of legal entities, local government or the Estonian state.

The right of inheritance is guaranteed.

Art. 33. The home is inviolable. No one may forcibly enter or search anyone's dwelling, property or place of work, except in such cases and in accordance with procedures determined by law for the protection of public order or health, or the rights and liberties of others, or in order to prevent a criminal act, to capture a criminal offender or to establish facts in a criminal investigation.

Art. 34. All persons legally present in Estonia shall have the right to freedom of movement and choice of abode. The right to freedom of movement may be restricted only in cases and in accordance with procedures determined by law for the protection of the rights and liberties of others, in the interest of national defense, in the event of a natural disaster or a catastrophe, or in order to prevent the spread of infectious diseases, to protect the environment, to avoid leaving a juvenile or mentally ill person without supervision or to ensure criminal proceedings.

Art. 35. Everyone shall have the right to leave Estonia. This right may be restricted in cases and in accordance with procedures determined by law for the purpose of ensuring court or pre-trial proceedings or the execution of a judgement.

Art. 36. No Estonian citizen may be deported from Estonia or prevented from settling in Estonia.

No Estonian citizen may be extradited to a foreign state, except in cases prescribed by a foreign treaty, and in accordance with procedures determined by the applicable treaty and law. Extradition shall be decided by the Government of the Republic. Anyone whose extradition is sought shall be entitled to contest the extradition in an Estonian court.

Every Estonian shall have the right to settle in Estonia.

Art. 37. Everyone shall have the right to an education. Education shall be compulsory for school-age children to the extent specified by law, and free of school fees in state and local government general education schools.

In order to make education available, state and local governments shall maintain the necessary number of educational institutions. As determined by law, other educational institutions may be established, including private schools.

Parents shall have the final decision in choosing education for their children.

Everyone shall have the right to instruction in Estonian. Educational institutions established for minorities shall choose their own language of instruction.

The provision of education shall be supervised by the state.

Art. 38. Science and the arts, and their instruction, shall be able to exist freely.

Universities and research institutions shall be autonomous, within the limits prescribed by law.

Art. 39. Authors shall have the inalienable right to their work. The state shall protect intellectual property rights.

Art. 40. Everyone shall have freedom of conscience, religion and thought.

Everyone may freely belong to a church or a religious association. There shall be no state church.

Everyone shall have the freedom, either alone or in community with others and in public or private to practise his or her religion, unless it endangers public order, health or morals.

Art. 41. Everyone shall have the right to hold his or her opinions and persuasions. No one may be coerced to change them.

Persuasions cannot be pleaded as an excuse for a legal offence.

No one may be legally charged because of his or her persuasions.

Art. 42. No state or local government authority or their officials may collect or store information on the persuasions of any Estonian citizen against his or her free will.

Art. 43. Everyone shall be entitled to secrecy of messages transmitted by him or to him by post, telegram, telephone or other generally used means. Exceptions may be made on authorization by a court, in cases and in accordance with procedures determined by law in order to prevent a criminal act or for the purpose of establishing facts in a criminal investigation.

Art. 44. Everyone shall have the right to freely receive information circulated for general use.

At the request of Estonian citizens, and to the extent and in accordance with procedures determined by law, all state and local government authorities and their officials shall be obligated to provide information on their work, with the exception of information which is forbidden by law to be divulged, and information which is intended for internal use only.

Estonian citizens shall have the right to become acquainted with information about themselves held by state and local government authorities and in state and local government archives, in accordance with procedures determined by law. This right may be restricted by law in order to protect the rights and liberties of other persons, and the secrecy of children's ancestry, as well as to prevent a crime, or in the interests of apprehending a criminal or to clarify the truth for a court case.

Unless otherwise determined by law, the rights specified in paragraphs 2 and 3 of the present Article shall exist equally for Estonian citizens and citizens of other states and stateless persons who are present in Estonia.

Art. 45. Everyone shall have the right to freely circulate ideas, opinions, persuasions and other information by word, print, picture and other means. This right may be restricted by law for the purpose of protecting public order or morals, or the rights and liberties, health, honor and reputation of others. The law may likewise restrict this right for state and local government officials, for the purpose of protecting state or business secrets or confidential communication, which due to their service the officials have access to, as well as of protecting the family life and privacy of other persons, and in the interests of justice.

There shall be no censorship.

Art. 46. Everyone shall have the right to petition state and local government authorities and their officials with memoranda and applications. Procedures for responding shall be determined by law.

Art. 47. Everyone shall have the right, without prior permission, to peacefully assemble and conduct meetings. This right may be restricted in cases and in accordance with procedures determined by law for the purpose of national security, public order or morals, traffic safety and the safety of the participants in such meetings or to prevent the spread of infectious diseases.

Art. 48. Everyone shall have the right to form non-profit associations and leagues. Only Estonian citizens may be members of political parties.

The establishment of associations and leagues possessing weapons or organized in a military fashion or conducting military exercises requires a prior permit, the issuing of which shall be in accordance with conditions and procedures determined by law.

Associations, leagues or political parties whose aims or activities are directed towards the violent change of the Estonian constitutional system or otherwise violate a criminal law shall be prohibited.

The termination or suspension of the activities of an association, a league or a political party, and its penalization, may only be invoked by a court, in cases where a law has been violated.

Art. 49. Everyone shall have the right to preserve his or her ethnic identity.

Art. 50. Ethnic minorities shall have the right, in the interests of their national culture, to establish institutions of self-government in accordance with conditions and procedures determined by the Law on Cultural Autonomy for Ethnic Minorities.

Art. 51. Everyone shall have the right to address a state or local government authority and their officials in Estonian, and to receive answers in Estonian.

In localities where at least half of the permanent residents belong to an ethnic minority, everyone shall have the right to receive answers from state and local government authorities and their officials in the language of that ethnic minority.

Art. 52. The official language of state and local government authorities shall be Estonian.

In localities where the language of the majority of the population is other than Estonian, local government authorities may use the language of the majority of the permanent residents of that locality for internal communication to the extent and in accordance with procedures determined by law.

The use of foreign languages, including the languages of ethnic minorities, by state authorities and in court and pre-trial proceedings shall be determined by law.

Art. 53. Everyone shall be obligated to preserve human and natural environment and to compensate for damages caused by him or her to the environment. The procedures for compensation shall be determined by law.

Art. 54. It shall be the duty of every Estonian citizen to be loyal to the constitutional system of government and to defend the independence of Estonia.

Where no other means are available, every Estonian citizen shall have the right to take spontaneous action against any forcible change of the constitutional system. Art.

Art. 55. Citizens of foreign states and stateless persons present in Estonia are obligated to respect the Estonian constitutional system of government.

CHAPTER III
The People

Art. 56. The people shall exercise their supreme power through citizens who have the right to vote by:

1) electing the Riigikogu;
2) participating in referenda;

Art. 57. The right to vote shall belong to every Estonian citizen who has attained the age of eighteen.

An Estonian citizen who has been declared mentally incompetent by a court of law shall not have the right to vote.

Art. 58. The participation in elections of Estonian citizens who have been convicted by a court of law and who are serving a sentence in a place of detention may be restricted by law.

CHAPTER IV
The Riigikogu

Art. 59. Legislative power shall rest with the Riigikogu.

Art. 60. The Riigikogu shall be comprised of one hundred and one members. Members of the Riigikogu shall be elected in free elections on the principle of proportionality. Elections shall be general, uniform and direct. Voting shall be secret.

Every citizen entitled to vote who has attained 21 years of age may be a candidate for the Riigikogu.

Regular elections to the Riigikogu shall be held on the first Sunday in March every fourth year following the year of previous elections to the Riigikogu.

Early elections to the Riigikogu shall be held, in the cases prescribed by Articles 89, 97, 105 and 119 of the Constitution, no earlier than twenty, and no later than forty days after elections have been declared.

The procedures for the election of the Riigikogu shall be determined by the Law On the Riigikogu Elections.

Art. 61. The authority of the members of the Riigikogu shall commence on the day the results of the elections have been announced. The authority of the previous complement of the Riigikogu shall cease from that same day.

Before beginning to fulfil his or her duties, a member of the Riigikogu shall take an oath of office affirming his or her loyalty to the Republic of Estonia and its constitutional system.

Art. 62. A member of the Riigikogu shall not be tied to his or her mandate, nor be held legally responsible for his or her votes or political statements which he or she has made in the Riigikogu or any of its bodies.

Art. 63. A member of the Riigikogu may not hold any other public office.

A member of the Riigikogu shall be released from the responsibility to serve in the defense forces for the duration of his or her term.

Art. 64. The authority of a member of the Riigikogu shall be suspended on his or her appointment as a member of the Government of the Republic, and shall be restored on his or her being released from the duties as a member of government.

The authority of a member of the Riigikogu shall be prematurely terminated:

1) on he or she assuming another public office;

2) on a guilty verdict by a court against him or her entering into force;

3) on he or she resigning in accordance with procedures determined by law;

4) if the National Court has pronounced him or her to be permanently incapable of fulfilling his or her duties;

5) on his or her death.

When the authority of a member of the Riigikogu has been suspended or prematurely terminated, an alternate member shall assume his or her seat, in accordance with procedures determined by law. The alternate member shall have all the rights and duties of a member of the Riigikogu.

The authority of an alternate member shall cease when a member of the Riigikogu resumes his or her authority.

Art. 65. The Riigikogu shall:

1) adopt laws and resolutions;

2) decide on the conducting of referenda;

3) elect the President of the Republic in accordance with Article 79 of the Constitution;

4) ratify and denounce foreign treaties in accordance with Article 121 of the Constitution;

5) authorize the candidate for Prime Minister to form the Government of the Republic;

6) adopt the national budget and approve the report on its execution;

7) appoint, on proposal by the President of the Republic, the Chairman of the National Court, the Chairman of the Council of the Bank of Estonia, the Auditor-General, the Legal Chancellor and the Commander or Commander-in-Chief of the Defense Forces;

8) appoint, on proposal by the Chairman of the National Court, judges for the National Court;

9) appoint members of the Council of the Bank of Estonia;

10) decide, on proposal by the Government, on the issue of Government loans and the undertaking of other financial obligations by the state;

11) present statements, declarations and appeals to the Estonian people, foreign states and international organizations;

12) establish national orders of merit and military and diplomatic ranks;

13) decide on votes of no-confidence in the Government of the Republic, the Prime Minister or individual ministers;

14) declare a state of emergency in the nation in accordance with Article 129 of the Constitution;

15) on proposal by the President of the Republic declare a state of war, order mobilization and demobilization.

16) resolve all issues of government which, according to the Constitution, are not to be resolved by the President of the Republic, the Government of the Republic, other state bodies or local government.

Art. 66. The first session of the complement of the new Riigikogu shall take place within ten days of the announcement of the results of the Riigikogu elections. The first session shall be convened by the President of the Republic.

Art. 67. Regular sessions of the Riigikogu shall take place from the second Monday of January to the third Thursday of June, and from the second Monday of September to the third Thursday of December.

Art. 68. Extraordinary sessions of the Riigikogu shall be convened by the Speaker of the Riigikogu, on the demand of the President of the Republic, the Government of the Republic or at least one fifth of the complement of the Riigikogu.

Art. 69. The Riigikogu shall elect from among its members the Chairman of the Riigikogu (Speaker) and two Deputy Chairmen (Deputy Speakers), who shall direct the work of the Riigikogu, in accordance with the Law On the Riigikogu By-Laws and the Law On the Riigikogu Proceedings.

Art. 70. The quorum for the Riigikogu shall be determined by the Law On the Riigikogu By-Laws. In an extraordinary session, the Riigikogu shall have a quorum when over half of its complement is present.

Art. 71. The Riigikogu shall establish committees.

Members of the Riigikogu shall have the right to form factions.

Procedures for establishing committees and factions, and their powers, shall be determined by the Law On the Riigikogu By-Laws.

Art. 72. Riigikogu sessions shall be public, unless the Riigikogu, by a majority of two-thirds, decides otherwise.

Voting in the Riigikogu shall be public. Voting by secret ballot shall only be held in cases prescribed by the Constitution or the Riigikogu By-Laws in matters concerning the election or appointment of officials.

Art. 73. Legal acts of the Riigikogu shall be adopted with a majority of yes-votes, unless otherwise prescribed by the Constitution.

Art. 74. Members of the Riigikogu shall have the right to request explanations from the Government of the Republic and its members, the Chairman of the Council of the Bank of Estonia, the President of the Bank of Estonia, the Auditor- General, the Legal Chancellor and the Commander or Commander- in-Chief of the Defense Forces.

Requests for explanations must be answered at a session of the Riigikogu within twenty session days.

Art. 75. The remuneration of members of the Riigikogu and restrictions on other income shall be determined by law, which may be amended for the next complement of the Riigikogu.

Art. 76 A member of the Riigikogu enjoys immunity. Criminal charges can only be brought against him or her on proposal by the Legal Chancellor and with the consent of the majority of the complement of the Riigikogu.

ANNEX 1

CHAPTER V

The President of the Republic

Art. 77. The President of the Republic is the Head of State of Estonia.

Art. 78. The President of the Republic shall:

1) represent the Republic of Estonia in international relations;

2) appoint and recall, on proposal by the Government, diplomatic representatives of the Republic of Estonia and accept letters of credence of diplomatic representatives accredited in Estonia;

3) declare regular Riigikogu elections, and early elections for the Riigikogu, in accordance with Articles 89, 97, 105 and 119 of the Constitution;

4) convene the new complement of the Riigikogu in accordance with Article 66 of the Constitution, and shall open its first session;

5) propose to the Speaker of the Riigikogu to convene an extraordinary session of the Riigikogu in accordance with Article 68 of the Constitution;

6) proclaim laws in accordance with Articles 105 and 107 of the Constitution and shall sign documents of ratification;

7) issue edicts in accordance with Articles 109 and 110 of the Constitution;

8) initiate amendments to the Constitution;

9) determine the candidate for Prime Minister in accordance with Article 89 of the Constitution;

10) appoint and recall members of the Government, in accordance with Articles 89, 90 and 92 of the Constitution;

11) present proposals to the Riigikogu for appointments to the offices of the Chairman of the National Court, the Chairman of the Council of the Bank of Estonia, the Auditor-General, the Legal Chancellor and the Commander or the Commander-in-Chief of the Defense Forces;

12) appoint, on proposal by the Council of the Bank of Estonia, the President of the Bank of Estonia;

13) appoint judges on proposal by the National Court;

14) appoint and recall from office the Government of the Republic and, on proposal by the Commander of the Defense Forces, officers in the Defense Forces;

15) confer civil and military honors and diplomatic ranks;

16) be the Supreme Commander of Estonia's national defense;

17) present proposals to the Riigikogu on declarations of a state of war, on orders for mobilization and demobilization and, in accordance with Article 129 of the Constitution, on proclamations of a state of emergency;

18) declare, in cases of armed aggression against Estonia, a state of war, shall issue orders for mobilization and shall appoint a Commander-in-Chief of the Defense Forces, in accordance with Article 128 of the Constitution;

19) grant mercy, on the request of prisoners, by freeing those sentenced or reducing the sentence;

20) initiate the placing of criminal charges against the Legal Chancellor, in accordance with Article 145 of the Constitution.

Art. 79. The President of the Republic shall be elected by the Riigikogu, or, in the case described in the fourth paragraph of the present Article, by the Electoral Body.

The right to present a candidate for President of the Republic shall rest with at least one-fifth of the complement of the Riigikogu.

Any Estonian citizen by birth, who is at least forty years of age, may be presented as a candidate for President of the Republic.

The President of the Republic shall be elected by secret ballot. Each member of the Riigikogu shall have one vote. A candidate who is supported by a two-thirds majority of the complement of the Riigikogu shall be considered to be elected. Should no candidate receive the required majority, then a new vote shall be organized on the next day. Before the second round of voting, there shall be a new presentation of candidates. Should no candidate receive the required majority in the second round, then a third round of voting shall be organized on the same day between the two candidates who received the most votes in the second round. Should the President of the Republic still not be elected in the third round of voting, the Speaker of the Riigikogu shall convene, within one month, an Electoral Body to elect the President of the Republic.

The Electoral Body shall be comprised of the members of the Riigikogu and representatives of the local government Volikogus. Each local government Volikogu shall elect at least one representative, who must be an Estonian citizen, to the Electoral Body.

The Riigikogu shall present to the Electoral Body as candidates for President the two candidates who received the greatest number of votes in the Riigikogu. The right to present a presidential candidate shall also rest with at least twenty-one members of the Electoral Body.

The Electoral Body shall elect the President of the Republic with a majority of those members of the Electoral Body who are present. Should no candidate be elected in the first round, a second round of voting shall be organized on the same day between the two candidates who received the highest number of votes.

Further procedures for the election of the President of the Republic shall be determined by the Law On Electing the President of the Republic.

Art. 80. The President of the Republic shall be elected for a term of five years. No person may be elected to the office of President of the Republic for more than two consecutive terms.

The regular election for President of the Republic shall be held no earlier than sixty and no later than ten days before the end of the term of the President of the Republic.

Art. 81. The President of the Republic shall assume office by swearing the following oath of office to the Estonian people before the Riigikogu: "In assuming the office of President of the Republic, I (given- and surname) hereby solemnly swear that I will unswervingly defend the Constitution and the laws of the Republic of Estonia, exercise the power entrusted to me in a just and equitable manner, and honorably fulfil my duties to the best of my ability and to the best of my understanding, for the benefit of the Estonian people and the Republic of Estonia."

Art. 82. The authority of the President of the Republic shall terminate on:

1) resigning from office;
2) being convicted of an offense;
3) his or her death;
4) a new President of the Republic assuming office.

Art. 83. If the President of the Republic, according to a resolution by the Riigikogu, is continuously unable to fulfil his or her duties due to the state of health, or he or she is unable to fulfil them temporarily, in cases specified by law, or his or her term has ended prematurely, his or her duties shall temporarily be transferred to the Speaker of the Riigikogu.

During the period when the Speaker of the Riigikogu is fulfilling the duties of the President of the Republic, his or her authority as a member of the Riigikogu shall be suspended.

The Speaker of the Riigikogu as acting President of the Republic shall not have the right to declare early elections for the Riigikogu or to refuse to proclaim laws, without the consent of the National Court.

Should the President of the Republic be unable to fulfil his or her duties for over three consecutive months, or if his or her authority has terminated prematurely, the Riigikogu shall elect a new President of the Republic within fourteen days, in accordance with Article 79 of the Constitution.

Art. 84. Upon assuming office, the authority and duties of the President of the Republic in all elected and appointed offices shall cease, and he or she shall suspend his or her membership in political parties.

Art. 85. The President of the Republic may be charged with a criminal offence only on proposal by the Legal Chancellor, with the consent of the majority of the complement of the Riigikogu.

CHAPTER VI
The Government of the Republic

Art. 86. Executive power shall be held by the Government of the Republic.

Art. 87. The Government of the Republic shall:

1) implement national domestic and foreign policies;

2) direct and coordinate the work of government institutions;

3) organize the implementation of legislation, the resolutions of the Riigikogu, and the edicts of the President of the Republic;

4) submit draft legislation to the Riigikogu, as well as foreign treaties for either ratification or denunciation;

5) prepare a draft of the national budget and present it to the Riigikogu, shall administer the implementation of the national budget, and present a report on the implementation of the budget to the Riigikogu;

6) issue ordinances and directives for fulfillment in accordance with the law;

7) organize relations with foreign states;

8) declare, in the case of natural disasters and catastrophes or in order to impede the spread of infectious diseases, a state of emergency throughout the nation or in parts thereof;

9) fulfil other tasks which have been placed under its jurisdiction by the Constitution and laws.

Art. 88. The Government of the Republic shall be comprised of the Prime Minister and Ministers.

Art. 89. The President of the Republic, within fourteen days after the Government of the Republic has resigned, shall nominate a candidate for Prime Minister, who shall be tasked with forming a new government.

The candidate for Prime Minister shall report to the Riigikogu, within fourteen days of being assigned the task of forming a government, the bases for the formation of the new government, after which the Riigikogu shall decide, without negotiation and by an open vote, on giving the candidate for Prime Minister the authority to form a Government.

The candidate for Prime Minister who has received authority from the Riigikogu to form a government, shall present, within seven days, the composition of the Government to the President of the Republic, who shall appoint the Government within three days.

If the candidate for Prime Minister, nominated by the President of the Republic, does not receive the majority of yes-votes in the Riigikogu, or is unable to form a Government, or abstains, the President of the Republic shall have the right to present another candidate for Prime Minister within seven days.

If the President of the Republic does not present another candidate for Prime Minister within seven days, or abstains, or if this candidate is unable to obtain authority from the Riigikogu, in accordance with the conditions and time restraints in Paragraphs 2 and 3 of the present Article, or is unable to form a Government, or abstains, the right to present a candidate for Prime Minister shall be transferred to the Riigikogu.

The Riigikogu shall present a candidate for Prime Minister, who shall present the composition of the Government to the President of the Republic. If, within fourteen days from the transfer of the right to present a candidate for Prime Minister to the Riigikogu, the composition of the Government has not been presented to the President of the Republic, the President of the Republic shall declare early elections for the Riigikogu.

Art. 90. Changes to the composition of those appointed to the Government of the Republic shall be made by the President of the Republic, on proposal by the Prime Minister.

Art. 91. The Government shall take office by swearing an oath of office before the Riigikogu.

Art. 92. The Government of the Republic shall resign:

1) on the new complement of the Riigikogu convening;

2) on the resignation or death of the Prime Minister;

3) when the Riigikogu expresses no-confidence in the Government or the Prime Minister;

The President of the Republic shall discharge the Government of the Republic when the new Government assumes office.

Art. 93. The Prime Minister shall represent the Government of the Republic and shall direct its work.

The Prime Minister shall appoint two Ministers who shall have the right to substitute for the Prime Minister during his or her absence. The procedures for the substitution shall be determined by the Prime Minister.

Art. 94. Appropriate Ministries shall be established in accordance with the law, for the purpose of executing particular functions of government.

A Minister shall head a Ministry, organize the handling of issues which belong to the sphere of activity of the Ministry, shall issue directives and ordinances to be fulfilled on the basis of the law, and shall fulfil other duties which have been imposed, on the basis and in accordance with procedures determined by law.

Should the Minister be temporarily unable to fulfil his or her duties, due to illness or other hindrances, the Prime Minister shall transfer the Minister's duties to another Minister for that time period.

The President of the Republic may appoint, on proposal by the Prime Minister, other Ministers who do not head Ministries.

Art. 95. A State Chancellery shall be within the Government, and shall be headed by the State Secretary.

The State Secretary shall be appointed and recalled by the Prime Minister.

The State Secretary shall participate in Government sessions, with the right to speak.

The State Secretary shall have the same rights in heading the State Chancellery which are specified by law for a Minister in heading a Ministry.

Art. 96. Sessions of the Government of the Republic shall be closed, unless the Government decides otherwise.

The Government shall make decisions on proposal by the Prime Minister or by the appropriate Minister.

Ordinances by the Government shall be in effect when they carry the signatures of the Prime Minister, the appropriate Minister and the State Secretary.

Art. 97. The Riigikogu may express no-confidence in either the Government of the Republic, the Prime Minister or a Minister by a resolution adopted by the majority of the complement of the Riigikogu.

The issue of no-confidence may be initiated by at least one-fifth of the complement of the Riigikogu by submitting a written motion at a session of the Riigikogu.

The issue of expressing no-confidence may come up for resolution no earlier than two days after its being submitted, unless the Government demands speedier resolution.

In the case of no-confidence being expressed in the Government or the Prime Minister, the President of the Republic may, on proposal by the Government and within three days, declare early elections.

In the case of no-confidence being expressed in a Minister, the Speaker of the Riigikogu shall notify the President of the Republic, who shall recall the Minister from office.

The expression of no-confidence on the same grounds may be re-initiated no earlier than three months after the previous no-confidence vote.

Art. 98. The Government of the Republic may tie the adoption of a draft, which it has presented to the Riigikogu, with the issue of no-confidence.

Voting may not take place any earlier than two days after the tying of the draft with the issue of no-confidence. Should the Riigikogu reject the draft, the Government shall resign.

Art. 99. Members of the Government of the Republic may not hold any other public office or belong to the leadership or council of a commercial enterprise.

Art. 100. Members of the Government of the Republic may participate, with the right to speak, in sessions of the Riigikogu and its committees.

Art. 101. A member of the Government of the Republic may be charged with a criminal offence only on proposal by the Legal Chancellor, with the consent of the majority of the complement of the Riigikogu.

The authority of a member of the Government shall terminate when a guilty verdict comes into effect.

CHAPTER VII

Legislation

Art. 102. Laws shall be adopted in accordance with the Constitution.

Art. 103. The right to initiate laws shall rest with:

1) members of the Riigikogu;
2) factions of the Riigikogu;
3) Riigikogu committees;
4) the Government of the Republic;
5) the President of the Republic for amendments to the Constitution.

The Riigikogu shall have the right, with a resolution adopted by a majority of its complement, to propose to the Government of the Republic that it initiate a draft desired by the Riigikogu.

Art. 104. Procedures for the adoption of laws shall be determined by the Law On the Riigikogu By-Laws.

The following laws may be adopted or amended only by a majority of the complement of the Riigikogu:

1) Law On Citizenship;
2) Law On the Riigikogu Elections;
3) Law On Electing the President of the Republic;
4) Law On Local Government Elections;
5) Referendum Law;
6) Law On the Riigikogu By-Laws and Law On the Riigikogu Procedures;
7) Law On the Salaries of the President of the Republic and the Members of the Riigikogu;
8) Law On the Government of the Republic;
9) Law On Court Procedures Against the President of the Republic and the Members of the Government;
10) Law On Cultural Autonomy For Ethnic Minorities;
11) Law On the National Budget;
12) Law On the Bank of Estonia;
13) Law On the State Audit Office;
14) Law On the Organization of the Courts and On Court Procedures;
15) Laws pertaining to external and internal loans, and state asset obligations;
16) Law on A State of Emergency;
17) Law on Peacetime National Defense and Wartime National Defense.

Art. 105. The Riigikogu shall have the right to put draft legislation or other national issues to a referendum.

The decision of the people shall be determined by the majority of those participating in the referendum.

A law which has been adopted by referendum shall be immediately proclaimed by the President of the Republic. The referendum decision shall be binding on all state bodies.

Should the draft law which has been put to referendum not receive a majority of yes-votes, the President of the Republic shall declare early elections for the Riigikogu.

Art. 106. Issues related to the budget, taxes, the financial obligations of the state, the ratification of foreign treaties, and the enactment and ending of a state of emergency may not be put to referendum.

Procedures for referenda shall be determined by the Referendum Law.

Art. 107. Laws shall be proclaimed by the President of the Republic.

The President of the Republic shall have the right not to proclaim a law adopted by the Riigikogu, and to return the law to the Riigikogu, within fourteen days of receiving it, together with the reasons for its rejection. If the Riigikogu adopts a law which has been returned by the President of the Republic, without amendments, the President of the Republic shall proclaim the law, or propose to the National Court that it declare the law to be in conflict with the Constitution. If the National Court declares the law to be in accordance with the Constitution, the President of the Republic shall proclaim the law.

Art. 108. A law shall come into force on the tenth day after its publication in the "Riigi Teataja", unless the law itself determines otherwise.

Art. 109. If the Riigikogu is prevented from convening, the President of the Republic shall have the right, in matters of national interest which cannot be postponed, to issue edicts which have the force of law, and which shall bear the co- signatures of the Speaker of the Riigikogu and the Prime Minister.

When the Riigikogu convenes, the President of the Republic shall present such edicts to the Riigikogu, which shall immediately adopt a law either confirming or repealing the edicts.

Art. 110. Neither the Constitution, the laws listed in Article 104 of the Constitution, nor laws determining state taxes or the national budget can be enacted, amended or repealed by edicts issued by the President of the Republic.

CHAPTER VIII
Finance and the National Budget

Art. 111. The sole right to issue currency in Estonia shall rest with the Bank of Estonia. The Bank of Estonia shall organize currency circulation, and promote the stability of a good national currency.

Art. 112. The Bank of Estonia shall operate in accordance with the law, and shall report to the Riigikogu.

Art. 113. State taxes, fees, levies, penalties and compulsory insurance payments shall be determined by law.

Art. 114. Procedures for the control, use and command of national assets shall be determined by law.

Art. 115. The Riigikogu shall adopt, as a law, a budget for all state income and expenditure for each year.

The Government of the Republic shall present a draft national budget to the Riigikogu no later than three months before the commencement of the budget year.

On proposal by the Government, the Riigikogu may adopt a supplementary budget during the budget year.

Art. 116. Proposed amendments to the national budget or to its draft, which require a decrease in income, an increase of expenditures, or a re-distribution of expenditures, as prescribed in the draft national budget, must be accompanied by the necessary financial calculations, prepared by the initiators, which indicate the sources of income to cover the proposed expenditures.

The Riigikogu may not eliminate or reduce in the national budget or its draft those expenditures which have been prescribed by other laws.

Art. 117. The procedures for the preparation and adoption of the budget shall be determined by law.

Art. 118. The national budget adopted by the Riigikogu shall enter into force from the beginning of the budget year. If the Riigikogu does not adopt the national budget by the beginning of the budget year, it shall be permitted to make expenditures each month up to one-twelfth of the expenditures of the previous budget year.

Art. 119. If the Riigikogu has not adopted the budget within two months of the beginning of the budget year, the President of the Republic shall declare early elections for the Riigikogu.

CHAPTER IX
Foreign Relations and Foreign Treaties

Art. 120. Procedures for the relations of the Republic of Estonia with other states and with international organizations shall be determined by law.

Art. 121. The Riigikogu shall ratify and denounce treaties of the Republic of Estonia:

1) which amend state borders;
2) the implementation of which requires the adoption, amendment or annulment of Estonian laws;
3) by which the Republic of Estonia joins international organizations or leagues;
4) by which the Republic of Estonia assumes military or assets obligations;
5) where ratification is prescribed.

Art. 122. The land border of Estonia shall be determined by the Tartu Peace Treaty of February 2, 1920, and other international border treaties. The sea and air borders of Estonia shall be determined on the basis of international conventions.

A two-thirds majority of the complement of the Riigikogu shall be mandatory for the ratification of treaties which amend Estonian state borders.

Art. 123. The Republic of Estonia shall not conclude foreign treaties which are in conflict with the Constitution.

If Estonian laws or other acts are in conflict with foreign treaties ratified by the Riigikogu, the articles of the foreign treaty shall be applied.

ANNEX 1

CHAPTER X
National Defense

Art. 124. Citizens of the Republic of Estonia shall be obligated to participate in national defense, in accordance with the bases and procedures determined by law.

Those who refuse service in the Defense Forces for religious or ethical reasons shall be obligated to participate in alternative service, in accordance with the procedures prescribed by law.

Unless the law, considering the special interests of the service, determines otherwise, persons in the Defense Forces or in alternative service shall have all constitutional rights, liberties and obligations. The rights and liberties prescribed in Article 8 par. 3 and 4, Articles 11-18, Article 20 par. 3, Articles 21-28, Article 32, Article 33, Articles 36-43, Article 44 par. 1 and 2, Articles 49-51 of the Constitution may not be restricted. The legal status of persons in the Defense Forces and alternative service shall be determined by law.

Art. 125. A person in active service may not hold elected or appointed office nor participate in the activities of any political party.

Art. 126. The organization of the Estonian Defense Forces and the national defense organizations shall be determined by law.

The organization of national defense shall be determined by the Peacetime National Defense Law and the Wartime National Defense Law.

Art. 127. The supreme commander of national defense shall be the President of the Republic.

The National Defense Council shall be an advisory body for the President of the Republic, and its composition and tasks shall be determined by law.

The Estonian defense forces shall be headed by the Commander of the Defense Forces in peacetime, and the Commander-in-Chief of the Defense Forces during a state of war. The Commander and Commander-in-Chief of the Defense Forces shall be appointed and recalled by the Riigikogu, on proposal by the President of the Republic.

Art. 128. The Riigikogu shall declare, on proposal by the President of the Republic, a state of war, order mobilization and de-mobilization, and shall decide on the utilization of the Defense Forces to fulfil the international obligations of the Estonian nation.

In the case of aggression directed against the Republic of Estonia, the President of the Republic shall declare a state of war and mobilization, and shall appoint the Commander-in-Chief of the Defense Forces, without waiting for a resolution to be adopted by the Riigikogu.

Art. 129. In the case of a threat to the Constitutional system of government, the Riigikogu may declare, on proposal by the President of the Republic or the Government of the Republic and with a majority of its complement, a state of emergency in the whole country, with a duration of no longer than three months.

Regulations for a state of emergency shall be determined by law.

Art. 130. During a state of emergency or a state of war, the rights and liberties of persons may be restricted, and obligations placed upon them, in the interests of national security and public order, in the cases, and in accordance with procedures prescribed by law. Rights and liberties determined by Article 8, Articles 11-18, Article 20 par. 3, Article 22, Article

23, Article 24 par. 2 and 4, Article 25, Article 27, Article 28, Article 36 par. 2, Article 40, Article 41, Article 49 and Article 51 par.1 of the Constitution may not be restricted.

Art. 131. During a state of emergency or a state of war there shall be no elections for the Riigikogu, the President of the Republic or representative bodies of local government, nor can their authority be terminated.

The authority of the Riigikogu, the President of the Republic, and representative bodies of local government shall be extended if they should end during a state of emergency or state of war, or within three months of the end of a state of emergency or state of war. In these cases, new elections shall be declared within three months of the end of a state of emergency or a state of war.

CHAPTER XI
State Audit Office

Art. 132. The State Audit Office shall be an independent state institution with responsibility for economic control.

Art. 133. State Audit Office shall supervise:

1) the economic activity of state institutions, state enterprises and other organizations;
2) the use and preservation of state assets;
3) the use and control of state assets which has been transferred to the jurisdiction of local government;
4) the economic activity of such enterprises where the state has over half of the votes determined by the shares or stocks, or whose loans or contractual obligations are guaranteed by the state.

Art. 134. The State Audit Office shall be headed by the Auditor-General, who shall be appointed and recalled by the Riigikogu, on proposal by the President of the Republic.
The term of office for the Auditor-General shall be five years.

Art. 135. The Auditor-General shall present to the Riigikogu an annual report on the use and preservation of state assets during the previous budget year at the time of the debate in the Riigikogu on the implementation of the national budget.

Art. 136. The Auditor-General shall have the right to participate in sessions of the Government of the Republic with the right to speak on issues related to his or her duties.

The Auditor-General shall have, in heading his or her office, the same rights which are specified by law for a Minister in heading a Ministry.

Art. 137. The organization of the State Audit Office shall be determined by law.

Art. 138. The Auditor-General may be charged with a criminal offence only on proposal by the Legal Chancellor, with the consent of the majority of the complement of the Riigikogu.

CHAPTER XII
The Legal Chancellor

Art. 139. The Legal Chancellor shall be, in conducting his or her work, an independent official supervising the accordance with the Constitution and legislation of the legal acts issued by the state legislature and executive, as well as by local government bodies.

The Legal Chancellor shall analyze the proposals made to him or her for amending legislation and adopting new laws, as well as for the work of government institutions, and, if necessary, shall present a report to the Riigikogu.

The Legal Chancellor shall, in the cases referred to in Articles 76, 85, 101, 138, 153 of the Constitution, propose to the Riigikogu to bring criminal charges against a member of the Riigikogu, the President of the Republic, a member of the Government of the Republic, the Auditor-General, the Chairman of the National Court or a member of the National Court.

Art. 140. The Legal Chancellor shall be appointed by the Riigikogu, on proposal by the President of the Republic, for a term of seven years.
The Legal Chancellor may be removed from office only by a Court decision.

Art. 141. The Legal Chancellor, in heading his or her office, shall have all the rights which are accorded to a Minister in heading a Ministry.

The Legal Chancellor shall have the right to participate in sessions of the Riigikogu and in sessions of the Government of the Republic, with the right to speak.

Art. 142. If the Legal Chancellor considers that a legal act issued by the state legislature or executive or by a local government is in conflict with the Constitution or a law, he or she shall propose to the body which has adopted that act to bring the act into accordance with the Constitution or law within twenty days.

If the act is not brought into accordance with the Constitution or law within twenty days, the Legal Chancellor shall apply to the National Court to declare the act null and void.

Art. 143. The Legal Chancellor shall present an annual report to the Riigikogu on the accordance with the Constitution and legislation of legal acts issued by the state legislature and executive and by local government.

Art. 144. The legal status of the Legal Chancellor and the organization of his or her office shall be determined by the law.

Art. 145. The Legal Chancellor may be charged with a criminal offence only on proposal by the President of the Republic and with the consent of the majority of the complement of the Riigikogu.

CHAPTER XIII
The Courts

Art. 146. Justice shall be administered only by the Courts. The Courts shall be independent in their work and shall administer justice in accordance with the Constitution and laws.

Art. 147. Judges shall be appointed for life. The bases and procedures for recalling judges shall be determined by law.

Judges may be recalled only by a Court decision.

Judges may not hold any other elected or appointed office, except in cases prescribed by law.

Guarantees for the independence and the legal status of judges shall be determined by law.

Art. 148. The court system shall be comprised of:

1) rural and city courts, as well as administrative courts;
2) district courts;
3) the National Court.

The creation of special courts to handle some categories of court cases shall be determined by law.
The establishment of emergency courts shall be prohibited.

Art. 149. Rural and city courts, as well as administrative courts shall be first level courts.

District courts shall be second level courts, and they shall examine the decisions of the first level courts as appeal procedures.

The National Court is the highest court in the land, which examines court decisions as appeal procedures. The National Court is also the court for constitutional supervision.

The court system and court proceedings shall be regulated by law.

Art. 150. The Chairman of the National Court shall be appointed by the Riigikogu, on proposal by the President of the Republic.

Members of the National Court shall be appointed by the Riigikogu, on proposal by the Chairman of the National Court.

Other judges shall be appointed by the President of the Republic, on proposal by the National Court.

Art. 151. The organization of representation, defense, state prosecution and supervision of legality in Court procedures shall be determined by law.

Art. 152. If any law or another legal act is in conflict with the Constitution, it shall not be applied by the Court in trying a case.

If any law or other legal act is in conflict with the provisions and spirit of the Constitution, it shall be declared null and void by the National Court.

Art. 153. A judge may be charged with a criminal offence during his or her term of office only on proposal by the National Court and with the consent of the President of the Republic.

The Chairman of the National Court and its members may be charged with a criminal offence only on proposal by the Legal Chancellor and with the consent of the complement of the Riigikogu.

CHAPTER XIV
Local Government

Art. 154. All local issues shall be resolved and regulated by local government, which shall operate independently in accordance with the law.

Obligations may be imposed upon local government only in accordance with the law or in agreement with local government. Expenditures related to the obligations imposed on local government by law shall be covered from the national budget.

Art. 155. The units of local government are districts and towns. Other units of local government may be formed in accordance with the bases and procedures determined by law.

Art. 156. The representative body of local government shall be the Volikogu, which shall be elected in free elections for a term of three years. The elections shall be general, uniform and direct. Voting shall be secret.

In the election of the local government Volikogu, all persons who have reached the age of eighteen years and who reside permanently on the territory of that local government unit shall have the right to vote, in accordance with conditions determined by law.

Art. 157. Local government shall have independent budgets, for which the principles of formation and procedures shall be determined by law.

Local governments shall have the right, based on the law, to impose and collect taxes and to impose fees.

Art. 158. Borders of local government units may not be altered without taking into consideration the opinion of the respective local governments.

Art. 159. Local governments shall have the right to form leagues and joint institutions together with other local governments.

Art. 160. The organization of local government and the supervision of its work shall be determined by law.

CHAPTER XV

Amendments to the Constitution

Art. 161. The right to initiate amendments to the Constitution shall rest with at least one-fifth of the complement of the Riigikogu and with the President of the Republic.

Amendments to the Constitution may not be initiated, nor the Constitution amended, during a state of emergency or a state of war.

Art. 162. Chapter I 'General Provisions' and Chapter XV 'Amendments to the Constitution' of the Constitution may be amended only by referendum.

Art. 163. The Constitution may be amended by a law which is adopted by:

1) referendum;
2) two successive complements of the Riigikogu;
3) the Riigikogu, in matters of urgency.

A draft law to amend the Constitution shall be considered during three readings in the Riigikogu, whereby the interval between the first and second readings shall be at least three months, and the interval between the second and third readings shall be at least one month. The manner in which the Constitution is amended shall be decided at the third reading.

Art. 164. In order to put a proposed amendment to the Constitution to referendum, the approval of a three-fifths majority of the complement of the Riigikogu shall be mandatory. The referendum shall not be held earlier than three months from the time that such a resolution is adopted in the Riigikogu.

Art. 165. In order to amend the Constitution by two successive complements of the Riigikogu, the draft law to amend the Constitution must receive the support of the majority of the complement of the Riigikogu.

If the next complement of the Riigikogu adopts the draft which received the support of the majority of the previous complement, without amendment, on its first reading and with a three-fifths majority of its complement, the law to amend the Constitution shall be adopted. Art. 166. A proposal to consider a proposed amendment to the Constitution as a matter of urgency shall be adopted by the Riigikogu by a four-fifths majority. In such a case the law to amend the Constitution shall be adopted by a two-thirds majority of the complement of the Riigikogu.

Art. 167. The law to amend the Constitution shall be proclaimed by the President of the Republic and it shall enter into force on the date determined by the same law, but not earlier than three months after its proclamation.

Art. 168. An amendment to the Constitution dealing with the same issue may not be re-introduced within one year of the rejection of the respective draft by referendum or by the Riigikogu.

ANNEX 2

LAW
ON CONSTITUTIONAL REVIEW COURT PROCEDURE

(Unofficial translation)

I. GENERAL PROVISIONS

Article 1. Task of the Law
This Law shall establish the procedures of the constitutional review court and the authority of the courts

Article 2. The Constitutional Review Court
(1) The National Court shall be the constitutional review court. The constitutional review court panel shall be formed within the National Court.

(2) The procedures for the formation and the number of members in the constitutional review panel shall be established by the Law on Courts.

(3) In the cases stipulated in paragraph 3 of Article 9 of this law, the general assembly of the National Court shall try constitutional review cases.

(4) The rules for the work of the constitutional review panel and the general assembly shall be established by the Rules of the National Court.

Article 3. The Principle of Constitutional Review
(1) The National Court shall declare any legal act to be null and void, wholly or in part, if it contradicts the provisions and spirit of the Constitution.

(2) The National Court shall not try legal disputes, which in accordance with the law are within the authority of other courts, as constitutional review cases.

Article 4. The Authority of the National Court in Constitutional Review
(1) The National Court, in the cases and in accordance with procedures stipulated in this law, shall try:

1) whether laws adopted by the *Riigikogu* and which have entered into force are in accordance with the Constitution, and whether resolutions adopted by the *Riigikogu* and which have entered into force are in accordance with the Constitution and the law;
2) in accordance with Article 107 of the Constitution, whether laws which have not been proclaimed and have not entered into force are in accordance with the Constitution;
3) whether the edicts issued by the President of the Republic in accordance with Article 109 of the Constitution and which have entered into force are in accordance with the Constitution;

4) whether legislative acts adopted by the executive and local government representative bodies and which have entered into force are in accordance with the Constitution and the law;
5) whether foreign treaties concluded by the Republic of Estonia, but which have yet to enter into force, are in accordance with the Constitution;
6) in accordance with Article 2 of the Law on the Application of the Republic of Estonia Constitution, whether legal acts adopted prior to the entering into force of the Constitution are in accordance with the Constitution.

(2) The National Court shall not express a prior opinion on whether laws which are being drafted or the drafts of other legal acts or foreign treaties are in accordance with the Constitution and the law.

(3) The National Court shall try a constitutional review case in regard to whether a legal act or foreign treaty stipulated in this Article is in accordance with the Constitution and the law, only to the extent as this requested in the petition.

Article 5. Constitutional Review in the Trial of Court Cases

(1) If in the trial of a case, a court concludes that the applicable law or other legal act contradicts the Constitution, the court shall declare it to be in contradiction with the Constitution and shall not apply it.

(2) If a court with its decision has declared a law or other legal act to be in contradiction with the Constitution and has refused to apply it, the court shall so inform the National Court and the Legal Chancellor, by which constitutional review proceedings in the National Court shall be initiated.

Article 6. Who Has the Right to Directly Petition the National Court for Constitutional Review

(1) The following shall have the right to directly petition the National Court for the court to determine whether a law, other legal act or foreign treaty is in accordance with the Constitution or the law:

1) the President of the Republic, in the cases stipulated in Article 107 of the Constitution;
2) the Legal Chancellor, in the cases stipulated in Article 142 of the Constitution and to determine whether a foreign treaty is in accordance with the Constitution;
3) any court, in the cases stipulated in Article 5, paragraph 2 of this Law.

(2) The proposal shall be made to the National Court in the form of a motivated petition.

II. RULES OF PROCEDURE

Article 7. Public Trials

(1) The trial of constitutional review cases shall be public.

(2) The court may decide to hold its session, wholly or in part, in closed session, if this is necessary to protect a state secret.

(3) The court, after issuing a warning, may remove persons from the courtroom who disturb order in the court and thereby obstruct the trial of the case.

(4) Persons present in the courtroom may make tape recordings of the session and may make written notes.

(5) Court permission shall be required to film, photograph, videotape or transmit radio and television broadcasts.

(6) The secretary of the panel or of the general assembly may be present during the adoption of a court decision, who shall be prohibited from disclosing any opinions or positions expressed in the course of deliberation and voting.

Article 8. Language of Court Proceedings

(1) Court proceedings shall be held in the official language of the state.

(2) Documents composed in other languages shall be made public as translations in the official language of the state.

(3) Parties to the case who do not have a command of the official language of the state may appear before the court through an interpreter in their native language or in another language which they command.

Article 9. Collectiveness

(1) The National Court shall resolve constitutional review cases collectively, in the sessions of either the constitutional court panel or the general assembly.

(2) The constitutional court panel shall try cases in a composition of at least three members.

(3) A case may be transferred to the general assembly for trial, if at least one judge on the panel has a dissenting opinion.

(4) The general assembly of the National Court shall have a quorum if at least eleven of its members are present, including at least three members of the constitutional review panel.

Article 10. Due Dates for Submitting Petitions and the Trial of a Case

(1) A petition to the National Court to determine whether a law or other legal act is in accordance with the Constitution or any other law may be made as of the day the same enter into force. In cases stipulated in Article 107 of the Constitution, a petition for constitutional review may be made in regard to a law which has not yet entered into force.

(2) A petition to determine whether a foreign treaty is in accordance with the Constitution or the law may be made as of one day after the day of its signing.

(3) The court shall try the case and shall announce its decision within two months from the time a petition is correctly filed with the National Court. This due date may be extended by the general assembly of the National Court by no longer than two months.

(4) In cases stipulated in Article 107 of the Constitution, the court shall try the case and shall announce its decision within one month from the time a petition is correctly filed with the National Court. This due date may not be extended.

Article 11. The Content and Form of Petitions to the National Court

(1) Petitions to determine whether a disputed law, other legal act or foreign treaty is in accordance with the Constitution or the law must indicate:

1) to whom the petition is addressed;
2) name and mailing address of the petitioner;
3) the exact title and provisions of the law, other legal act or foreign treaty which allegedly contradict the Constitution, its date of adoption, date of signing or date of conclusion and place of publication;
4) the provisions of the Constitution which the disputed law, legal act or foreign treaty contradicts;
5) motivation for the petition.

(2) The text of the disputed law, other legal act or foreign treaty shall be included with the petition together with other documents on which the petition is based. The petition shall be signed by the official stipulated in Article 6 or, in the cases stipulated in Article 5, by the chairman of the respective court.

(3) The National Court shall have the right to demand supplementary documents and explanations from the petitioner.

(4) Eight copies of the petition and supplementary documents shall be included with the originals.

Article 12. Refusal to Accept a Petition

(1) The National Court shall justifiably refuse to accept or review a petition, if:

1) the petition is not within the authority of the court of constitutional review;
2) the petition is filed by a person not stipulated in Article 6 of this Law;
3) the petition does not meet the requirements established in Article 11. The court may demand that inaccuracies in content and form be corrected on a petition. If the petitioner corrects inaccuracies in content and form, the National Court shall accept the case for trial.

Article 13. Demand for the Position of the Body Which Adopted the Legal Act

The National Court shall send a copy of the petition to the body which adopted the law or other legal act and may demand that the body present its position within a determined period of time.

Article 14. Parties to the Case

(1) Parties to the trial of a petition in the National Court shall be:

1) the official who filed the petition or his or her representative;
2) a representative of the body which adopted the disputed law of other legal act.

(2) Parties to the case shall be notified of the time and place of the trial, however their absence from the trial shall not obstruct the trial of the case.

(3) If the National Court deems the appearance of a party to the case to be obligatory, the court, in the event of the party's failure to appear, may postpone the trial of the case.

(4) In their capacity of office, the Legal Chancellor and the Minister of Justice, or their representatives, may participate in the court sessions of a constitutional review case, with the right to speak.

Article 15. Preparations for Trial

(1) The following shall be subpoenaed or summoned to court:
1) the parties to the case;
2) experts to give testimony, as the National Court sees fit.

(2) Persons who are to appear in court shall be sent a subpoena or summons in due time before the trial. The subpoena or summons shall indicate that appearance before the court is obligatory and the consequences for failure to appear.

(3) The National Court shall have the right:
1) to demand additional documentation and explanations from the body which adopted the legal act;
2) to appeal to international organisations for consultation;

(4) The courts and state and local government bodies shall be obligated to present required documentation and explanations to the National Court within a determined period of time.

Article 16. Trial Procedures

(1) Trial procedures shall be determined by law and by the Rules of the National Court.

(2) The chairman of the constitutional review panel shall be the Chairman of the National Court, or, in his or her absence, the senior member of the panel.

(3) Sessions of the constitutional court panel or of the general assembly of the National Court shall open with a presentation by a member of the court panel and with a statement by the petitioner or his or her representative.

(4) Experts summoned to court shall present an opinion and the parties to the case shall have the right to question the expert.

(5) Members of the National Court may in the course of the trial question the member who makes the presentation, the parties to the case, and the experts.

Article 17. Trial Records

A record of the course of the trial and of statements made shall be made in accordance with procedures established in the Rules of the National Court.

Article 18. Passing and Announcing a Decision

(1) Decisions shall be made with justification and in observance of the confidentiality of meetings.

(2) Judges shall resolve any disagreement in regard to a decision through a vote. No judge shall have the right to refuse to vote or to abstain. In the case of a tied vote, the deciding vote shall be cast by the chairman, who shall vote last.

(3) Decisions shall be recorded in writing and shall be signed by the Chairman of the National Court, or, in the case of his or her absence, by the senior member of the panel who participated in the trial of the case.

(4) The dissenting position of a judge in the minority, which must be submitted by the time the decision is announced, shall be included with the decision.

(5) Parties to the case shall be notified of the time of the announcement of the court decision after the trial of the case has concluded. The decision shall be announced no later than two weeks after the trial concludes.

(6) A copy of the decision shall be forwarded to the parties to the case.

Article 19. Authority of the National Court in the Trial of a Case

(1) The Court shall have the right:

1) to decide against a petition;
2) to decide for a petition and to declare a law or other legal act null and void, either wholly or in part;
3) declare a foreign treaty to be in contradiction with the Constitution;
4) declare a law to be in contradiction with the Constitution, in the trial of cases stipulated in Article 107 of the Constitution.

(2) If a law or other legal act is declared null and void in part, the court decision must indicate exactly which parts of the law or other legal act are declared null and void.

Article 20. The Entering Into Force of a Decision

(1) A decision shall enter into force as of the day of its announcement.

(2) Decisions shall be final and shall not be subject to appeal.

Article 21. Interpretation of National Court Decisions

(1) Decisions made in constitutional review cases shall be interpreted by the National Court.

(2) The interpretation shall be recorded in writing.

Article 22. Correction of Errors

(1) After a decision has been announced, the court which adopted the decision shall have the right, on its own initiative or at the request of a party to the case, to correct spelling errors in the decision, inadequate phrasing or apparent inaccuracies.

(2) All erroneous copies which have been issued shall be recalled and shall be corrected or substituted by the court which made the decision.

Article 23. Obligatory Force of Court Decisions

National Court decisions shall have obligatory force for all Republic of Estonia state and government bodies, local governments, courts, officials, legal persons and natural persons.

Article 24. Publication of Decisions

(1) National Court decisions shall be published in the *Riigi Teataja*.

(2) If the National Court deems necessary, decisions shall be released to the press for publication.

Article 25. Trial Expenses
Expenses related to the trial of a case shall be defrayed from the state budget.

Article 26. Fines
(1) If a person who is obligated to appear before the court fails to appear before the court without a justifiable excuse, or if a person obstructs or disrupts the work of the court or displays apparent disrespect for the court, the National Court may impose a fine of up to 200 days salary.

(2) The order to fine shall be executed in accordance with procedures established by law for executing court decisions.

Article 27. The Entering Into Force of this Law
This Law shall enter into force as of the day of its publication in the *Riigi Teataja*.

Tallinn, May 5, 1993

U. Nugis
Chairman of the *Riigikogu*

ANNEX 3

LAW
ON THE APPLICATION OF THE CONSTITUTION OF THE REPUBLIC OF ESTONIA

Article 1
The Constitution shall enter into force on the day following its adoption by referendum and shall be applied in accordance with procedures established by this law.

The authority of the Republic of Estonia Supreme Council and the Congress of Estonia shall cease upon the announcement of the results of the *Riigikogu* elections.

Until the results of the *Riigikogu* elections have been announced, the Republic of Estonia Supreme Council shall carry out the functions of the legislative body.

The Government of the Republic, confirmed into office by the Supreme Council, shall be released from office upon the assumption of office of a government formed by the *Riigikogu.*

Article 2
Legal acts currently in force in the Republic of Estonia shall continue to be in force after the Constitution enters into force, insofar as they do not contradict the Constitution or of the Law on the Application of the Constitution and until such a time as they are voided or brought into full accordance with the Constitution.

In cases of dispute, the National Court shall decide whether a legal act is in accordance with the Constitution and with the Law on the Application of the Constitution.

Article 3
Elections to the *Riigikogu* and for the President of the Republic shall be announced by the Supreme Council after the adoption of the Constitution, whereby the schedule for the election shall be determined. The elections must be held no later than September 27, 1992.

The authority of the first complement of the *Riigikogu* elected after the adoption of the Constitution shall extend, as an exception, up to three years.

The first session of the *Riigikogu* shall be convened by the Chairman or Vice-Chairman of the Republic of Estonia Electoral Committee within ten days after the announcement of the election results.

The Chairman or Vice-Chairman of the Republic of Estonia Electoral Committee shall lead the work of the *Riigikogu* until the election of the Chairman of the *Riigikogu.*

Until the adoption of the Law on the *Riigikogu* Standing Orders and Law on *Riigikogu* Procedure, the *Riigikogu* shall have a quorum if at least one half of its members are present at a session.

For the purposes of the Constitution, the following shall mean:

- majority of affirmative votes — more affirmative votes than negative votes are cast;
- two thirds majority of votes — at least twice as many affirmative votes than negative votes are cast;
- four fifths majority of votes — at least four times as many affirmative votes than negative votes are cast;

- majority of the members of the *Riigikogu* — over one half of the members of the *Riigikogu* cast an affirmative vote;
- two thirds majority of the members of the *Riigikogu* — at least two thirds of the members of the *Riigikogu* cast an affirmative vote;
- three fifths majority of the members of the *Riigikogu* — at least three fifths of the members of the *Riigikogu* cast an affirmative vote.

Prior to the announcement of the elections to the *Riigikogu* and for the President of the Republic, the Supreme Council shall enact legal acts on electing the President of the Republic and on the remuneration and social security for members of the *Riigikogu* and the President of the Republic.

Article 4
Point 11 of Article 78 and Article 79 of the Constitution shall be applied after the President of the Republic, elected on the basis of the present Article, assumes office.

In applying the Constitution, the President of the Republic, as an exception, shall be elected simultaneously with the election of the *Riigikogu* through a general, uniform and direct election, by secret ballot, by a majority of votes cast, for a term of four years. If no one candidate receives over one half of the votes cast, the President of the Republic shall be elected by the *Riigikogu* from amongst the two candidates who receive the greatest number of votes within ten days of the convention of the *Riigikogu*. Detailed procedures for the election of the President of the Republic shall be established by the Presidential Electoral Law.

The right to nominate candidates for President shall rest with at least ten thousand Republic of Estonia citizens, who have the right to vote.

Any persons who is a candidate for the office of President of the Republic may not simultaneously be a candidate for the *Riigikogu*.

Article 5
The entering into force of the Constitution shall not in itself bring about the end of the employment relations of existing employees of government bodies.

The authority of the Auditor-General, the President of the Bank of the Estonia, the Chairman of the National Court and the members of the National Court, appointed to office for a term by the Supreme Council, shall extend until the end of their appointed term.

Candidates for the offices listed in point 11 of Article 78 of the Constitution, and which are not specified in paragraph 2 of the present article, shall be presented by the President of the Republic to the ***Riigikogu*** within 60 days after assuming office.

Article 6
Until December 31, 2000, candidates for the office of President of the Republic, the ***Riigikogu*** or local government councils, as well as persons who seek the office of Prime Minister, minister, Chairman of the National Court, member of the National Court, judge, Legal Chancellor, Auditor-General, President of the Bank of Estonia, Commander or Commander-in-Chief of the Defence Forces or any other government or local government office filled by election or appointment must take a written oath of conscience that they have not been in the service or an agent of security organizations, military intelligence or counter intelligence services of states which have occupied Estonia and that they have not participated in the persecution or repression of citizens for their political convictions, disloyalty, social class or service in the government or defence services of the Republic of Estonia.

If a court determines that the information confirmed by the oath is untrue, the candidate shall be excluded from the list of candidates or his or her mandate shall be voided, or the person shall not be appointed to the of offices noted in paragraph 1 of the present Article or the person shall be dismissed from of office.

Article 7

Persons who wish to remain in the offices specified in paragraph 1 of Article 6, which they have assumed prior to the convention of the *Riigikogu,* must take the written oath of conscience within 30 days after the convention of the Riigikogu. If a person refuses to take the oath or if a court determines that the information confirmed by the oath is untrue, the person shall be dismissed from office.

Regulations for taking the oath shall be enacted by the Supreme Council prior to the declaration of the elections to the *Riigikogu* and for the President of the Republic.

Article 8

During the three years following the adoption of the Constitution by referendum, the *Riigikogu* shall have the right to make urgent amendments to the Constitution with a two thirds majority vote of the *Riigikogu.* The decision to consider a draft law to amend the Constitution as a matter of urgency shall be adopted by a majority of affirmative votes.

The right to initiate amendments to the Constitution during the three years after the adoption of the Constitution by referendum shall also rest with public initiative, in the form of at least ten thousand citizens, who have the right to vote. The proposal to amend the Constitution by public initiative shall be entered into the agenda of the *Riigikogu* as a matter of urgency and shall be resolved in accordance with procedures established in paragraph 1 of the present Article.

Article 9

This law is adopted together with the Constitution, by referendum on June 28, 1992. The law shall enter into force simultaneously with the Constitution.

The Law on the Application of the Constitution may be amended in accordance with procedures prescribed for amendments to the Constitution.

3. Incorporation and Implementation of Human Rights in Latvia

by Ineta Ziemele,
University of Latvia

1. INTRODUCTION

The methods and means of implementation and incorporation of human rights depend upon various factors which are not necessarily based on legal considerations. In the case of the Baltic states, and particularly of the Republic of Latvia, when talking about the application of human rights standards one should take into consideration the framework of the country concerned - the historical, political, and economic factors as well as legal traditions and the significant role of the socio-ethnic aspect.

Some points have to be emphasized about the Latvian framework in order to understand why international law has been applied in one particular way and not in another, as well as to predict about possible future developments.

Obviously, the historical factor plays an important role in many ways. The fact that the Republic of Latvia lost her sovereignty for a long period of time prevented Latvia from taking part in the developing process of international law and from considering this issue at all. Today, international affairs in general, and human rights in particular are new fields of interest for the State and her people.

Furthermore, as a consequence of the events in 1940 the socio-ethnic picture of society in the Baltic countries have changed considerably, especially in Latvia (*Table 1*).

M. Scheinin (ed.), International Human Rights Norms in the Nordic and Baltic Countries, 73–110.

Table 1. The National/Ethnic Composition of the Population (by percentages)

	1935	1959	1979	1989
Latvians	75.5	62	53.7	52
Non-Latvians	24.5	38	46.3	48

The 50 years of foreign domination and the considerable changes in the population of the country, as well as the comparatively small size and the strategic location of the country, are aspects decisive to the political factor that should be considered when discussing Latvia's approach to human rights. Keeping in mind the factors mentioned above, some variables of Latvia's possible activities in the field of human rights implementation within the framework of international law might be illustrated as follows:

1) Because the question of sovereignty appears to be very important to a country which recently regained her independence, the country will probably not show much enthusiasm *vis-a-vis* the principle of international law supremacy over national legislation as the word 'national' is assumed to mean maintaining sovereignty;

2) Due to the long period of prohibition to participate in international activities, the country may enter into a process of extensive internationalization which will involve the acceptance of various international law standards and consequently, the country may accept a lot of international commitments without even considering that this may interfere with the state's sovereignty. This process is likely to be regarded as the major guarantee to ensure the sovereignty of the country.

Finally, the changes in the socio-ethnic picture of the country and the course of those changes have an impact on the methods and means to implement human rights. What we are dealing with in Latvia, and this is fully acknowledged in Europe, is the question of the survival of the Latvian nation.

One cornerstone of Latvia's legal system today is for the country to continue to fulfill international rights and duties due to the very fact that the extinction of the Republic of Latvia did not take place. The threat by the USSR to use force used in 1940 *vis-a-vis* all three Baltic states, as well as the armed invasion of the territories of these independent states, were already at that time illegal according to international law and also according to certain bilateral agreements between the countries in question. The very principle of *ex injura non oritur jus* is, therefore, applicable in this case. Consequently, Latvia regards all international instruments to be binding if they were binding before 1940 and if they are still in force.[1] These treaties were *de facto* suspended during the illegal occupation of the country. International treaties that remained *de jure* binding on Latvia are listed in the L.N.T.S. and in the U.N.T.S. National legislation in Latvia continues on the basis of the legislation that existed before the illegal occupation in 1940. Since the re-establishment of the independent Latvia laws have of course been revised and adopted for the present situation and, finally, abolished due to the fact that new acts are coming into force which may replay old acts on the same subject. The continuity of the pre-existing legal order is, hereby, being maintained by the state.

2. THE STATUS OF HUMAN RIGHTS NORMS IN LATVIA

2.1 Constitutional Provisions. The constitutional basis of the Republic of Latvia is the Constitution of 1922, the Constitutional Act On the Rights and Obligations of Citizens and Persons, and the Constitutional Act On the Republic of Latvia Status as a State, as well as the Declaration of the Supreme Soviet of the Latvian SSR on the Renewal of the Independence of the Republic of Latvia. It is a question for the Constitutional Court to interpret the legal status of the latter declaration. However, there is little doubt about the constitutive effect of the declaration with relation to the re-establishment of the state.

The declaration announced *de jure* independence of the state and re-established the authority of the Constitution of 1922 in Latvia. Equally, it had legitimate authority to suspend the Constitution during the transitional period for the re-establishment of the *de facto* independence of the state. Although the transitional period ended with the convening of the Parliament of Latvia on July 5-6, 1993, the declaration might not be considered as a matter of history. Apart from

[1] Republic of Latvia Supreme Council (1993) 'Resolution On Multilateral Treaties which the Republic of Latvia has Ratified or which It has Acceded up until 1940', *Latvijas Republikas Augstâkâs Padomes un Valdìbas Ziņotâjs,* January 5.

setting up the constitutional development of the state, the declaration also puts forward some basic principles for the framework of the re-established country. It recognizes the supremacy of the fundamental principles of international law over national law and guarantees social, economic and cultural rights as well as political rights and freedoms to citizens and permanent residents of the country. It is worthwhile noticing that the Constitution does not contain such principles.

Declaration on the Renewal of the Independence of the Republic of Latvia, 4 May 1990 (Annex 1). Article 1 of the Declaration recognizes "the supremacy of the fundamental principles of international law over national law".[2] However, according to Article 38, paragraph 1 of the Statute of the International Court of Justice, the scope of international law includes not only general principles of law but also international conventions, international custom, etc. The question here is how to interpret Article 1 of the Declaration. What is meant by the term 'fundamental principles of international law'? Does this mean the scope of international law as it is mentioned in the Statute of ICJ, or does it also include the general standards or understandings that have been worked out on an intergovernmental level. In the absence of an authoritative statement on this question by the Constitutional Court, the status and the interpretation of the declaration remains uncertain.

*Declaration on the Accession of the Republic of Latvia to International Instruments Relating to Human Rights, 4 May 1990 (Annex 2).*The general attitude of Latvia *vis-a-vis* human rights is reflected in the Declaration. In the Preamble of the Declaration, Latvia affirms its wish to respect and guarantee human rights in its legislation. However, the Declaration talks about "norms of international law relating to human rights"[3] and it is to a certain extent unclear if it also includes international customary law and non-legally binding standards.

Again, it is a question for the Constitutional Court to decide on the legal status of the Declaration and the extent of legal or political

[2] 5th Saeima-Republic of Latvia Standing Commission on Human Rights (1993) 'Declaration of the Supreme Soviet of the Latvian SSR on the Renewal of the Independence of the Republic of Latvia', *Human Rights Issues* 58-59.

[3] *Ibid.*, p. 60.

commitment under the Declaration. In practice, the Declaration has been seen as a parliamentary consent to to the fact that Latvia is bound by the various instruments listed in the Declaration. The necessary acts of ratification were passed according to the Declaration. It must be assumed that within the given context the expressed desire to harmonize domestic legislation with international human rights instruments is a legal commitment or at least a binding method to create domestic law.

Constitution (Satversme), 7 November 1922 (Annex 3). The Constitution of the Republic of Latvia was adopted by the first Latvia's People's Assembly - Latvia's Constituent Assembly on 15 February 1922 and it came into force on 7 November 1922. It did not have any provisions on human rights or a Bill of Human Rights. Law-makers did, however, intend to draft a section in the Constitution on this subject-matter, but obviously they never succeeded. The Constitution of the Republic of Latvia was restored in full in July 1993 at the end of the transition period; the sovereignty of the state was unquestionable, democratic elections were held and a new Parliament was formed by Latvia's citizens.

Constitutional Law on the Rights and Obligations of Citizens and Persons, 10 December 1991 (Annex 4). There are two contravening interpretations as to what is the status of the Constitutional Law in the hierarchy of the national legal norms. According to the first interpretation, the Constitutional Law is a natural part of the Constitution. According to the second interpretation, the Constitutional Law has no prevailing status with respect to the other national Acts of Parliament because the Constitution does not provide for the adoption of "constitutional laws" in general. It is being argued that the Constitution of Latvia needs some revision in order to grant constitutional status to human rights and some other important legal instruments like the Constitutional Court. The Constitutional Law is supposed to function as a Bill of Human Rights. On the one hand, it directly lists the majority of human rights already listed in existing human rights conventions. On the other hand, as the Law is part of the Constitution, it also declares the basic principles of the state's constitutional order, dealing with the relationship between the state and its citizens. However, it is a clear disadvantage that the

Constitutional Law lacks means of implementation. For instance, a procedure to bring a claim on human rights violations does not exist. The option to claim a violation of the law concerned does not exist either. It is, nevertheless, possible to state that the Constitutional Law complies with the two Covenants on human rights in both spirit and letter, but it must be observed that the rights declared are not made justiciable and self-executing within the domestic legal system. In the absence of a national mechanism for supervision and control, one has access to international procedures established in various human rights instruments to which the state has acceded.

2.2 Human rights implementation procedures. Latvia applies two different methods to implement international law. A treaty does not become binding on Latvia before it has been ratified by Parliament or accepted by the Cabinet. A treaty obtains the same status as the Constitution with respect to ordinary acts and ordinances in the domestic law hierarchy. The provisions of a treaty must be followed as soon as the treaty becomes legally binding on Latvia usually after parliamentary ratification. However, there is no domestic procedure to handle non-observance of such a treaty, even if it has become a genuine part of domestic law.

In fact, "adoption" as the main method of implementation of international law instruments in Latvia has developed by coincidence. Specifically within the Latvian framework, this method of implementation might be called "quasi-adoption" because national consent that international treaties form part of domestic law has not yet been expressed.

The main reason for using some elements of the so-called adoption method has been the absence of domestic acts at the time of the re-establishment of the state. These gaps have been filled by international norms and standards. At least, among lawyers the opinion prevailed that if a question cannot be solved by any domestic act then one should apply international law by analogy. Furthemore, due to staff shortage it has been impossible to enact each and every international treaty through drafting and approving relevant national acts. This does not mean that there is no need for separate domestic legislative measures.

The other method of implementation used in Latvia is to enact clauses requiring relevant state authorities to initiate amendment to and changes of existing national acts. Such clauses are inserted into acts on the ratification of international treaties in order to harmonize domestic law with the treaty.

International treaties do not directly form part of the national legal system. They do it only by reference or by analogy.

Law On Judicial Power, 15 December 1992. Previously, Latvia had the following court system:

1) District Courts and City District Courts;
2) the Supreme Court; and
3) the Commercial Court.

The first instance courts dealt with civil and criminal cases. The Supreme Court served as a court of appeal. The Commercial Court heard disputes of a commercial nature between two or more legal persons under its jurisdiction.

According to the act passed on December 1992, the court system is now under reform. It is being re-organized as follows:

1) District, City, and City District Courts as first instance courts;
2) Regional Courts that generally serve as appellate courts, but in some specific cases as courts of first instance; and
3) the Supreme Court which, according to this act,[4] includes the Constitutional Court Panel with the right to review constitutional issues.

According to Article 9[5], the Constitutional Court Panel is entitled to review the constitutionality, legality and treaty-conformity of acts and other decrees of state authorities. No individual complaint procedure is mentioned.

---

[4] During the court reform in Latvia the initial idea to establish a separate Constitutional Court Panel within the Supreme Court system has been abandoned.

[5] Law on Judicial Power: Article 9. Adjudication on issues of constitutional review. On issues of constitutional review, judgments are passed by the Supreme Court, which reviews and resolves, by trial, matters related to the conformity of the Republic of Latvia's acts and the normative acts of the Saeima (Parliament), local governments, State authority institutions and other organisations with the Satversme (Constitution), the Constitutional Acts, and the interstate agreements concluded by the Republic of Latvia, as well as cases concerning the violations of the Satversme of which the highest officials of the State are guilty.

According to the criminal procedure, civil procedure or administrative procedure, a person can lodge a complaint against a government official if he/she has not complied with the competence given by law and the person feels that his/her rights have been violated. However, it is a question of civil, criminal or administrative law respectively which has always been regulated within the state and by the state in order to maintain public order in society. On the other hand, when it comes to human rights, as long as the law within the state protects her residents according to already established principles within the domestic legal order (e.g. the principle of innocence), one may argue that the implementation of human rights is effected due to the fact that the domestic acts by their very nature guarantee a certain protection for the individual. The result is all the same. One can call it passive transformation of human rights into domestic legislation because there is no need to amend the domestic acts in question. They already provide the necessary rights and guarantees.

Draft Law On Constitutional (Satversmes) Court[6]. At the present time, the work on the Act On the Constitutional (Satversme) Court is being conducted both in Parliament and by the Cabinet. One of the questions to be answered in this act is what the procedure for human rights complaints will be.

According to draft Article 11, paragraph 6, the Constitutional Court is entitled to review administrative enactments. An individual whose constitutional rights have been violated by the executive power may bring a case before the Constitutional Court. The definition of constitutional rights in the draft makes reference to human rights guaranteed by the 1991 Constitutional Act. It is not possible only to base a complaint upon international human rights instruments.

A document issued by any of the state authorities or any other legal person under public law that contradicts any of the constitutional provisions on human rights (administrative enactment)[7] is the necessary element for someone to base his or her complaint on.

Hopefully, the interpretation of the notion of an administrative document, which is unavoidable in such cases, will not be too narrow.

---

[6] Republic of Latvia Cabinet Session's *Record* Nr. 11, para. 13, 22.02.94.

[7] Article 47 of the draft Act on the Constitutional Court.

The Constitutional Court must establish that all prospective issues submitted to the court are considered within the context of international treaties, custom and fundamental principles of international law as a basic method of its work due to the fact that Latvia has declared international law to be binding.[8]

One may already predict some disharmony in the system. For instance, Article 4, paragraph 1 of the Act on Religious Organisations establishes a prohibition of direct or indirect restrictions in a resident's rights or the creation of privileges due to his/her attitude of religion. The Act stipulates that in the case of a violation of this Article, someone who is responsible for an illegal act should be held liable. This Act does not create any mechanism to establish a violation of the Article, and neither does any other act. Unfortunately, the Constitutional Court procedure will deal with cases arising from violations of the Constitution or the Constitutional Act. The conclusion is that if one wants to protect his/her rights guaranteed by specific acts, he/she has to look in the Constitutional Act and find a relevant provision in said act.

*2.3 Conclusions.*To sum up this brief survey of the basic legislative acts in Latvia, it is possible to conclude, *first*, that the Declaration on the Renewal of the Independence of the Republic of Latvia confirms that Latvia accepts that international law has priority over national law. Moreover, a vast amount of domestic acts do contain provisions to this end. If one looks at Article 9 of the Act On Judicial Power, it states explicitly that ordinary acts should comply with the Constitution, the Constitutional Act and the international treaties of the Republic of Latvia.

It must, however, be assumed that the principles enacted in the Declaration give Latvia recourse to the principles of international law that are not yet codified. The Declaration sets up the general tendency in Latvia's attitude *vis-a-vis* the question of the status of international law within the national legal system, including among other things the status of international human rights treaties. The priority principle might not raise any doubt, but the relationship between the

[8] Article 1 of the Declaration on The Renewal of the Independence of the Republic of Latvia; The Preamble of the Declaration on The Accession of the Republic of Latvia to International Instruments Relating to Human Rights; Article 1 of the Act on Religious Organisations.

Constitution and international treaties is uncertain and consequently also the constitutional status of international treaties. At the same time, as long as the Constitutional Court has not made an authoritative decision, the problem can only be assessed from a personal point of view.

Second, the Declaration on the Accession of the Republic of Latvia to International Instruments Relating to Human Rights specifies one particular issue: - that national law must comply with human rights treaties. The Declaration states that Latvia commits herself to be bound by those international treaties listed in the declaration. Latvia's legislative power has to draw up acts that are in conformity with those documents.

Third, the Constitutional Act on the Rights and Obligations of Citizens and Persons provides for the rights of individuals in the state. The act is an example of a relevant national act transforming the norms of international treaties on human rights into national law.

Due to the fact that the Constitutional Act forms the constitutional basis, human rights have become protected constitutional rights in Latvia.

By means of reference used in the already analyzed basic domestic acts, international law has been given equal status with the Constitution and the Constitutional acts within the hierarchy of the domestic legal system. For instance, according to the draft Act on the Constitutional Court, the President of the State, one third of the Members of Parliament, the Cabinet and the relevant lower courts shall have the right to bring a case before the Constitutional Court if a national legal norm is in contradiction to international treaties binding upon Latvia[9]. Of course, the main concern of the Constitutional Court will be the constitutionality of national law.

Transformation of human rights into the Constitutional Act does not change the special status of international human rights instruments within the hierarchy of law due to the fact that they have been transformed into the Constitutional Act and not into an ordinary act. This immediately brings up two problems. Firstly, what will happen if an international treaty is transformed into an ordinary act? Secondly, what about the uncertain relationship between the two pillars of the

---

[9] Article 11, para. 7.

legal system, that is the Constitution and international law? Lawmakers do not agree on which approaches and methods should be applied with respect to international law, and consequently, contradictions will appear in different ways.

Finally, it would be incorrect to assume that Latvia has acceded solely to either monism or dualism because for the time being it is not stated anywhere that international law forms part of domestic law. Within the domestic legal system, international law remains a statement of good intentions or a framework to comply with.

At the same time, legal norms in domestic normative enactments may be interpreted in accordance with international law and most importantly, cases concerning contradictions between domestic law and international law may become a subject-matter for the Constitutional Court to decide on and it might be claimed then that international law is one of the factors influencing domestic law.

3. METHODS APPLIED IN THE PROCESS OF INTERNATIONAL LAW ASSESSMENT AND IMPLEMENTATION

3.1 Consequences of parliamentary consent to the ratification of treaties

The Act on International Treaties of the Republic of Latvia, 26 January 1994. The act in question establishes the procedure for the relevant state authorities to deal with international treaties, beginning with the decision on negotiations, the negotiations themselves, a signature and consent to a treaty by Parliament or the Cabinet. At the same time, it does not elaborate on the status and the application of international treaties in Latvia. Nevertheless, the drafting history of this act shows an interesting approach to international law.

As a consequence of Parliament's consent expressed on 6 April 1993 to ratify the Vienna Convention on the Law of Treaties of May 23 1969, the Convention came into force in accordance with international procedure on 3 June 1993. If Latvia had clearly accepted that international treaties become part of domestic law after domestic consent and international ratification, no domestic act on the same issue would have had to be adopted. This act is an example of a separate domestic act dealing with the same subject-matter as the Convention in question. The difference between the two documents is that our national act does not cover as broad a scope of issues as the Convention does. Obviously, one may assume that if a question which is not covered by the national act arises, it will be solved by reference to the Convention.

The opinion of the Supreme Court of Latvia is that if domestic legislation has not been brought into harmony with international law, international instruments must be applied directly.

As already mentioned above, this practice is not followed consistently. Some acts adopted by Parliament on the approval of international treaties explicitly state that the relevant national acts should be brought into harmony with the treaties in question. In this case, the process of harmonizing national law with international law is the second step after the country has consented to be bound by the international treaty.

International Treaties Priority Clause and Domestic Legislation. In order to understand how the international treaties priority clause works within domestic law, it is necessary to analyse some national acts. The following is the most commonly used legislative formulation of the priority clause:

> "In case of divergence between the norms of the law and an international treaty to which the Republic of Latvia is a party, the norms of the international treaty shall apply".[10]

This clause is written into many acts, for instance, the Act on Patent Rights, the Act on Copyrights, the Act on the Entry and Residence of Foreign Citizens and Stateless Persons in the Republic of Latvia, etc. Article 13, paragraph 1 of the Act on Amendments to the Act on Public Organisations and their Associations stipulates that if the aim of the organisation, as stated in the Statutes of such an organisation, contradicts the Constitution, this act and other national acts as well as ratified conventions or international treaties, the public organisation and its associations shall not be registered.

---

[10] Republic of Latvia Supreme Council (1992) Act 'On the Entry and Residence of Foreign Citizens and Stateless Persons in the Republic of Latvia', *Latvijas Republikas Augstâkâs Padomes un Valdìbas Ziņotâjs* No 27/28 p. 1416.

3.2 Conclusions on the implementation methods used. The legislative power in Latvia tries to create a national legal system which is as complete as possible and which complies with Latvia's international obligations. The process is rather fast, and therefore due to lack of time legislative drafters are perhaps sometimes unable to bring national legislation into harmony with Latvia's international obligations already in the draft stage. Besides lack of time, Latvia also lacks the necessary manpower, information, and technical equipment to speed-up the process. However, it is Latvia's intention to create a legal system that complies with international law, which is also pointed out in the Declaration on the Renewal of the Independence of the Republic of Latvia.

The drafting stage of a domestic piece of legislation consists of two interrelated steps: *first,* while drafting all possible domestic acts, existing international norms are to be kept in mind. *Second,* a comprehensive assessment of the international law binding upon Latvia, including both conventions and customary rules must be carried out. However, the second step is, in fact still, lagging behind the first one, although they are supposed to be simultaneous and supplement each other.

The picture gets even more complicated when the act has been adopted and the priority clause is in force, but no international treaty is binding upon the state. In this respect, the priority clause becomes a statement of good intentions. However, one should keep in mind that in such cases there are no legally binding obligations with respect to the state, but still political commitments and guidelines exist. This is a gap which must be filled by custom or relevant principles of international law.

Overlapping between an international treaty and a domestic act is not something which should be avoided completely as long as they do not contradict each other. However, if the two legal systems contradict each other, the priority clause has to be applied. Another possible problem arises when an already adopted act in its very essence contradicts international standards. In order to solve this problem, the national act must be amended and changed. However, a lot of amendments create a complicated legislative system. Therefore, it is very important to sustain the mutual work mentioned above.

The quite extensive usage of the priority clause in separate domestic acts shows that Latvia's law-makers intend to apply the so-called method of reference when dealing with international law implementation.

Ratification or acceding to any international treaty does not in itself provide for the self-executing status of the norms of a particular treaty. This is part of the whole process to assess of international law. According to some constitutional provisions mentioned before, this does not exclude a situation where a binding treaty or even a custom will be applicable if there is no domestic legislation on a particular matter.

4. CONSEQUENCES OF THE DECLARATION ON THE ACCESSION OF THE REPUBLIC OF LATVIA TO INTERNATIONAL INSTRUMENTS RELATING TO HUMAN RIGHTS

The Declaration deserves some attention not only because of its constitutional status but also because the document includes an extensive list of all the international instruments which Latvia intends to follow. Of course, legally non-binding international instruments do not need to be ratified or acceded to, but nothing prevents the state from expressing its position in a very precise and binding manner. This is exactly what Latvia has done with respect to international declarations and other documents of a political nature. The Declaration recognizes 51 documents to be binding upon Latvia, including the Final Act of the Helsinki Meeting of Representatives of the Participating States on Security and Cooperation in Europe of 1975, the Concluding Document of the Madrid Meeting 1980 of Representatives of the Participating States of the Conference on Security and Cooperation in Europe of 1983, and the Concluding Document of the Vienna Meeting 1986 of Representatives of the Participating States of the Conference on Security and Co-operation in Europe of 1989.

According to the Declaration, Latvia has committed itself to be legally bound even by CSCE/OSCE documents. Obviously, when adopting the Declaration and thus establishing the degree of legal commitment with respect to international human rights, Latvia's law-makers did not draw a distinction between the legal burden of international political commitments, soft law, and international treaties. This means that the general policy and the legislative activities of the state should be governed by these documents. As a consequence of the lack of a clear statement from Parliament on the status of international documents after they have been ratified by Latvia, it is difficult to assume that they directly form part of domestic law, that is article by article. At the same time, they obviously have some impact on the legal system. One can conclude from the previous discussion and the examples being put forward that international treaties and other documents have a certain status within the domestic legal system. However, the scope of the legal or/and judicial nature of these norms within the domestic system remains to be decided by an authoritative institution.

If an individual claims that a principle of soft law which is binding on the state subject to the adopted Declaration has been violated the courts will be expected to decide that the principle in question shall be complied with.

The norms contained in the international instruments listed in the Declaration are made legally binding within the domestic legal system. However, the Declaration is, regardless the question of its constitutional status a unilateral legal act adopted by the highest legislative authority of the state concerned and has a certain position within the hierarchy of domestic law.

Article 9 of the Act on Judical Power stipulates that this particular matter is under the jurisdiction of the Constitutional Court when actions of the state authorities do not comply with the Constitution, the Constitutional Acts or international treaties. Now the question is what relation the Declaration might have with respect to Article 9? First of all, the court would be expected to take due account of soft law also.

Following a communication stating that Latvia has fulfilled its constitutional requirements in order to make the two International Covenants on Human Rights binding, these documents became binding on Latvia on 14 July 1992. The next step taken by the law-makers was the adoption of the Constitutional Act on The Rights and Obligations of Citizens and Persons. In this context, it was discussed to what extent civil and political rights as well as economic, social and cultural rights are justiciable in Latvia due to the binding status of the two Covenants and the constitutional status of domestic law on this issue. Much evidence shows that civil and political rights are covered by domestic judical procedure. These rights are elaborated further in the following domestic legislative acts:

the Criminal Code;

the Civil Code;
the Labour Code;
the Code of Administrative Violations, and
the Criminal Procedure Code.

The Civil Procedure Code that is presently under amendment and revision by the working groups as well as the Criminal Code, and the Code of Administrative Violations[11], make civil and political rights justiciable to a large extent[12].

5. GENERAL CONCLUSIONS

There are two prospective methods to deal with human rights. The one is the so-called formal method which requires that the status of international treaties becomes clear and that the question on how to apply the treaties in the country is answered. The second method is to deal with the substance of human rights - an approach which is of course, connected with the first method. It implies that a procedure or

---

[11] The work is being performed on Administrative Procedure Code and Penal Code.

[12] The right to life (Covenant on Civil and Political Rights (CCPR), Art. 6) is elaborated on in detail in the majority of the articles of the Criminal Code forbidding any arbitrary interference with the right to life. No one shall be subjected to torture (CCPR Art. 7): The procedure of an investigation is prescribed by the relevant articles in the Criminal Procedure Code, Article 111 of the Criminal Code establishes criminal liability for performing torture. Right to liberty (CCPR Art. 9): Article 125 of the Criminal Code establishes criminal liability for unlawful depriviation of liberty, the grounds for detention are set forth in detail by the Criminal Procedure Code, maximum period for the accused juvenile to be detained in custody is 6 months, Article 252 of the Code of Administrative Violations establishes the ground of the depriviation of liberty and Article 253 establishes the terms of the depriviation. (CCPR Art. 11): This is not a ground for imprisonment according to Latvian legislation. (CCPR Art. 12 & 13): Very detailed domestic legislation on how to move within the country, how to enter the country with the possibility to claim one's right to remain or enter the country being violated with the relevant state authority and court. (CCPR Art. 14): All principles are put into the Criminal Procedure Code and non-compliance with it is entitled to retrial, and many other procedures that guarantee rights of the parties in a court. (CCPR Art. 15): The principle of non-retroactivity of the law is a basic principle of criminal law in Latvia. (CCPR Art. 17): Article 132 of the Criminal Code establishes criminal liability for unlawful interference with correspondence or home. (CCPR Art. 18): Violation of the right to freedom of religion is punishable according to Article 137 of the Criminal Code. (CCPR Art. 24): Article 22 of the Law on The Civil Status of a Person obliges for the registration of a new-born child within one month and further articles provides with the mechanism for giving a name and citizenship to a child.

a mechanism to make human rights justiciable is established. Today, the situation is quite complicated due to the fact that a lot of acts and different procedures may to some extent be relevant when blaiming a human rights violation but they are not based on human rights instruments. What is needed if human rights are to be protected as constitutional rights because of the adoption of the Constitutional Act is a procedure that enables an individual to claim a violation of his/her constitutional rights. Due to the fact that the constitutional status of the Constitutional Act on the Rights and Obligations of Citizens and Persons is somewhat open, the intention of the law-makers in Latvia is to include this act in the Constitution as a second part of the Constitution.

To sum up the situation envisaged above, it is possible to say that Latvia's law-makers have to agree upon principles which will be given attention in the process of developing the domestic legal system. A specific act on the status and application of international law or an extra article in the Constitution which provides whether Latvia accedes to monism or dualism when applying international law is needed. Because the principle on the priority of international treaties over national law has become very well established in the legal system of Latvia, the adoption of an ordinary act on the status of international treaties in Latvia would compromise the principle with respect to any national law. Therefore, the established status of international treaties in the Constitution seems to be the right approach.

If review of normative enactments in administrative cases becomes an established competence of the Constitutional Court, it will mark a step forward in setting up a local procedure enabling individuals to base complaints on the Constitutional Act on the Rights and Obligations of Citizens and Persons or a prospective second part of the Constitution. At the present stage, it is worthwhile to point out that the Constitutional Act is a rather precise copy of the European Convention on Human Rights.[13]

As Latvia has acceded to the Optional Protocol to the Covenant On Civil and Political Rights on 26 May 1994, and accordingly to the complaint procedure before the Human Rights Committee, there is an

---

[13] *Editor's note:* On 10 February 1995, Latvia became a member of the Council of Europe and signed the European Convention on Human Rights. See, Council of Europe Press Release 68 (95).

urgent need to clarify the status of this accession with respect to the various domestic legal procedures. Obviously, the method of implementation of the Covenant in question, as well as of other human rights instruments, depends on Latvia's choice between a monistic or a dualistic approach to international law. Until now the development with respect to international law, as well as to human rights instruments has been of an accidental nature in the most cases because the decision on the relations between international law and national law is still to be made and the establishment of the mechanism of implementation and application of national laws, as well as international norms is still in the process. Still, the development is governed by the clear wish of the state to comply with international standards.

REFERENCES

Act On Judicial Power, 15 December 1992.

Act On Republic of Latvia International Treaties, 26 January 1994.

Act On Religious Organisations, 11 September 1990.

Draft Act On the Constitutional (Satversme) Court, (submitted for first reading at the Parliamentary Plenary Session, Document No. 608).

Draft Act On Religious Organisations, (revised version of the Parliamentary Human Rights Committee prepared for second reading, not yet submitted).

First Draft of the Initial Report of the Republic of Latvia On the International Covenant on Civil and Political Rights, July 1994.

Report On Children's Rights in Latvia, 21 July 1994, (assessment of situation under the auspicies of the Governmental Commission On Defence on Children's Rights).

Republic of Latvia 5th Saeima Standing Commission on Human Rights (eds.) (1993): *Human Rights Issues*, Compilation of documents and materials.

ANNEXES

1. Declaration of the Supreme Soviet of the Latvian SSR on the Renewal of the Independence of the Republic of Latvia.

2. Declaration on the Accession of the Republic of Latvia to International Instruments Relating to Human Rights.
3. Constitution of the Republic of Latvia.
4. Constitutional Law: The Rights and Obligations of a Citizen and a Person.
   - Resolution on the Order in Which the Republic of Latvia Constitutional Law "The Rights and Obligations of a Citizen and a Person" Takes Effect.

Annex 1

DECLARATION

OF THE SUPREME SOVIET OF THE LATVIAN SSR ON THE RENEWAL OF THE INDEPENDENCE OF THE REPUBLIC OF LATVIA

The independent state of Latvia, founded on November 18, 1918, was granted international recognition in 1920 and became a member of the League of Nations in 1921. The Latvian Nation's right to self-determination was implemented in April, 1920, when the people of Latvia gave their mandate to the Constituent Assembly chosen by universal, equal, direct and proportional elections. In February, 1922, the Assembly adopted the Constitution of the Republic of Latvia, which is still in effect *de jure*. The ultimatum of June 16, 1940, from the Stalinist government of the USSR to the Latvian Government, asking for its resignation, and the following military aggression, constitute international crimes, which resulted in the occupation of Latvia and the liquidation of its statehood. The new government of Latvia was formed by the dictate of the government of the USSR. According to international law, this government did not represent the executive authority of the sovereign Republic of Latvia, since it represented the interests of the USSR instead of those of Latvia.

The elections of July 14 and 15, 1940, to the Parliament (Saeima) of occupied Latvia were held under conditions of political terror after an illegal and unconstitutional election law had been adopted. Of the 17 lists of candidates submitted, only one was permitted in the elections - the list of the Working People's Bloc. The pre-election platform of this bloc did not include any demand to establish Soviet power in Latvia or to join the Soviet Union. Moreover, the results of the elections were falsified. Thus, the illegally and fraudulently formed Parliament did not represent the will of the Latvian people. It had no constitutional powers to change the governmental system and liquidate the sovereignty of Latvia. Only the people had the right to decide on these matters, but no referendum was held. Hence, according to international law, the incorporation of Latvia into the Soviet Union is invalid. Accordingly, the Republic of Latvia continues to exist *de jure* as a subject of international law and is recognized as such by more than 50 nations of the world.

Taking into account the "Declaration on the Sovereignty of the Latvian State" adopted by the Supreme Soviet of the Latvian SSR on July 28, 1989; the "Declaration on the Question of the Independence of the Latvian State" adopted by the Latvian Supreme Soviet on February 15, 1990; and the "Appeal of the All-Latvia Meeting of People's Deputies" of April 21, 1990;

Observing the will of the inhabitants of Latvia, which was unmistakably expressed by the election to the Latvian Supreme Soviet of a majority of deputies who had expressed the determination to restore the independence of the Republic of Latvia;

Being determined to restore *de facto* the free, democratic and independent Republic of Latvia,

The Supreme Soviet of the Latvia SSR d e c i d e s:

1. To recognize the supremacy of the fundamental principles of international law over national law and to consider illegal the treaty of August 23, 1939, between the USSR and Germany, and the subsequent liquidation of the sovereignty of the Republic of Latvia on June 17, 1940, which was the result of Soviet military aggression.

2. To declare null and void from the moment of inception the decision of July 21, 1940, by the Parliament of Latvia: "On the Republic of Latvia's Joining the USSR".

3. To re-establish the authority of the Constitution of the Republic of Latvia, adopted by the Constituent Assembly on February 15, 1922, in the entire territory of Latvia. The official name of the Latvian state is "The Republic of Latvia", abbreviated as "Latvia".

4. Until the adoption of a revised constitution, to suspend the Constitution of the Republic of Latvia, except for the articles expressing the constitutional and legal foundation of the Latvian state, which, according to Article 77 of the Constitution, can be changed only by popular referendum:
Article 1 - Latvia is an independent, democratic republic;
Article 2 - The sovereign power of the Latvian state belongs to the people of Latvia;
Article 3 - The territory of the Latvian state shall consist of Vidzeme, Latgale, Kurzeme and Zemgale, within the boundaries stipulated by international treaties;
Article 6 - The Saeima is elected by universal, equal, direct and secret vote on the basis of proportional representation.

The application of Article 6 will follow the renewal of those state and adminsitrative structures of Latvia which guarantee free elections.

5. To set a transition period for the re-establishment of the *de facto* independence of the Republic of Latvia, which will conclude with the convening of the Parliament of Latvia. During the transition period, supreme state power in Latvia is held by the Parliament of Latvia.

6. During the transition period, to implement those constitutional and other legal acts of the Latvian SSR which are in effect in Latvia when this Declaration is adopted, insofar as they do not contradict Articles 1, 2, 3 and 6 of the Constitution of the Republic of Latvia. Conflicts of law are resolved by the Constitutional Court of Latvia.

7. To form a commission for revising the Constitution of the Republic of Latvia, so that it corresponds to the present political, economic and social situation in Latvia.

8. To guarantee citizens of the Republic of Latvia and those of other nations permanently residing in Latvia social, economic and cultural rights, as well as those political rights and freedoms which are defined in international human rights instruments. To apply these rights also to those citizens of the USSR who express the desire to continue living in the territory of Latvia.

9. To develop relations between Latvia and the USSR in accordance with the Peace Treaty between Latvia and Russia of August 11, 1920, which is still in force and which recognizes the independence of Latvia for all time. To establish a Government Commission for conducting negotiations with the USSR.

This act takes effect from the moment of its adoption.

May 4, 1990, in Riga

A. Gorbunovs
Chairman of the Supreme Soviet
of the Latvian SSR

I. Daudišs
Secretary of the Supreme Soviet
of the Latvian SSR

ANNEX 2

REPUBLIC OF LATVIA
SUPREME COUNCIL

DECLARATION
ON THE ACCESSION OF THE REPUBLIC OF LATVIA TO INTERNATIONAL INSTRUMENTS RELATING TO HUMAN RIGHTS

Recognizing that all human beings are born free and equal in rights;

Mindful of the determination proclaimed by the people of the world in the Charter of the United Nations to affirm faith in fundamental human rights, in the worth of the human person, in the equality and right to self-determination of nations large and small;

Considering it necessary to promote social progress and justice;

Conscious of the need for the creation of conditions of stability and well-being and peaceful and friendly relations, and of the observance of human rights and freedoms for all without distinction as to race, sex, language, religion, or national or social origin;

Considering the important role of the United Nations in assisting the movement for independence in Trust and Non-Self-Governing Territories;

Convinced of the right of all peoples to freely determine their political status and to pursue their economic, social and cultural development;

Considering that all armed actions or repressive measures of all kinds directed against dependent peoples should cease in order to enable them to exercise peacefully and freely their right to complete independence, and that the integrity of their national territory should be respected;

Recognizing what was declared in the Act of Proclamation of the Republic of Latvia of 18 November, 1918: "... all citizens, irrespective of nationality, are asked to help, for the rights of all peoples will be guaranteed in Latvia. It will be democratic and just state where oppression and injustice will not exist...";

Desiring that the laws of the Republic of Latvia conform to the norms of international law relating to human rights;

the Supreme Council of the Republic of Latvia p r o c l a i m s :

I

Acknowledging the special significance in guaranteeing human rights of international instruments adopted by the UN and its specialized agencies, as well as those adopted at the Helsinki, Madrid and Vienna meetings of the Conference on Security and Cooperation in Europe, the Republic of Latvia accedes to the following international instruments:

1. Universal Declaration of Human Rights 10 December 1948
2. International Covenant on Economic, Social and Cultural Rights 16 December 1966
3. International Covenant on Civil and Political Rights 16 December 1966
4. Declaration on the Granting of Independence to Colonial Countries and Peoples 14 December 1960
5. International Convention on the Elimination of all Forms of Racial Discrimination 21 December 1965
6. International Convention on the Suppression and Punishment of the Crime of *Apartheid* 30 November 1973
7. International Convention against *Apartheid* in Sports 10 December 1985
8. Convention against discrimination in Education 14 December 1960
9. Equal Remuneration Convention 29 June 1951
10. Convention on the Elimination of All Forms of Discrimination against Women 18 December 1979
11. Convention on the Elimination of All Forms of Intolerance and Discrimination Based on Religion or Belief 25 November 1981
12. Declaration on the Fundamental Principles concerning the Contribution of the Mass Media to Strengthening Peace and International Understanding, to the Promotion of Human Rights and to Countering Racialism, *Apartheid* and Incitement to War 28 November 1968
13. Convention on the Prevention and Punishment of the Crime of Genocide 9 December 1948
14. Convention on the Non-Applicability of Statutory Limitations to War Crimes and Crimes against Humanity 26 November 1968
15. Principles of international co-operation in the detection, arrest, extradition and punishment of persons guilty of war crimes and crimes against humanity 3 December 1973
16. Supplementary Convention on the Abolition of Slavery, the Slave Trade, and Institutions and Practices Similar to Slavery 7 September 1956
17. Abolition of Forced Labour Convention 25 June 1957
18. Convention for the Suppression of the Traffic in Persons and of the Exploitation of the Prostitution of Others 2 December 1949
19. Standard Minimum Rules for the Treatment of Prisoners 30 August 1955
20. Convention against Torture and Other Cruel, Inhuman or Degrading Treatment or Punishment 10 December 1984
21. Code of Conduct for Law Enforcement Officials 17 December 1979
22. Principles of Medical Ethics relevant to the Role of Health Personnel, particularly Physicians, in the Protection of Prisoners and Detainees against Torture and Other Cruel, Inhuman or Degrading Treatment or Punishment 18 December 1982
23. Safeguards guaranteeing protection of the rights of those facing the death penalty 25 May 1984
24. United Nations Standard Minimum Rules for the Administration of Juvenile Justice ("The Beijing Rules") 29 November 1985
25. Declaration of Basic Principles of Justice for Victims of Crime and Abuse of Power 29 November 1985
26. Basic Principles on the Independence of the Judiciary 29 November 1985
27. Convention on the Nationality of Married Women 29 January 1957
28. Convention on the Reduction of Statelessness 20 August 1961
29. Declaration on the Human Rights of Individuals Who are not Nationals of the Country in which They Live 13 December 1985
30. Convention on the International Right of Correction 16 December 1952

31. Freedom of Association and Protection of the Right to Organise Convention 9 July 1948
32. Right to Organise and Collective Bargaining Convention 1 July 1949
33. Workers' Representatives Convention 23 June 1971
34. Labour Relations (Public Service) Convention 27 June 1978
35. Employment Policy Convention 9 July 1964
36. Convention on the Political Rights of Women 20 December 1952
37. Declaration of the Rights of the Child 20 November 1959
38. Declaration on the Protection of Women and Children in Emergency and Armed Conflict 14 December 1974
39. Declaration on the Promotion among Youth of the Ideals of Peace, Mutual Respect and Understanding between Peoples 7 December 1965
40. Declaration on Social and Legal Principles relating to the Protection and Welfare of Children, with Special Reference to Foster Placement and Adoption Nationally and Internationally 3 December 1986
41. Declaration on the Rights of Mentally Retarded Persons 20 December 1971
42. Universal Declaration on the Eradication of Hunger and Malnutrition 16 November 1974
43. Declaration on the Rights of Disabled Persons 9 December 1975
44. General Assembly Resolution 41/114 4 December 1986
45. Declaration on the Right of Peoples to Peace 12 November 1984
46. Declaration on the Right to Development 4 December 1986
47. General Assembly Resolution 41/117 4 December 1986
48. Declaration of the Principles of International Cultural Co-operation 4 November 1966
49. The Final Act of the Helsinki Meeting of Representatives of the Participating States of the Conference on Security and Co-operation in Europe 1975
50. The Concluding Document of the Madrid Meeting 1980 of Representatives of the Participating States of the Conference on Security and Co-operation in Europe 1983
51. The Concluding Document of the Vienna Meeting 1986 of Representatives of the Participating States of the Conference on Security and Co-operation in Europe 1989

II

Acknowledging the role of the Council of Europe and the European Parliament in guaranteeing human rights, the Supreme Council of the Republic of Latvia will be guided in its legislative activities by the documents relating to human rights adopted by these organisations.

Riga, May 4, 1990

A. Gorbunovs
Chairman, Supreme Council
Republic of Latvia

I. Daudišs
Secretary, Supreme Council
Republic of Latvia

The authenticity of the translation is confirmed by Secretary of the Supreme Council of the Republic of Latvia. For purposes of interpretation, the original Latvian text is to be regarded as official.

I. Daudišs

ANNEX 3

CONSTITUTION
OF THE REPUBLIC OF LATVIA

Passed by the Constituent Assembly at its meeting of February 15th, 1922, and come into force on November 7th, 1922.

The Latvian people have adopted, through their freely elected Constituent Assembly, the following Constitution:

SECTION 1
General Regulations

1. Latvia shall be an independent democratic Republic.

2. The sovereign power of the Latvian State shall belong to the People of Latvia.

3. The territory of the Latvian State shall consist of Livonia, Latgale, Courland and Zemgale, within the boundaries stipulated by international treaties.

4. The national flag of the Latvian State shall be red with a white stripe.

SECTION 2
The Saeima (Parliament)

5. The Saeima shall consist of one hundred representatives of the people.

6. The Saeima shall be elected by universal, equal, direct and secret vote, on the basis of proportional representation.

7. Latvia being divided into separate electoral districts, the number of parliamentary representatives to be elected from each district shall be proportionate to the number of electors in that district.

8. Latvian citizens of both sexes, who are in possession of all rights and who are over twenty-one years of age on the first day of polling, shall have the right to vote.

9. Any Latvian citizen who is over twenty-one years of age on the first day of voting, may be elected to the Saeima.

10. The Saeima shall be elected for a period of three years.

11. The parliamentary elections shall take place on the first Sunday in october and on the preceding Saturday.

12. The newly-elected Saeima shall hold its first sitting on the first Tuesday in November, on which day the powers of the previous Saeima shall have expired.

13. Should the parliamentary election, by reason of the dissolution of the previous Saeima, take place at another season of the year, the Saeima thus elected shall assemble not later than one month after its election, and its powers shall expire after two years, on the first Tuesday in November, on which day a new Saeima shall assemble.

14. The electors may not recall any Members of the Saeima.

15. The Saeima shall assemble in Riga. It may assemble elsewhere only in extraordinary circumstances.

16. The Saeima shall elect its Board, which shall consist of the President, his two Deputies and Secretaries. The Board of the Saeima shall carry on its work uninterrupted throughout the duration of the legislative period.

17. The first sitting of the newly-elected Saeima shall be opened by the President of the preceding Saeima or by any other member of the Board charged by the Board.

18. The Saeima itself shall examine the mandates of its members.

19. The Board shall convene sessions and decree ordinary and extraordinary sitting.

20. The Board shall convoke a sitting of the Saeima at the request of either the President of the State, the Prime Minister, or not less than one-third of the Members of the Saeima.

21. The Saeima shall draw up the Standing Orders for the regulation of its activities and its internal procedure.

22. The sitting of the Saeima shall be public. At the request of ten Members of the Saeima, the President of the State, the Prime Minister or any one Minister, the Saeima may decide, by a majority of not less than two-thirds of the members present, to sit in camera.

23. The sittings of the Saeima may take place if at least one-half of the members are present.

24. Except in cases otherwise provided for by the Constitution, the Saeima shall pass its resolutions by the absolute majority vote of the members present.

25. The Saeima shall elect Committees, determine the number of their members and their duties. The Committees shall be entitled to request the respective Ministers and Local Authorities to supply any information necessary for their work, and also to invite responsible representatives of the respective Ministries and Local Authorities to their meetings, for the purpose of obtaining explanations. The Committees may carry on their work between the Sessions.

26. At the request of not less than one-third of its members, the Saeima shall appoint parliamentary Enquiry Committees to deal with special cases.

27. The Saeima shall have the right to address to the Prime Minister, or to any other Minister, interpellations or questions to which they, or responsible officials empowered by them, shall reply.

At the request of either the Saeima or its Committees, the Prime Minister, or any other Minister, shall place at their disposal relevant papers and documents.

28. The Members of the Saeima shall be exempt from judicial, administrative and disciplinary prosecution, in connection with their voting and with ideas expressed in the execution of their duties. Member of the Saeima, even in their public capacity, are liable to prosecution, if - 1) they wilfully spread defamatory information, or - 2) they spread defamatory information about private or family life.

29. Members of the Saeima may not be arrested or searched, nor may their personal liberty be restricted in any way, without the sanction of the Saeima. Members of the Saeima shall be liable to arrest if apprehended in the act of committing a crime. The arrest of a Member of the Saeima shall be brought to the notice of the Board of the Saeima within twenty-four hours. A report shall be presented by the Board at the next sitting of the Saeima, whereupon the Saeima shall decide as to whether the member shall be retained under arrest or liberated. During the period between the sessions, the Board of the Saeima shall decide the question of the retention under arrest of a Member of the Saeima.

30. A Member of the Saeima shall not be liable to judicial or administrative prosecution for criminal actions, without the consent of the Saeima.

31. The Member of the Saeima shall have the right to withhold evidence:

1) concerning persons who have entrusted him, as a Representative of the People, certain facts or data;

2) concerning persons to whom he, as a Representative of the People, has entrusted certain facts or data;

3) concerning such facts and data.

32. Members of the Saeima may not undertake Government Contract or receive Government concessions in their name or in that of any other person. The stipulations of this Article shall refer to Ministers, even if they are not members of the Saeima.

33. Members of the Saeima shall receive remuneration from State funds.

34. No person shall be prosecuted for circulating reports about sittings of the Saeima or its Committees, if such reports correspond to facts. Accounts of sittings in camera, of either the Saeima or its Committees, may only be published with the sanction of the Board of either the Saeima or the respective Committees.

SECTION 3

The President of the State

35. The President of the State shall be elected by the Saeima for a period of three years.

36. The President of the State shall be elected by secret ballot with a majority of not less than fifty-one votes.

37. No person who is under forty years of age may be elected President of the State.

38. The office of President of the State shall not be compatible with any other office. If the elected President be a member of the Saeima, he shall resign his membership.

39. The same person cannot hold office as President of the State for more than six consecutive years.

40. On assuming office at the first meeting of the Saeima after his election, the President of the State shall make the following solemn declaration: "I swear that all my work shall be devoted to the good of the Latvian people. I will do everything in my power to promote the welfare of the State of Latvia and its inhabitants. I will heed and keep sacred the Constitution of Latvia and its laws. I will be just to everyone and will fulfill my duties to the best of my ability".

41. The President of the State shall represent the State in an international capacity: he shall accredit Latvian representatives abroad, and receive accredited representatives of foreign States. He shall carry out the decisions of the Saeima concerning the ratification of international treaties.

42. The President of the State shall be the chief of the armed forces of the State. In the time of war, he shall appoint a Commander-in-Chief.

43. The President of the State shall declare war on the strength of the decision of the Saeima.

44. The President of the State shall have the right to take steps indispensable to the military defence of the country if another State shall have declared war on Latvia, or if the enemy shall be attacking Latvian frontiers. At the same time, the President of the State shall immediately convoke the Saeima, which shall decide upon the declaration of war and opening of hostilities.

45. The President of the State shall have the right to pardon criminals undergoing penal sentences. This right of pardon shall not refer to cases for which the Law provides a different mode of pardon. Amnesty shall be granted by the Saeima.

46. The President of the State shall have the right to convoke extraordinary meetings of the Cabinet for the discussion of an agenda prepared by him, and to preside over such meetings.

47. The President of the State shall have the right of legislative initiative.

48. The President of the State shall have the right to propose the dissolution of the Saeima. This shall be followed by a referendum. If in the referendum more than one-half of the votes are cast in favour of dissolution, the Saeima shall be considered as dissolved and new elections shall be proclaimed. These elections shall take place within two months of the dissolution of the Saeima.

49. On the dissolution of the Saeima, its members shall retain their powers until the newly-elected Saeima shall have assembled. The former Saeima may only assemble on being convoked by the President of the State, who shall draw up agenda for its sitting.

50. If the dissolution of the Saeima is opposed by more than one-half of the votes cast when the referendum is taken, the President of the State shall be considered as having resigned, and the Saeima shall elect a new President of the State for the duration of the unexpired of office of the President who has resigned.

51. On the motion of not less than one-half of the Members of the Saeima, the Saeima, at the sitting to which the public is not admitted, may decide by a majority of not less than two-thirds of their number, to dismiss the President of the State. After this decision, the Saeima shall immediately elect a new President of the State.

52. Should the President of the State resign his office, die or be dismissed before the expiry of his term of office, the duties shall be carried out by the President of the Saeima, pending the election of a new President of the State. Likewise the President of the Saeima shall take the place of the President of the State, should the latter be absent from Latvian territory, or in any other way prevented from exercising his functions.

53. The President of the State shall not be held responsible for his activities. All decrees of the President of the state shall be countersigned by the Prime Minister, or by the Minister concerned, who shall thereby assume full responsibility for the decrees, except in cases foreseen by Articles forty-eight and fifty-six.

54. The President of the State may be prosecuted for criminal offences with the sanction of the Saeima, by a majority of not less than two-thirds of its members.

SECTION 4
The Cabinet

55. The Cabinet shall consist of the Prime Minister and Ministers invited by him.

56. The Cabinet shall be formed by a person entrusted who that task by the President of the State.

57. The number of Ministers and the scope of their activities, as the mutual relations of Government Departments shall be fixed by Law.

58. The administrative institutions shall be subordinated to the Cabinet.

59. In the execution of their functions, the Prime Minister and Ministers shall by necessity enjoy the confidence of the Saeima and shall be responsible to the Saeima for their activities. Should the Saeima defeat the vote of confidence in the Prime Minister, the whole Cabinet shall resign. Should the Saeima defeat the vote of confidence in any particular Minister, that Minister shall resign and the Prime Minister shall invite another person to take his place.

60. The meetings of the Cabinet shall be presided over by the Prime Minister, or, in his absence, by another Minister so empowered by the Prime Minister.

61. The cabinet shall discuss all Bills drawn up by the separate Ministries and all questions concerning the activities of various ministries; likewise all questions of State policy, put forward by individual members of the Cabinet.

62. If the State be threatened by foreign invasion, or, if in the State or part thereof, disorders endangering the existing order of the State arise, the Cabinet shall have the right to proclaim a state of enforced defence. The Cabinet shall notify such a proclamation of the Board the Saeima within twenty-four hours, and the Board shall put it before the Saeima without delay.

63. Ministers, even if they are not Members of the Saeima, and responsible State officials empowered by Ministers, shall have the right to be present at the sittings of the Saeima or its Committees, and to introduce additions and amendments to Bills.

SECTION 5
Legislation

64. The right of legislation shall belong to both the Saeima and to the people, within the limits laid down in this Constitution.

65. Bills may be presented to the Saeima by the President of the State, the Cabinet, the Committees of the Saeima, not less than five Members of the Saeima or, in cases and in a manner provided for in this Constitution, by one-tenth of the electors.

66. Before the commencement of each financial year, the Saeima shall pronounce on the State Revenue and Expenditure Budget, the draft of which shall be submitted by the Cabinet.
If the Saeima pass a resolution involving expenditure not foreseen in the Budget, it shall likewise specify in this resolution the sources of revenue with which to meet such expenditure. After the expiry of the financial year, the Cabinet shall submit, for the confirmation of the Saeima, a statement showing the actual realisation of the Budget.

67. The Saeima shall decide on the strength of the armed forces of the State in time of peace.

68. The ratification of the Saeima shall be indispensable to all international agreements dealing with questions to be settled by legislation.

69. The President of the State shall promulgate laws passed by the Saeima not before the seventh and not later than twenty-first day after their adoption. If no other term be fixed, the laws shall come into force fourteen days after their promulgation.

70. The President of the State shall promulgate laws by means of the following formula: "The Saeima (or the People) have adopted and the President of the State promulgates the following law:" (text of the law).

71. Within seven days of the adoption of a law by the Saeima, the President of the State shall be entitled to ask, by means of explanatory letter addressed to the President of the Saeima, for the revision of that law. If the Saeima leave the law unaltered, the President of the State shall not have the right to raise any further objections.

72. The President of the State shall have the right to withhold the promulgation of a law for a period of two months. He shall postpone the promulgation at the request of not less than one-third of the Members of the Saeima. This right shall be exercised by the President of the State or by one-third of the Members of the Saeima within seven days of the adoption of the law by the Saeima. The law, the promulgation of which has been thus postponed, shall be submitted to a referendum, if not less than one-tenth of the electors so desire. Should such request not be formulated within the period of two months as mentioned above, the law shall be promulgated at the expiry of that period. The referendum shall not be taken, however, if the Saeima put this law to the vote once more and if then not less than three-fourths of all the members be in favour of its adoption.

73. The following matters shall not be submitted to a referendum: the budget, laws concerning loans, taxes, custom's duties, railway tariffs, military service, the declaration and commencement of war, the conclusion of peace, the promulgation of a state of enforced defence termination, mobilisation, demobilisation, foreign treaties.

74. A law adopted by the Saeima and postponed in the manner set forth in Article 72, may be annulled by a referendum, if at least one-half of those who have the right to vote shall take part in the suffrage.

75. Should the Saeima adopt the urgency of a law with a majority of not less than two-thirds, the President of the State may not demand a second examination of the law; it may not be submitted to a referendum and shall be promulgated within three days of its transmission to the President.

76. The Saeima may modify the Constitution at sittings at which at least two-thirds of its members shall be present. The modification shall be passed in the course of three readings, by a majority of not less than two thirds of the members present.

77. If the Saeima has modified the first, second, third or sixth Articles of the Constitution, such amendments, in order to acquire the force of Law, shall be submitted to a referendum.

78. Not less then one-tenth of the electors shall have the right to submit to the President of the State a fully elaborated scheme for the revision of the Constitution, or a Bill, which shall be submitted to the Saeima by the President. Should it not be accepted by the Saeima without substantial amendments, it shall be submitted to a referendum.

79. Such amendments to the Constitution as shall have been submitted to a referendum shall be adopted if at least one-half of those who have the right to vote shall have declared themselves in their favour.

80. All Latvian citizens who have the right to vote in the election of the Saeima are entitled to take part in the referendum.

81. In cases of urgent necessity between session, the Cabinet shall have the right to issue regulations which shall have the force of Law. These regulations shall not modify: the law of election to the Saeima, laws bearing on judicial constitution and procedure, the budget rights, and laws passed by the Saeima then in power; they shall not refer to amnesty, the issue of Treasury notes, State taxes, custom's duties, railway tariffs, loans and they shall be annulled if not presented to the Saeima within three days of the opening of the following session.

SECTION 6

Courts of Justice

82. All citizens shall be equal before the Law and the Courts of Justice.

83. The judges shall be independent and bound only by Law.

84. The appointment of judges shall be confirmed by the Saeima and they may not be dismissed. Judges may not be dismissed from their office against their will, unless it be the decision of the Courts of Justice. The retiring age limit for judges may be fixed by Law.

85. Trial by jury shall exist in Latvia in accordance with a special Law.

86. Justice shall be administered solely by such institutions as shall have been so entitled by Law and in such a manner as shall have been specified by Law. The Courts-Martial shall function in accordance with a special law.

SECTION 7
State Control

87. The state control shall be an independent collegiate institution.

88. The State Controllers shall be appointed and confirmed in the same manner as the judges, but only for a definite period. During the period their appointment shall not be revoked, except by the decision of the Courts of Justice. The organisation of the State Control and the competency thereof shall be fixed by a special law.

J. Tschakste
President of the
Constituent Assembly

R.Ivanovs
Secretary of the
Constituent Assembly

ANNEX 4

REPUBLIC OF LATVIA
SUPREME COUNCIL

CONSTITUTIONAL LAW
THE RIGHTS AND OBLIGATIONS OF A CITIZEN AND A PERSON

(Translation)

SECTION I
General Regulations

Article 1. A person, his/her existence, freedom, honor and rights are the highest fundamental values of the State of Latvia.

Article 2. Each person has the right to all actions which are not prohibited by law.

Article 3. The State's responsibility is to protect each person, his/her existence, freedom, security, honor, rights and property.

SECTION II
Citizenship, the Rights and Obligations of a Citizen

Article 4. Republic of Latvia citizenship is a person's stable political and legal link with the Republic of Latvia.

The content of citizenship is shaped by the totality of the mutually binding rights and responsibilities of the citizen and the State.

Article 5. The rights and responsibilities of all citizens are equal, regardless of the manner in which citizenship is obtained.

Republic of Latvia citizenship may be obtained, maintained and lost only according to the procedures stipulated by law.

Upon becoming a Republic of Latvia citizen, dual citizenship cannot be created.

Article 6. The Republic of Latvia does not extradite its citizens.

Article 7. Republic of Latvia citizens abroad are under the protection of the State of Latvia.

Article 8. Citizens participate in the determination of state and social issues directly or through the mediation of freely-elected representatives.

Citizens have equal rights to hold state office. Citizens have the right to establish political parties.

Article 9. Land and other natural resources may be transferred into ownership or sold only to citizens, except for those cases for which international treaties signed by the Republic of Latvia determine a different procedure.

Article 10. A citizen may freely choose his/her residence in any part of Latvia's territory.

Citizens have the right to freely leave Latvia and to freely return to Latvia.

Article 11. A citizen must be loyal to the Republic of Latvia and has the right and responsibility to defend its freedom, independence and democratic parliamentary system.

A citizen must fulfill mandatory state service and other obligations to the state as determined by law.

A citizen has the right to possess registered weapons.

SECTION III
Rights and Obligations of a Person

Article 12. All persons in Latvia are equal under the law regardless of race, nationality, sex, language, party affiliation, political and religious persuasion, social, material and occupational standing and origin.

Article 13. The death penalty can be determined by a court only in exceptional cases for particularly serious crimes.

Article 14. Each person has the right to resist unlawful violence with all existing legal means at his/her disposal.

Article 15. Detainment, imprisonment, searches or other restrictions of a person's freedom are permissible only in accordance with the procedures stipulated by law.

Each person is guaranteed the right to an attorney upon the moment of his/her detention.

The law determines the maximum terms of detainment, imprisonment and preliminary investigation.

Within seventy-two hours from a person's detention, a judge must issue a court order to sanction the person's arrest and further detention or to order the immediate release of such person.

Torture or other cruel, inhumane or degrading treatment of a person is prohibited.

Unlawful forced medical treatment, as well as the forced use of medicine for the purpose of obtaining from a person his/her testimony, his/her refusal to testify his/her statement of a particular viewpoint, or for the purpose to restrict the person's freedom of expression, is prohibited.

Article 16. A person's residence is inviolable.

No person has the right to enter a residence without the permission of its residents or to conduct a search without the order of a judge, except for those instances when a person is being detained at the scene of a crime or the lives of other persons are endangered.

Article 17. The State guarantees the confidentiality of correspondence, telephone conversations, telegraph and other communications.

These rights may be restricted by a judge's order for the investigation of serious crimes.

Article 18. Each person has the right to defend his/her rights and interests in court.

Each person is presumed innocent as long as his/her guilt is not proven in court in accordance with law.

Only the court may find a person guilty of a crime in accordance with the laws in effect at the time of the offense.

Each person has the right to a just, public review of his/her matter by a competent, independent and objective court, which is formed in accordance with law.

Each person has the right to the assistance of an attorney, as well as the right not to testify against him/herself and his/her family members.

Criminal responsibility may only be individual.

Each unlawfully arrested or convicted person has the right to compensation for his/her material and moral injuries.

Article 19. Convicted persons have all the human rights mentioned in this Law, except those which are restricted by law or by the court's order.

Each convicted person must work according to his/her physical and mental abilities.

Convicted persons may not be deprived of their rights to paid employment, as well as to rest, health care, the exercise of established cultural values, education and personal development.

Article 20. Forced labour is prohibited.

Mandatory state service involvement in the liquidation of disastrous effects and reformatory labour prescribed in accordance with a court order are not considered to be forced labour.

Article 21. The State recognizes and protects property and its rights of inheritance.

A person may own any property, except for property referred to in the restrictions stated in Article 9.

The forced expropriation of property shall occur solely by a court decision in accordance with the procedures prescribed by law. If the property is expropriated for the realization of a public project, then appropriate compensation is due to the owner.

Article 22. Each person has the right to engage in entrepreneurial activity which is not contrary to law.

Article 23. Each person has the right to freely choose his/her profession, occupation and employer.

Article 24. Each person has the right, in accordance with an employment contract, to such wages which are not less than the state-determined minimum wage.

Article 25. The maximum length of the work week is determined by law.

Employees have the right to weekly days off and to annual paid vacations.

Article 26. Employees have the right to strike in order to protect their economic or professional interests.

These rights are restricted by law in order to guarantee the operation of necessary services to the public.

Article 27. Each person has the right to material security in old age, during illness, or in the event of total or partial disability, as well as in the case of the loss of the breadwinner.

Each person has the right to unemployment benefits if he/she has no other means of subsistence and if the unemployment has arisen due to circumstances beyond his/her control.

Article 28. Each person has the right to freely depart for or emigrate to foreign countries.

These rights may not be restricted on the basis of political or ideological motives.

Article 29. Each person has the right to freely move within the territory of Latvia.

Article 30. Each person has the right to freely acquire and disseminate information, to express his/her views and ideas in oral, written or any other form. The realization of these rights must not be restricted by censorship.

No one may be forced to express his/her political, religious, ethical or other views, as well as his/her party affiliation.

Article 31. All people have the right to form public organisations and to participate in their activities if the goals and practical actions of such organisations are not contrary to law.

It is prohibited to form secret organisations and armed units which are not subject to the jurisdiction of the Republic of Latvia Government and administrative institutions.

Article 32. The State guarantees freedom of assembly for previously-announced peaceful gatherings, meetings, street processions and demonstrations.

The local government may change the time or place of such events, if such is required in the interests of public safety and order.

Article 33. The State guarantees freedom for creative work and protects patent rights and copyrights.

Article 34. Each person has the right to turn to the institutions of the State government and administration with individual or collective submissions or proposals and to receive an answer in accordance with the procedures prescribed by law.

Article 35. The State is separate from the church.

The State guarantees the freedom of religious persuasion.

People or their associations have the right to practice religious rituals and ceremonies.

No one may be forced to participate in religious rituals and ceremonies, or to learn religious doctrine.

Religious or ideological motives do not free anyone from their responsibilities to the State and the necessity of observing the law.

Article 36. Family and marital rights, as well as the rights of mothers and children are protected by the State.

The basis of marriage is the voluntary union of a woman and a man, as well as their legal equality.

The care and upbringing of children is in the first instance the right and responsibility of the parents or the guardians.

Society and the State provide that the parents or the guardians are able to fulfill their responsibilities to their children.

Children born within wedlock and those born out of wedlock have equal rights.

The State guarantees special assistance and protection to children who are left without the care of their parents.

Article 37. Everyone has the right to medical care.

Everyone has the responsibility to care for their own health and that of their family and society.

The State protects the health of the public and guarantees each person with the minimum level of medical assistance determined by law.

Article 38. Each person has the right to an education.

The State guarantees the opportunity to acquire an education free of charge, as well as to secure further education appropriate to each person's capabilities.

Article 39. The parents' responsibility is to secure their children's education appropriate to their capabilities and the requirements of mandatory education.

Article 40. Persons and their societies have the right to establish educational institutions of various levels with any language of instruction. The acquisition of education in such schools is under the State's supervision.

Article 41. Each person has the responsibility to observe the laws of the Republic of Latvia, to respect the customs and traditions of the Latvian people and of the national and ethnic groups living in Latvia, as well as to respect the national pride of other persons.

Article 42. Everyone participates in the discharge of State and local government expenses, by paying taxes and levies in accordance with the procedures set by law.

Article 43. The protection of nature, cultural centers, historical and architectural monuments and the environment is the responsibility of each person, the entire society and the State.

Article 44. Necessary restrictions on people's rights and freedom may be determined by law in order to:

1) protect the rights, honor, health and morals of other people;
2) guarantee State security, public order and peace.

Riga, December 10, 1991

A. Gorbunovs
Chairman, Supreme Council
Republic of Latvia

I. Daudišs
Secretary, Supreme Council
Republic of Latvia

The authenticity of the translation is confirmed by Secretary of the Supreme Council of the Republic of Latvia. For purposes of interpretation, the original Latvian text is to be regarded as official.

I. Daudišs

Supreme Council
Republic of Latvia

RESOLUTION
ON THE ORDER IN WHICH THE REPUBLIC OF LATVIA CONSTITUTIONAL LAW "THE RIGHTS AND OBLIGATIONS OF A CITIZEN AND A PERSON" TAKES EFFECT

(Translation)

The Supreme Council of the Republic of Latvia r e s o l v e s :

1. To establish that Article 11, Part 2, of the Republic of Latvia Constitutional Law "The Rights and Obligations of a Citizen and a Person", which provides for a citizen's responsibility to fulfill mandatory state service, take effect on completion of the registration of Republic of Latvia citizens and will be regulated by the law on mandatory state service.

2. To establish that Article 15, Part 4, of this Law which provides that decisions about a detained person's arrest and further detention are made by a court judge, Article 16, Part 2, on the right to conduct searches only based on a judge's decision, as well as Article 17, Part 2, which provides for a citizen's rights to the privacy of correspondence, telephone conversations, telegraph and other communications can only be restricted by a judge's decision, take effect simultaneously with the adoption date of the corresponding Republic of Latvia criminal procedure law.

Riga, December 10, 1991

A. Gorbunovs
Chairman, Supreme Council
Republic of Latvia

I. Daudišs
Secretary, Supreme Council
Republic of Latvia

The authenticity of the translation is confirmed by Secretary of the Supreme Council of the Republic of Latvia. For purposes of interpretation, the original Latvian text is to be regarded as official.
I. Daudišs

4. INCORPORATION AND IMPLEMENTATION OF HUMAN RIGHTS IN LITHUANIA

by Vilenas Vadapalas,
Vilnius University

1. INTRODUCTION

On 11 March 1990, the Supreme Council (Parliament) of the Republic of Lithuania passed the Act on the Re-Establishment of the Independent State of Lithuania proclaiming *inter alia* as follows:

> "The State of Lithuania stresses its adherence to universally recognized principles of international law, recognizes the principle of inviolability of borders as formulated in the Helsinki Final Act of the Conference on Security and Co-operation in Europe of 1975, and guarantees human, civil and ethnic community rights." [1]

After the re-establishment of independence, Lithuania has signed or acceded to many international treaties, either bilateral or multilateral. Being a small country and living through the period of post-communist transition, Lithuania attaches great importance to international treaties which play a significant role particularly in areas such as protection of human rights and promotion of development of the national economy. One may mention, for example, Lithuania's accession to the main international instruments on human rights. On 12 March 1991, Lithuania acceded to the two International Covenants on Human Rights and to the Optional Protocol to the International Covenant on Civil and Political Rights of 1966 (accession effective from 20 February 1992); on 14 May 1993, Lithuania signed and on 27 April 1995 ratified the European Convention for the Protection of Human Rights and Fundamental Freedoms (accession effective from 20 June 1995).

---

[1] English text from: *The Road to Negotiations with the U.S.S.R. Volume One. March 1990 - May 1991. Second revised edition. Vilnius: State Publishing Centre, 1991,* p. 70.

M. Scheinin (ed.), International Human Rights Norms in the Nordic and Baltic Countries, 111–167.

Lithuania has also acceded to the International Convention on the Prevention and Punishment of the Crime of Genocide, to the Convention against Torture and other Cruel, Inhuman or Degrading Treatment or Punishment, to the Convention on the Rights of the Child, etc.

2. STATUS OF HUMAN RIGHTS TREATIES - GENERAL CONSIDERATIONS

The provisional Constitution (the Provisional Basic Law of the Republic of Lithuania) adopted by the Supreme Council on 11 March 1990[2], the day of the restoration of independence, left out a provision on the interrelation between the domestic law of Lithuania and international law. Due to the absence of relevant constitutional rules, it was necessary to pass a statute regulating this issue. The Law on International Treaties of the Republic of Lithuania adopted by the Supreme Council on 21 May 1991[3], provides for a monistic approach to international treaties within the Lithuanian legal system:

> *Article 12*
> International treaties of the Republic of Lithuania shall have the force of law on the territory of the Republic of Lithuania.

The Law defines international treaties of the Republic of Lithuania ("Article 1. For the purposes of the present Law an international treaty of the Republic of Lithuania means an agreement concluded in written form by the Republic of Lithuania with foreign States or international organisations whatever of its particular designation"). The Law of 1991 (Article 7) established a category of treaties calling for Parliament's ratification: Treaties on political co-operation or mutual assistance, on the renunciation of the use or threat of force, on the stationing abroad of Lithuanian armed forces or of foreign troops on Lithuanian territory, on the participation of Lithuania in both universal and regional international organisations, peace, defence or border treaties, as well as

---

[2] English text see in: Selected Anthology of Institutional, Economic and Financial Legislation. Vilnius: *State Publishing Centre, 1991*, pp 6 - 28.

[3] *Parliamentary Record of the Supreme Council of the Republic of Lithuania* (referred below as *Parliamentary Record*), 1992 No. 5, pp. 2-5.

treaties establishing norms differing from those of Lithuanian laws, and multilateral and long-term economic agreements. According to the Law on International Treaties, such negotiations and conclusions fall under the competence of Parliament which takes the decision to negotiate, to deliver the full powers to sign such a treaty, to ratify it and so on. Treaties which do not require ratification, are within the terms of reference of Government.

On 7 January 1992, the Government passed the Decree on the Application of the Law on International Treaties of the Republic of Lithuania.[4] In the first instance, the Decree is aimed at interpreting the internal procedure of conclusion and application of international treaties of Lithuania within the terms of reference of Government (treaties exempted from ratification) and provided a mechanism to entitle various bodies and officials to deliver full powers to negotiate and sign or initial a treaty (competence of the Government), to sign the document providing with full powers (competence of the Prime Minister and Minister of Foreign Affairs) as well as the procedure of registration and publication of treaties.

The Constitution of the Republic of Lithuania adopted by Referendum of 25 October 1992[5], changed many rules and principles called into question prior to the Referendum. Firstly, the Constitution changed the general monistic approach to international treaties.[6] Article 138, part 3 of the Constitution stipulates:

> "International agreements which are ratified by the Seimas of the Republic of Lithuania shall be the constituent part of the legal system of the Republic of Lithuania."

This constitutional provision means that the ratification of a treaty makes it directly applicable in the Lithuanian legal system. It seems that the general monistic approach to international treaties ("treaties ... have the legal force of laws" - Article 12 of the Law on International

---

[4] *Zinios* (referred to below under its recent title as *Valstybes zinios*), 1992, No. 12-31.

[5] *Parliamentary Record*, 1992, No. 11, pp. 2-30.

[6] It should be noted also that the Constitution of 1992 created the institution of the President and provides that "the President shall represent the State of Lithuania" (Article 77, part 2), "settle basic foreign policy issues and, together with the Government, implement foreign policy" (Article 84, alinea 1), "sign international treaties of the Republic of Lithuania and submit them to the Seimas for ratification" (Article 84, alinea 2).

Treaties of 1991) was substituted by a more limited approach according to which only ratified treaties form a constituent part of the Lithuanian legal system. Parliament ratifies a treaty through enacting a resolution on its ratification and this resolution (in case of ratification of the European Convention on Human Rights - the Law on Ratification) makes a treaty directly applicable in domestic law.

The method of domestic implementation of ratified treaties in Lithuania is adoption: international treaties are part of domestic law as a consequence of ratification. It seems that treaties exempt from ratification do not have direct effect on the Lithuanian legal system without a separate domestic enactment (incorporation) or an amendment of special domestic laws (transformation). Anyway, without the appropriate amendments to the Law of 1991, the question of legal effect of such treaties is still unresolved. The contradictions between Article 12 of the Law on International Treaties providing for a general monistic approach and Article 138 of the Constitution limiting this approach have not yet been resolved because the Law on the Procedure for the Enforcement of the Constitution of the Republic of Lithuania of 6 November 1992 (Article 2) [7] stipulates:

> "Laws, other legal acts, or parts thereof which were in effect on the territory of the Republic of Lithuania prior to the adoption of the Constitution of the Republic of Lithuania, shall be effective provided that they do not contradict the Constitution and this law, and shall remain effective until they are either declared null and void or coordinated with the provisions of the Constitution."

On 12 March 1991, the Parliament (at this time - the Supreme Council) of the Republic of Lithuania passed a Resolution stipulating that it "decides to accede to the International Covenant on Economic, Social and Cultural Rights, to the International Covenant on Civil and Political Rights and to the Optional Protocol to the International Covenant on Civil and Political Rights."[8] This Resolution of accession does not contain a formal ratification of these instruments. Nevertheless, the International Covenants and the Optional Protocol have the legal force of acts of Parliament (Laws) in Lithuania according to the Law on International Treaties of 1991.

---

[7] *Parliamentary Record*, 1992, No. 11, pp. 30-31.

[8] *Lietuvos Respublikos Aukscíausiosios Tarybos ir Lietuvos Respublikos Prezidiumo dokumentu rinkinys. T. 3, Vilnius: Valstybinis leidybos centras, 1991*, pp. 25-26.

The European Convention for the Protection of Human Rights and Fundamental Freedoms was ratified by Parliament on 27 April 1995. It means that the European Convention after its international ratification is a constituent part of the Lithuanian legal system.[9]

Some Lithuanian statutes related to human rights contain general references to international treaties. For example, Article 36 of the Law on Citizenship[10] entitled "Application of International Treaties on Questions of Citizenship" stipulates:

> "If an international treaty to which the Republic of Lithuania is a party prescribes rules other than those established by this Law, the provisions of the international treaty shall prevail."

The same provision is provided by Article 39 of the Law on the Legal Status of Foreigners in the Republic of Lithuania.[11]

The question of priority relationships between domestic enactments and rules of international law has no direct answer in the Lithuanian legal system. Of course, it could be taken into account that constitutional provisions have priority over all other legal acts according to Article 7 of the Constitution:

> "Any law or other legal statute which contradicts the Constitution shall be invalid."

It seems, however, that the term "other legal statute" does not cover the international treaties of Lithuania.

3. DIRECT APPLICABILITY OF HUMAN RIGHTS TREATIES

In general, Lithuanian courts seem to be rather conservative to change their traditional jurisprudence based exclusively on domestic sources of law. Until now there is no Lithuanian case law from domestic courts with regard to the application of human rights treaties, except from some recent cases before the Constitutional Court.

---

[9] The text of Parliament's ratification is presented as *Annex 4*, below.

[10] *Parliamentary Record*, 1992, No. 1, pp. 2-10.

[11] *Parliamentary Record*, 1992, No. 5, pp. 5-9.

The first case was the *Case on the compliance of the Law of the Republic of Lithuania on Appending and Amending the Law on the Procedure and Conditions of the Restoration of the Rights of Ownership to Existing Real Property*. In this case the Constitutional Court in its Ruling of 27 May 1994 referred to the Universal Declaration of Human Rights and to the First Protocol to the European Convention for the Protection of Human Rights and Fundamental Freedoms:

> "The right to possess property is one of the most significant human natural rights, and a person may not be arbitrarily deprived of it. It may only be seized for the needs of society according to the procedure established by law. Such a principle for the protection of property and rights to property is also formulated in international legal instruments. It is for instance specified in the second part of Article 17 of the Universal Declaration of Human Rights that: "No one shall be arbitrarily deprived of his property"; in the first part of Article 1 of Protocol 1 to the European Convention for the Protection of Human Rights and Fundamental Freedoms it is maintained that: "Every natural or legal person is entitled to the peaceful enjoyment of his possessions. No one shall be deprived of his possessions except in the public interest and subject to the conditions provided for by law and by the general principles of international law".[12]

The Ruling of the Constitutional Court of 18 November 1994 in the *Case of Conformity of Article 58 part 2 paragraph 3 of the Code of Penal Procedure with the Constitution of the Republic of Lithuania* contains several references to international human rights instruments, as well as to the case law of the European Court of Human Rights. The Court pointed out:

> "The right to defense is universally recognized and declared in international instruments. It is usually stipulated also by domestic law. Principle 17 of the Body of Principles for the Protection of All Persons under Any Form of Detention or Imprisonment adopted by the Resolution of 9 December 1988 (A/RES/43/173) proclaims that a detained person shall have the right to legal assistance of counsel; promptly after his arrest a competent authority shall inform him of this right and about the reasonable possibilities of having defense assigned to him.
>
> Article 6 paragraph 3 of the European Convention for the Protection of Human Rights and Fundamental Freedoms stipulates: "Everyone charged with a criminal offence has the following minimum rights: a. to be informed promptly, in a language which he understands and in detail, of the nature and cause of the accusation against him; b. to have adequate time and facilities for the preparation of his defence; c. to defend himself in person or through legal assistance of his own choosing or, if he has not sufficient means to pay for legal assistance, to be given it free when the interests of justice so require; d. to examine or have

[12] *Rulings and Decisions of the Constitutional Court of the Republic of Lithuania*. Vol. 2, p. 79.

examined witnesses against him and to obtain the attendance and examination of witnesses against him; e. to have the free assistance of an interpreter if he cannot understand or speak the language used in court."[13]

In the same Ruling, the Court also pointed out:

"Principle 15 of the Body of Principles for the Protection of All Persons under Any Form of Detention or Imprisonment stipulates that notwithstanding the exceptions contained in Principle 16, paragraph 4, and Principle 18, paragraph 3, communication of a detained or imprisoned person with the outside world, and in particular with his family or counsel, shall not be denied for more than a matter of days. Principle 18 pragraph 3 provides with the following exception: the right of a detained or imprisoned person to meet counsel, to ask his advice and to contact him immediately, without censorship, in full confidence cannot be temporarily abolished or restricted, except in exceptional circumstances, provided by law or by regulations established by law, when the court or another organ thinks that it is necessary for maintaof ining security and order.

The possibility to restrict the right of a defended person to meet his counsel was confirmed by the European Court of Human Rights in the *Case of Campbell and Fell v. United Kingdom* (1984). The European Court of Human Rights pointed out that the provisions of Article 6(3) (b) of the European Convention for the Protection of Human Rights and Fundamental Freedoms can be interpreted in a broad manner, i.e. in some exceptional circumstances the State is entitled to restrict confidentiality of legal advice.[14] When well-founded suspicions arise that a counsel misuses his procedural status and by his advice to the accused person misleads the court or hinders a normal course of procedure, a State is entitled to defer from the principle of the privacy of legal advice.

It may thus be concluded that the domestic law of most democratic countries, documents of international organisations and the European Court of Human Rights provide the prerequisites for restricting contact between suspected or accused persons and their counsel without supervision. Hovewer, there is also a general requirement: such restrictions can only be provided by law and keeping within the limits of what is reasonable." [15]

On 13 July 1994, the President of Lithuania appealed to the Constitutional Court for the conclusion of the Court in an inquiry on the conformity of certain provisions of the European Convention for the Protection of Human Rights and Fundamental Freedoms and of its

---

[13] Lietuvos Respublikos Konstitucinio Teismo nutarimas Del Lietuvos Respublikos Baudziamojo kodekso 58 straipsnio antrosios dalies 3 punkto atitikimo Lietuvos Respublikos Konstitucijai. - *Valstybes zinios*, 1994, No. 91, p. 42-43.

[14] *Editor's note:* In the *Case of Campbell and Fell* (Judgment of 28 June 1984, Series A No. 80), the European Court of Human Rights found a violation of ECHR Art. 6 (1) because Father Fell was refused to consult his solicitors without the absence of a prison officer. In this connection, the Court also stated: "there may well be security considerations which would justify some restriction on the conditions for visits by a lawyer to a prisoner" (§ 113).

[15] Ibid., p. 44.

Protocol No.4 with the Constitution of Lithuania. The inquiry deals with the penitentiary works (Article 4, para. 3a of the Convention), the right of arrested or detained persons to be brought promptly before a judge (Article 5, para. 3 of the Convention), the right to freedom of thought, conscience and religion (Article 9 of the Convention), the enjoyment of the rights and freedoms without discrimination (Article 14 of the Convention), the right to liberty of movement and freedom to choose one's residence (Article 2 of Protocol No. 4).

It should be noted that the Constitution of 1992 created a mechanism for the control of the constitutionality of international treaties. Article 105, part 3, alinea 3 of the Constitution provides that the Constitutional Court shall present the conclusions on "the conformity of international agreements of the Republic of Lithuania with the Constitution". According to article 106, part 5 of the Constitution, the right to apply to the Constitutional Court requesting it to make a conclusion on the constitutionality of an international treaty is vested only in the Seimas (Parliament) and the President. Article 107 of the Constitution stipulates:

> "Laws (or parts thereof) of the Republic of Lithuania or any other acts (or parts thereof) of the Seimas, acts of the President of the Republic of Lithuania, and acts (or parts thereof) of the Government may not be applied from the day of the official promulgation of the decision of the Constitutional Court that the act in question (or part thereof) is inconsistent with the Constitution of the Republic of Lithuania.
>
> The decisions of the Constitutional Court on issues assigned to its jurisdiction by the Constitution shall be final and may not be appealed.
>
> On the basis of the conclusions of the Constitutional Court, the Seimas shall have a final decision on the issues set forth in part 3 of Article 105 of the Constitution."

The interpretation *stricto sensu* of this Article should not lead to the conclusion that in the event of inconsistency between an international treaty and the Constitution, the conclusion of the Court will invalidate the treaty from the point of view of Lihuanian domestic law. An international treaty can thus neither be considered as "the law of the Republic of Lithuania" nor as "an act of the Seimas", nor as "an act of the Government". Nevertheless, the Court seems to be empowered to conclude, for example, that the resolution of the Seimas on the ratification of a treaty, as well as the decree by the Government to accede to the treaty are inconsistent with the Constitution. There is no doubt that the question of invalidity, suspension or extinction of international treaties is governed by international law, namely by the

Vienna Convention on the Law of Treaties to which Lithuania is a State Party. The inapplicability or invalidity of an international treaty in terms of the domestic law of a particular State does not affect *per se* the international obligations and responsibility of the State for non-respect of the treaty.

It is interesting to note that contrary to the Constitution, the Law on the Constitutional Court of 3 February 1993[16] (Article 63 of the Law entitled "The Constitutional Court's Jurisdiction in Cases concerning the Compliance of Legal Acts with the Constitution") does not give the Constitutional Court jurisdiction over the conformity of international treaties of Lithuania with its Constitution. However, Article 73 of the Law entitled "Conclusions presented by the Constitutional Court" stipulates that the Court shall present its ruling on "whether international treaties of the Republic of Lithuania are in conformity with the Constitution. A conclusion concerning an international treaty may also be requested prior to the ratification of the treaty in question by the Seimas." This could mean that the treaties calling for ratification may only be submitted for preventive constitutional control and are exempted from the competence of the Court after ratification. But the case of treaties falling under the second category of international treaties of Lithuania (treaties not to be ratified) still seems to be unresolved. *De lege ferenda* these treaties could be submitted to the Constitutional Court even after their entry into force according to the terms of the treaty in question.

As for the request of the President of Lithuania for the conclusion of the Constitutional Court on the conformity of some provisions of the European Convention on Human Rights with the Constitution, it could be noted that this request was aimed at bringing Lithuanian legislation into conformity with the European Convention. According to Article 107, part 3 of the Constitution, Parliament shall have the final decision in the matter of the request. The conclusion of the Constitutional Court on the merits of the case could have initiated relevant constitutional or other legislative amendments.[17]

---

[16] *Parliamentary Record*, 1993, No. 3, pp. 2-28.

[17] On the conclusion by the Lithuanian Constitutional Court, see Part 8 of this article.

4. REFERENCES TO INTERNATIONAL SOURCES OF HUMAN RIGHTS LAW OTHER THAN TREATIES

Some Lithuanian domestic enactments contain references to the Universal Declaration of Human Rights. According to the Resolution of the Supreme Council of 12 March 1991 on the accession of the Republic of Lithuania to the Instruments of The International Bill of Human Rights, Lithuania "solemnly undertakes to respect the Universal Declaration of Human Rights adopted by the United Nations General Assembly on December 10th, 1948".

The resolution of Parliament of 10 December 1991 on the accession to the Convention against Torture and Other Cruel, Inhuman or Degrading Treatment or Punishment of 1984 contains a reference in its Preamble according to which Parliament "recognizes the provisions of the Universal Declaration of Human Rights and the International Covenant on Civil and Political Rights prohibiting torture and other cruel, inhuman or degrading treatment or punishment." [18]

Lithuanian legislation does not contain any provisions on the applicabilty of general principles of international law or customary international law in domestic law. The reference to "the universally recognized principles and norms of international law" in Article 135 of the Constitution is only related to the foreign policy of Lithuania:

> "In conducting foreign policy, the Republic of Lithuania shall pursue the universally recognized principles and norms of international law, shall strive to safeguard national security and independence as well as the basic rights, freedoms and welfare of its citizens, and shall take part in the creation of sound international order based on law and justice."

5. ASSESSMENT OF LAW AND PRACTICE

It seems too soon to make general assessments of the effects of the system of implementation of international human rights standards in Lithuania. The entire Lithuanian legal system is going through a transition from communist law to a democratic legal system. It is evident that in the present situation the domestic legal system of

---

[18] *Lietuvos Respublikos AukscIausiosios Tarybos ir Lietuvos Respublikos Prezidiumo dokumentu rinkinys. T. 4, Vilnius: Valstybinis leidybos centras, 1992,* p. 21.

Lithuania can not secure an effective incorporation and implementation of international treaties into Lithuanian domestic law. Appropriate mechanisms of implementation should be created. Two ways are possible: either to pass effective adoption or incorporation clauses, or to create the mechanisms of transformation. The last option seems rather difficult due to the lack of appropriate legislative machinery and relevant experience.

6. RECENT DEVELOPMENTS AND REFORM

The Draft Amended Law on International Treaties was prepared by the Legal Department of the Ministry of Foreign Affairs together with the Office of the Prime Minister. In the opinion of the present author, the method of implementation of international treaties proposed by the drafters is too complicated and there is a risk that within the Lithuanian legal system ratified treaties will prevail over the treaties which do not require ratification, and that the acts of Lithuania will prevail over the last category of treaties. Article 12 of the Draft Amended Law on International Treaties stipulates:

> "International treaties of the Republic of Lithuania which have entered into force have binding force in the Republic of Lithuania.
> International treaties of the Republic of Lithuania ratified by the Seimas which have entered into force have the legal force of acts of Parliament (Laws) in the Republic of Lithuania.
> When a ratified international treaty of the Republic of Lithuania which has entered into force provides rules which differ from the laws of the Republic of Lithuania, the provisions of the international treaty of the Republic of Lithuania shall apply.
> When an international treaty of the Republic of Lithuania which has entered into force and does not require ratification provides rules which differ from legal instruments lower than acts of Parliament (Laws) of the Republic of Lithuania, the provisions of the international treaty of the Republic of Lithuania shall apply."[19]

The last paragraph in fact means that treaties exempt from ratification in the Lithuanian legal system, would be higher than so-called "regulations", i.e. instruments adopted by Parliament, Government or ministries that are lower than acts of Parliament. The clause implies that acts of Parliament (Laws) would prevail over such treaties.

---

[19] *Lietuvos Respublikos Istatymas del Lietuvos Respublikos Tarptaiutiniu sutarciu. Lietuvos Respublikos Seimas. Akto projekto No. 842,* 1994.03.23.

The revised Draft Article 12 together with Article 138 of the Constitution providing for the adoption method (i.e. international treaties ratified by Parliament are a constituent part of the legal system of Lithuania) could create a legislative minimum for domestic implementation of international treaties of Lithuania.

It also seems that without appropriate amendments to the Constitution, the question of the relationships between international treaties and domestic laws of Lithuania will still remain unresolved.

7. PRACTICAL ASPECTS OF IMPLEMENTATION

The Law on Publication and Entry into Force of the Laws and other Decrees of the Republic of Lithuania of 6 April 1993 (Article 29) provides that the international treaties ratified by Parliament are to be published by the "Valstybes Zinios", the official journal of Parliament and the Government. This provision contradicts Article 16 of the Law on International Treaties of 1991 stipulating that all treaties, i.e. the treaties ratified and approved as well as treaties to which Lithuania has acceded shall be published by the "Valstybes Zinios". In fact the "Valstybes Zinios" began to publish all international treaties. At this moment, however, a large number of international treaties of the Republic of Lithuania remain unpublished. International human rights instruments including human rights treaties to which Lithuania is a state party are published in different separate publications of the publishing house "Mintis". However it seems that official publication in "Valstybes Zinios" is necessary.

8. CONCLUSION BY THE CONSTITUTIONAL COURT OF LITHUANIA IN THE CASE CONCERNING COMPLIANCE OF THE EUROPEAN CONVENTION ON HUMAN RIGHTS WITH THE CONSTITUTION OF LITHUANIA

On 13 July 1994, the President of Lithuania appealed to the Constitutional Court for the conclusion of the court in an inquiry on the conformity of certain provisions of the European Convention for the Protection of Human Rights and Fundamental Freedoms and of its Protocol No. 4 with the Constitution of Lithuania.

The President concluded in his Request that comparative analysis of some corresponding Articles in the Convention and the Protocols and of the Constitution shows inconsistencies between the two (or differences in content). The President pointed out:

> "Therefore, once the Republic of Lithuania ratified the European Convention for the Protection of Human Rights and Fundamental Freedoms, it could not fulfill its international obligations because Article 7 of the Constitution of the Republic of Lithuania stipulates that "any law or other statute which contradicts the Constitution shall be invalid."[20]

The Conclusion of the Court may be divided into six parts: the first part is devoted to the question of applicability of international treaties in the Lithuanian domestic legal system in general, and of the ECHR in particular. The other five parts answer five points contained in the Request of the President.

8.1 General Problems of the Relationship between International Treaties and the Lithuanian Legal System. Starting with the examination of the legal nature of the provisions of the ECHR and referring to Article 1 of the Convention,[21] the Court stated:

> "Therefore every State should effectively implement the provisions of the Convention (or the protocols which the State has ratified) with the aim of fully fulfilling its obligations under the Convention.
>
> This general principle is directly linked with the relationship between international and internal (national) law of States in general, and in particular with the problem of human rights and freedoms. At present, the most expanded system in Europe is probably is the so-called parallel system of harmonisation of international and internal law, based on the principle that international treaties are transformed (incorporated) into internal law of a state. This method of implementation of international treaties is provided for by the Constitution of the Republic of Lithuania as well.
>
> The European Convention for the Protection of Human Rights and Fundamental Freedoms is a specific source of international law the aim of which differs from the aims of other international legal instruments. Such an aim is universal - to seek that the rights proclaimed in the Universal Declaration of Human Rights should be universally and fully recognized and respected in the protection and implementation of human rights and fundamental freedoms.

---

[20] See in: *Lietuvos Respublikos Konstitucinio Teismo Isvada "Del Europos Zmogaus teisiu ir pagrindiniu laisviu apsaugos konvencijos 4, 5, 9 ir 14 straipsniu ir jos Ketvirtojo protokolo 2 straipsnio atitikimo Lietuvos Respublikos Konstitucijai".* - *Valstybes Zinios* 1995, No. 9, § 199, pp. 22 - 30. An English text of the Conclusion will be published in *Rulings and Decisions of the Constitutional Court of the Republic of Lithuania,* Vol. 3 by the end of the year 1995.

[21] Article 1: "The High Contracting Parties shall secure to everyone within their jurisdiction the rights and freedoms defined in Section 1 of this Convention."

In this respect, the Convention plays the same role as the constitutional guarantees of human rights, because the Constitution provides such guarantees within the country whereas the Convention on the international level."

It should be noted that the general remark made by the Court about transformation as a method of implementation of international treaties used by the Lithuanian Constitution is correct in the sense that the act of ratification of the treaty incorporates it into the Lithuanian legal system (Article 138 of the Constitution provides that "international agreements *which are ratified* by the Seimas of the Republic of Lithuania shall be the constituent part of the legal system of the Republic of Lithuania." *(our emphasis added)*. I think that this method of domestic implementation of treaties is, rather, adoption as ratified treaties have direct effect in the Lithuanian legal system without separate domestic enactments or amendments of domestic acts (i.e. transformation). In other words, ratified international treaties should be directly applicable in Lithuanian law. As for the prevailing method of domestic implementation of the ECHR in Europe, it could be noted that the remark made by the Court that "the parallel system of harmonisation of international and internal law" prevailing in Europe does not seems to be quite exact. As far as the States Parties to the ECHR are concerned the treaty provisions are directly applicable as municipal law in most States.[22]

The Constitutional Court found that the provision in Article 138 of the Constitution about incorporation of ratified treaties into the Lithuanian legal system "means with regard to the Convention that, when ratified and entered into force in Lithuania, it will form a constituent part of the legal system of the Republic of Lithuania and should be implemented as the acts of Parliament (Laws) of the Republic of Lithuania. Its provisions correspond to the level of acts of parliament in the system of the sources of law of the Republic of Lithuania, since Article 12 of the Law on International Treaties of the Republic of Lithuania sipulates that 'the international treaties of the Republic of Lithuania shall have the force of law on the territory of the Republic of Lithuania'."

---

[22] See: *Jochen Abr. Frowein, European Convention on Human Rights (1950).* In: Encyclopedia of Public International Law. Vol. 8, p. 185; *Rudolf Bernhardt. The Convention and Domestic Law.* In: The European System for the Protection of Human Rights, ed. by R.St.J. Macdonald, F. Matscher, H.Petzold. Dordrecht/Boston/London: Martinus Nijhoff, 1994, pp. 28-29.

The Court reaffirmed a well-known general conclusion by the European Court of Human Rights that the ECHR does not provide how States Parties are to implement the relevant obligations undertaken through the Convention internally.[23] With regard to the means of implementation of the provisions of the ECHR the Constitutional Court referred to Article 13[24] of the ECHR, and pointed out:

> "Therefore, State authorities for legal protection should apply the norms of the Constitution directly, as well as implement the provisions of the Convention. Such provisions should become a constituent part of internal law, and there should be no room for obstacles to their application by the courts and other law enforcing bodies.
>
> Besides, it should be emphasised that the Convention does not require, which would also be impossible, that the norms of internal law are identical in their wording with the content of the norms of Convention. Neither does the Convention stipulate strictly the means by which the rights and freedoms established by the Convention should be implemented. In this connection, it is very important to determine the so-called margin of appreciation, i.e. to establish a sufficient and effective legislative protection of the rights defined in the Convention. The State bodies decide on the "margin of appreciation" within the framework of the jurisdiction given to them by the Constitution. (...)
>
> Nevertheless, the provisions in Sections II, III, IV and V of the Convention without any doubt mean that the rules of the Convention should really be implemented, and breach of any of the rights and freedoms cannot be justified by invoking that the laws of a State provide otherwise. This operation of the provisions of the Convention is based on the fact that a State Party to the Convention should secure the application of the rules of the Convention in its internal legal system. However, international treaties and this Convention as well, operate differently in different areas of legal life. Concrete means and forms of implementation are provided for by the laws of the Republic of Lithuania. Civil law provides for the direct applicability of international treaties by resolving any conflicts with the norms of the laws of the Republic of Lithuania in the following way: if international treaties of the Republic of Lithuania prescribe rules other than those established by the acts of Parliament (Laws) of the Republic of Lithuania, the provisions of the international treaty shall apply (Article 606 of the Civil Code and Article 482 of the Code of Civil Procedure). In criminal law this way of resolving conflicts between norms is not applicable. In such cases, the Penal Law and laws on criminal procedure of the Republic of Lithuania are directly applicable, and international treaties only apply in cases provided by such acts (Article 7-1 of the Penal Code and Articles 20, 21, 21-1, 21-2, 22, 22-1 and 22-2 of the Code of Penal Procedure). If when applying criminal law, there are doubts about the possibility of enforcing the human rights provided by the Convention, the question should be resolved by means of constitutional control, focussing on whether the law contradicts the Constitution or not. From another point

---

[23] *Swedish Engine Drivers' Union case*, Judgment of 6 February 1976, Publications of the European Court of Human Rights, Series A, 1976, Vol. 20, p.18.

[24] Article 13: "Everyone whose rights and freedoms as set forth in this Convention are violated shall have an effective remedy before a national authority notwithstanding that the violation has been committed by persons acting in an official authority".

> of view, the rights provided by the Convention cannot be ensured directly without applying the internal legal instruments. In other words, if only the direct applicability of the Convention was recognized, the abovementioned rights could not be ensured, because the Convention in itself establishes neither the means of implementation of such rights in States which have ratified the Convention, nor the responsibility of the persons violating the rights, nor the necessary procedures and special jurisdiction of the judicial authorities. In such cases, the rule of *ubi jus ibi remedium* is clearly applicable: when the law establishes a right, it also provides a remedy to protect it. Such remedies in the legal system of a State are established by the laws of the State in question. The Convention provides for such remedies only in cases where the dispute concerning the established rights becomes a matter of international jurisdiction."

The conclusion to be drawn from the lines of the Court is that Article 138 of the Constitution providing for the incorporation of international treaties into the Lithuanian legal system by way of ratification gives the ECHR the legal force of law. (According to the Court: "... when ratified and entered into force in Lithuania, it will form a constituent part of the legal system of the Republic of Lithuania and should be implemented as the acts of Parliament (Laws) of the Republic of Lithuania".) If so, it is unclear why the Court concluded that "if when applying criminal law there are doubts about the possibility of enforcing the human rights provided by the Convention, the question should be resolved by means of constitutional control focussing on whether the law contradicts the Constitution or not. From another point of view, the rights provided by the Convention can not be ensured directly without applying the internal legal instruments". Moreover, since the Court has implicitly recognized that the Convention applies directly in Lithuanian law and found that there is no inconformity between the ECHR and the Constitution, it is unclear why the Court left room for doubt about the possibility of direct effect of the ECHR without applying domestic legal instruments.

Next, the Constitutional Court turned to the examination of the role of Article 7 of the Constitution to the merits of the case ("Any law or other statute which contradicts the Constitution shall be invalid").

This, according to the Court, "cannot invalidate an international treaty - the Convention. However, it requires that the provisions of international treaties do not contradict the provisions of the Constitution, otherwise it would be uncertain how the Convention should be implemented in the internal law of the Republic of Lithuania."

It seems that the Court has found an interesting interpretation of the term "contradiction with the Constitution" by pointing out:

"The provisions of the Convention could be considered inconsistent with the Constitution, if:
1. The Constitution would etablish an exhaustive and full list of rights and freedoms, although the Convention would establish other rights and freedoms;
2. The Constitution would prohibit any acts, although the Convention would define these acts as rights or freedoms;
3. Any provision of the Convention could not be applied in the legal system of the Republic of Lithuania, because it was inconsistent with any provision of the Constitution."[25]

The Court found that there is no room for such inconsistencies in the sense of points 1 or 2 of this formula.

It should be emphasised that the Court's interpretation of conformity of the provisions of the ECHR and the Constitution is very distant from the formal linguistic interpretation of conformity in corresponding texts. As it stated, "the interpretation of the conformity (relationship) of the norms of the Constitution and the Convention should be essential, logical, but not identical in wording. A purely formal linguistic interpretation of human rights cannot be accepted by the very nature of human rights."

As for point 3, the Court decided on it when answering the concrete points of the Request by the President of Lithuania.

8.2 Answer to the first point of the Request. This point deals with the possible inconformity of Article 4, paragraph 3(a), of the ECHR with Article 48 of the Constitution (our emphases added):

ECHR, Article 4 (*extract*)
2. No one shall be required to perform forced or compulsory labour.
3. For the purpose of this Article the term 'forced or compulsory labour' shall not include:
a. *any work required to be done in the ordinary course of detention* imposed according to the provisions of Article 5 of this Convention or *during conditional release from such detention; ...*"

The Constitution, Article 48 (*extract*)
"... *Labour which is provided by law for persons convicted by a tribunal* shall not be deemed as forced labour either.[26]

[25] The last point of "inconsistency" would be more clear if the Court would use the expression "if it precludes the applicability of any provision of the Constitution because of its inconformity with the Constitution."

[26] *Editor's note:* The author's translation of the constitutional provision differs from the one given in Annex 1. The difference is related to the problem of interpretation involved in the case.

The President's Request. The Constitution contains a general provision that every criminal penalty may include mandatory labour for convicted persons. This principle is implemented *inter alia* by Article 29 of the Penal Code providing for such a criminal penalty as correctional work without deprivation of liberty. According to the President's Request:

> "The rule laid down by the Convention provides a duty to work only in the ordinary course of detention or during conditional release from detention. Thus, the rule provided by the Convention is more restricted in content than the Constitution and this allows one to make the conclusion that Article 4, paragraph 3(a), of the Convention is incompatible with Article 48, part 5, of the Constitution."

The Constitutional Court pointed out that it is erroneous to interpret Article 48 of the Constitution in such a way that it provides for correctional labour. This Article does not even mention correctional work as a criminal penalty. The expression *"labour which is provided by law for persons convicted by a tribunal"* does not mean that the law should establish correctional labour penalties.

The Court, making reference to the case law of the European Court of Human Rights[27], concluded that the provisions of Article 4, paragraph 3(a), of the Convention do not necessarily mean prohibition of involuntary labour without depriving persons convicted for criminal offences of their liberty. As the Court stated, Article 4 of the ECHR links work required to be done with the requirements of Article 5 of the Convention, i.e. with the legality of detention or conditional release from detention. It is important that the work should not lie outside the limits of what is usually required, and that the work to be done may be aimed at reintegrating a person into society.

Therefore, the Court came to the conclusion that Article 4, paragraph 3(a), of the Convention does not contradict the Constitution.

8.3 Answer to the second point of the Request. This point deals with the possible inconformity between Article 5, paragraphs 3 and 4, of the ECHR and Article 20 of the Constitution:

[27] *Van Droegenbgoek case*, Judgement of 24 June 1982, Publications of the European Court of Human Rights, Series A, 1982, Vol. 50, pp. 32-60.

ECHR, Article 5 (*extract*)

3. *Everyone arrested or detained* in accordance with the provisions of paragraph 1c of this Article *shall be brought promptly before a judge or other officer authorized by law to exercise judicial power* and shall be entitled to trial within a reasonable time or to release pending trial. (...)

4. Everyone who is deprived of his liberty by arrest or detention shall be entitled to take proceedings by which *the lawfulness of his detention shall be decided* speedily by a court and his release ordered if the detention is not lawful.

The Constitution, Article 20 (*extract*)

A person arrested in flagrante delicto must, within 48 hours, be brought to court for the purpose of determining, in the presence of the detainee, *the validity of the detention....*

The President's Request. The ECHR establishes a procedural guarantee which is broader than that of the Constitution because it provides that every arrested or detained person is brought before a court, although the Constitution deals only with a person arrested *in flagrante delicto*. Secondly, Article 5, paragraph 4, of the Convention stipulates that a judge should decide on the lawfulness of the arrest, although according to the Constitution the court must determine the validity of the arrest. This difference is essential, because a lawful arrest is *per se* always valid, although a valid arrest may be unlawful. Thirdly, it is doubtful whether the term "promptly" of the Convention is consistent with the rule of 48 hours provided by the Constitution. All this allows one to conclude that the rules established by Article 5, paragraph 4, of the Convention are inconsistent with Article 20 of the Constitution in their content, as well as in their scope.

First of all, the Constitutional Court noted that differences in the wording of corresponding provisions of the ECHR and the Constitution are not alone sufficient to conclude that they are inconsistent. The Court found:

"... if the Constitution does not establish any rights, freedoms or guarantees or constructs them in a different manner, it does not mean that such rights, freedoms or their enforcement could not be guaranteed in the legal system of the Republic of Lithuania. They could be and are indeed provided by other legal instruments and are implemented in practice. Besides, they could be ensured by applying the Convention on the basis of Article 138, part 3, of the Constitution. The provisions of the Convention are not applicable only if such provisions contradict the Constitution."

Comparing the formulas "*to bring promptly before a judge*" and "*to bring to court within 48 hours*", the Court concluded that there is no inconformity. The Court made reference to the relevant case law of the organs under the Convention recognizing that four days in ordinary cases and five days in exceptional cases correspond to the requirement of bringing an arrested person promptly before a judge. Likewise, the Court referred to the relevant Articles of the Constitutions of some States Parties to the Convention, providing the term of 48 hours (Article 28 of the Constitution of Portugal and Article 13 of the Constitution of Italy) or 72 hours (Article 17 of the Constitution of Spain).

In this connection, I should add that until now the rule to bring an arrested person to court within 48 hours as provided by Article 20 of the Constitution of Lithuania has not come into force yet. The Law on the Procedure for the Enforcement of the Constitution of the Republic of Lithuania of 6 November 1992 (Article 8) made the following reservation:

> "The provisions of part 3 of Article 20 of the Constitution of the Republic of Lithuania shall become applicable once the laws on the criminal procedure of the Republic of Lithuania are coordinated with this Constitution."

This has not been done yet. The rule which is still applicable stipulates that the lawfulness of any arrest must be decided within 72 hours by the procurator who is entitled to order an arrested person released or to prolong his/her arrest.

The Court further found no contradiction between the requirement that *"everone who is arrested or detained (...) shall be brought before a judge"* and the rule providing that *"a person detained in flagrante delicto must (...) be brought to court."* Applied simultaneously on the basis of Article 138 of the Constitution, the two provisions complement each other and form one legal guarantee.

Finally, the Court came to the conclusion that there is no contradiction between the provision of Article 5, paragraph 4, of the Convention which stipulates that a judge should decide on the *lawfulness* of the arrest, and Article 20 of the Constitution which requires that the court must determine the *validity* of the arrest. Both the Constitution and the Convention require that the court should decide on the lawfulness and validity of the arrest. The Court concluded:

> "However, one cannot interpret part 3 of Article 20 of the Constitution by separating it from the whole text of this Article, as well as of other provisions of the Constitution establishing

guarantees of legality. Part 2 of the Article mentioned above provides that: 'No person may be arbitrarily arrested or detained. No person may be deprived of freedom except on the bases, and according to the procedures, which have been established in laws.' Such provisions basically etablish the principle of the lawfulness of the detention of a person as a general rule. That is why the content of the term 'validity' employed by Article 20 is broader than the pure meaning of causality of facts; it means that it covers the term of 'lawfulness'.

Therefore, the Court concludes that Article 5 of the ECHR does not contradict the Constitution of the Republic of Lithuania."

8.4 Answer to the third point of the Request. This point deals with the possible inconformity of Article 9, paragraph 2, of the ECHR and Article 26 of the Constitution:

ECHR, Article 9 (*extract*)

2. *Freedom to manifest* one's religion or belief shall be subject only to such limitations as are prescribed by law and are necessary in a democratic society in the interest of public safety, for the protection of public order, health or morals, or for the protection of the rights and freedoms of others.

The Constitution, Article 26 (*extract*)

A person's *freedom to profess* and propagate his or her religion or faith may be subject only to those limitations prescribed by law and only when such restrictions are necessary to protect safety of society, public order, a person's health or morals, or the fundamental rights and freedoms of others.

The President's Request. Article 9, paragraph 2, of the Convention only allows for restrictions to the freedom to manifest religion or belief, while Article 26 of the Constitution stipulates that the freedom to both profess and manifest religion or belief could be restricted.

"It should be noted that the Convention, as well as the Constitution distinguish between the freedom to profess and the freedom to manifest one's religion or belief as two different freedoms, which allows one to conclude that the Convention does not provide for the possibility to restrict someone's freedom to profess (religion or belief - V.V.). Therefore, it may be concluded that the extent of Article 9, paragraph 2, of the Convention is in contradiction to part four of Article 26 of the Constitution."

The Court found that Article 9 of the ECHR does not distinguish between the right to profess and the freedom to manifest one's religion or belief. Although the Constitution provides for the possibility to establish limitations in the freedom *to profess and manifest* one's religion or belief, it is nothing more than a difference in wording. The Court pointed out that it is not possible to restrict the freedom to profess a religion or belief because it is impossible to restrict such a moral category as religious faith or belief. Here, the court referred to the English and French texts of Article 18 of the International Covenant on Civil and Political Rights where the corresponding wording "freedom to have" and "la liberté d'avoir" is used. This wording does not mean any external manifestation of religion or belief which could be subject to legal restrictions. *Lex non cogit ad impossibilia* - law does not require the impossible.

The Court concluded:

> "Therefore, this provision of the Constitution did not entail any negative consequences with regard to the freedom of religion and belief in the legal system of the Republic of Lithuania, and no act restricts the freedom to profess relifion or belief".

Thus, according to the Conclusion there is no contradiction between Article 9 of the ECHR and the Constitution.

8.5 Answer to the fourth point of the Request. This point deals with the possible inconformity between Article 14 of the ECHR and Article 29 of the Constitution:

> ECHR, Article 14
> The enjoyment of the rights and freedoms set forth in this Convention shall be secured without discrimination on any ground such as sex, race, *colour*, language, religion, political or other opinion, national or social origin, *association with a national minority*, property, birth or other status.
>
> The Constitution, Article 29 (*extract*)
> *A person may not* have his rights restricted in any way, or *be granted any privileges*, on the basis of his or her sex, race, nationality, language, origin, social status, religion, convictions, or opinions.

The President's Request:

> "The Convention only prohibits so-called 'negative' discimination, although the Constitution deals with both 'negative' and 'positive' (granting of privileges) discrimination. In addition, the Convention provides a more extensive list of grounds for discrimination, for example: the Constitution does not mention 'colour' and 'association with a national minority'. These two aspects allow one to conclude that Article 14 of the Convention is inconsistent with part two of Article 29 of the Constitution with regard to the scope of the protection."

The Court concluded that so-called positive discrimination does not amount to the granting of privileges. It does not imply inequality before the law. The Constitution does secure universally recognized specific rights inherent to some goups of persons, namely, to persons belonging to national minorities.

Article 29 of the Constitution stipulates that "a person may not have his rights restricted in any way, or be granted any privileges, ...". This formula corresponds to the expression used in Article 14 of the ECHR providing that "the enjoyment of the rights and freedoms set forth in this Convention shall be secured without discrimination on any ground...". The fact that the Constitution does not mention the terms "colour" and "association with a national minority" is simply a difference of wording. The Court has also mentioned some other differences in wording, for example, "social origin" (Convention) and "social status" (Constitution); This has no implication for the general principle of non-discimination provided by both the Convention and the Constitution.

The Court stated that Article 14 of the ECHR does not contradict the Constitution.

8.6 Answer to the fifth point of the Request. This point deals with the possible inconsistency between Article 2 of Protocol No. 4 to the ECHR and Article 32 of the Convention:

> Protocol No. 4 to the ECHR, Article 2 (*extract*)
> 1. *Everyone* lawfully within the territory of a State shall, within that territory, have the right to liberty of movement and freedom to choose his residence.

> The Constitution, Article 32 (*extract*)
> Cititens may move and choose their place of residence in Lithuania freely, and may leave Lithuania at their own will.

The President's Request. Protocol No. 4 guarantees everyone's right to liberty of movement and freedom to choose residence, while the Constitution guarantees this right for citizens of Lithuania.

> "The Constitutional Court notes that Article 2 of Protocol No. 4 to the ECHR containing the provision that 'everyone lawfully within the territory of a State shall, within that territory, have the right to liberty of movement and freedom to choose his residence' consists of two interrelated constituent parts. One of them covers the right of a person to move freely and to choose freely his residence; the other that this right is guaranteed only to persons lawfully residing within the territory of that State. Such persons could be nationals, as well as foreigners or stateless persons. The residence of a national within the territory of his State is always lawful. Article 32, part 3, of the Constitution stipulates: 'A citizen may not be prohibited from returning to Lithuania.' Meanwhile, the conditions of entry or of leaving the country by a foreigner or a stateless person are established by the internal law of the State.

Such conditions are established by the Law of the Republic of Lithuania on the Legal Status of Foreigners in the Republic of Lithuania.[28]

Foreigners, as well as stateless persons, residing lawfully in the Republic of Lithuania according to the Law mentioned above, enjoy the same rights and freedoms as citizens of the Republic of Lithuania unless the Constitution of the Republic of Lithuania, this act and other laws of the Republic of Lithuania, as well as international treaties of the Republic of Lithuania provide otherwise. Therefore, the provisions of Protocol No. 4, applied in the legal system of Lithuania together with the provisions of the Law on the Legal Status of Foreigners in the Republic of Lithuania, would overlap. One practical question still to be answered in a concrete case is whether a foreigner or a stateless person is lawfully within the territory of Lithuania for the purpose of full enjoyment of his his right to move and choose freely his residence.

Taking all this into consideration, it may be concluded that Article 2 of Protocol No. 4 of the ECHR does not contradict the Constitution of Lithuania."

It is without doubt that the Conclusion of the Constitutional Court on the conformity of the European Convention for the Protection of Human Rights and Fundamental Freedoms with the Constitution of Lithuania accelerated the accession of Lithuania to the Convention.

ANNEXES

1. Constitution of the Republic of Lithuania *(Parliamentary Record 1992, No. 11, pp. 2-30).*
2. Law on the Procedure for the Enforcement of the Constitution of the Republic of Lithuania *(Parliamentary Record 1992, No. 11, pp. 30-31).*
3. Law on International Treaties of the Republic of Lithuania *(Parliamentary Record 1992, No. 5, pp. 2-5).*
4. Law on the Ratification of the European Convention for the Protection of Human Rights and Fundamental Freedoms, and the Fourth, Seventh, and Eleventh Protocols to the Convention (*27 April 1995, No. I-865*).

---

[28] For the English text of the Act on the Legal Status of Foreigners in the Republic of Lithuania see in: *Parliamentary Record*/Seimas of the Republic of Lithuania. 1992, No. 5, pp. 5-10.

ANNEX 1

CONSTITUTION
OF THE REPUBLIC OF LITHUANIA

Approved by the citizens of the Republic of Lithuania in the Referendum on 25 October 1992

THE LITHUANIAN NATION

- having established the State of Lithuania many centuries ago,
- having based its legal foundations on the Lithuanian Statutes and the Constitutions of the Republic of Lithuania,
- having for centuries defended its freedom and independence,
- having preserved its spirit, native language, writing, and customs,
- embodying the inborn right of each person and the People to live and create freely in the land of their fathers and forefathers - in the independent State of Lithuania,
- fostering national concord in the land of Lithuania,
- striving for an open, just, and harmonious civil society and law-governed State, by the will of the citizens of the reborn State of Lithuania, approves and declares this

CONSTITUTION

CHAPTER 1
The State of Lithuania

Article 1
The State of Lithuania shall be an independent and democratic republic.

Article 2
The State of Lithuania shall be created by the People. Sovereignty shall be vested in the People.

Article 3
No one may limit or restrict the sovereignty of the People or make claims to the sovereign powers of the People.

The People and each citizen shall have the right to oppose anyone who encroaches on the independence, territorial integrity, or constitutional order of the State of Lithuania by force.

Article 4
The People shall exercise the supreme sovereign power vested in them either directly or through their democratically elected representatives.

Article 5
In Lithuania, the powers of the State shall be exercised by the Seimas, the President of the Republic and Government, and the Judiciary.

The scope of powers shall be defined by the Constitution.

Institutions of power shall serve the people.

Article 6
The Constitution shall be an integral and directly applicable statute.

Every person may defend his or her rights on the basis of the Constitution.

Article 7
Any law or other statute which contradicts the Constitution shall be invalid.

Only laws which are promulgated shall be valid.

Ignorance of the law shall not exempt a person from responsibility.

Article 8
The forced seizure of State power or any of its institutions shall be considered an anti-constitutional action, which is illegal and invalid.

Article 9
The most significant issues concerning the life of the State and the People shall be decided by referendum.

In the cases established by law, referendums shall be announced by the Seimas.

Referendums shall also be announced if no less than 300,000 of the electorate so request.

The procedure for the announcement and execution of a referendum shall be established by law.

Article 10
The territory of the State of Lithuania shall be integral and shall not be divided into any state derivatives.

The State borders may only be realigned by an international treaty of the Republic of Lithuania which has been ratified by four-fifths of all the Seimas members.

Article 11
The administrative divisions of the territory of the State of Lithuania and their boundaries shall be determined by law.

Article 12
Citizenship of the Republic of Lithuania shall be acquired by birth or on other bases established by law.

With the exception of cases established by law, no person may be a citizen of the Republic of Lithuania and another state at the same time.

The procedure for the acquisition and loss of citizenship of the Republic of Lithuania shall be established by law.

Article 13
The State of Lithuania shall protect its citizens abroad.

It shall be prohibited to extradite a citizen of the Republic of Lithuania to another state unless an international agreement whereto the Republic of Lithuania is a party establishes otherwise.

Article 14
Lithuanian shall be the State language.

Article 15
The colours of the State flag shall be yellow, green, and red.

The State emblem shall be a white Vytis on a red background.

The State flag and emblem and their use shall be established by law.

Article 16
The national anthem shall be Vincas Kudirka's "Tautiska Giesmes".

Article 17
The capital of the Republic of Lithuania shall be the city of Vilnius, the long-standing historical capital of Lithuania.

CHAPTER 2
The Individual and the State

Article 18
The rights and freedoms of individuals shall be inborn.

Article 19
The right to life of individuals shall be protected by law.

Article 20
Personal freedom shall be inviolable.

No person may be arbitrarily arrested or detained. No person may be deprived of freedom except on the bases, and according to the procedures, which have been established in laws.

A person detained in flagrante delicto must, within 48 hours, be brought to court for the purpose of determining, in the presence of the detainee, the validity of the detention. In the event that the court does not pass a decision to arrest the person, the detained individual shall be released immediately.

Article 21
The person shall be inviolable.

Human dignity shall be protected by law.

It shall be prohibited to torture, injure, degrade, or maltreat a person, as well as to establish such punishments.

No person may be subjected to scientific or medical testing without his or her knowledge thereof and consent thereto.

Article 22
The private life of an individual shall be inviolable.

Personal correspondence, telephone conversations, telegraph messages, and other intercommunications shall be inviolable.

Information concerning the private life of an individual may be collected only upon a justified court order and in accordance with the law.

The law and the court shall protect individuals from arbitrary or unlawful interference in their private or family life, and from encroachment upon their honour and dignity.

Article 23
Property shall be inviolable.

The rights of ownership shall be protected by law.

Property may only be seized for the needs of society according to the procedure established by law and must be adequately compensated for.

Article 24
A person's dwelling place shall be inviolable.

Without the consent of the resident(s), entrance into a dwelling place shall only be permitted upon a corresponding court order, or according to the procedure established by law when the objective of such an action is to protect public order, apprehend a criminal, or save a person's life, health, or property.

Article 25
Individuals shall have the right to have their own convictions and freely express them.

Individuals must not be hindered from seeking, obtaining, or disseminating information or ideas.

Freedom to express convictions, as well as to obtain and disseminate information, may not be restricted in any way other than as established by law, when it is necessary for the safeguard of the health, honour and dignity, private life, or morals of a person, or for the protection of constitutional order.

Freedom to express convictions or impart information shall be incompatible with criminal actions - the instigation of national, racial, religious, or social hatred, violence, or discrimination, the dissemination of slander, or misinformation.

Citizens shall have the right to obtain any available information which concerns them from State agencies in the manner established by law.

Article 26
Freedom of thought, conscience, and religion shall not be restricted.

Every person shall have the right to freely choose any religion or faith and, either individually or with others, in public or in private, to manifest his or her religion or faith in worship, observance, practice or teaching.

No person may coerce another person or be subject to coercion to adopt or profess any religion or faith.

A person's freedom to profess and propagate his or her religion or faith may be subject only to those limitations prescribed by law and only when such restrictions are necessary to protect the safety of society, public order, a person's health or morals, or the fundamental rights and freedoms of others.

Parents and legal guardians shall have the liberty to ensure the religious and moral education of their children in conformity with their own convictions.

Article 27
A person's convictions, professed religion or faith may justify neither the commission of a crime nor the violation of law.

Article 28
While exercising their rights and freedoms, persons must observe the Constitution and the laws of the Republic of Lithuania, and must not impair the rights and interests of other people.

Article 29
All people shall be equal before the law, the court, and other State institutions and officers.

A person may not have his rights restricted in any way, or be granted any privileges, on the basis of his or her sex, race, nationality, language, origin, social status, religion, convictions, or opinions.

Article 30
Any person whose constitutional rights or freedoms are violated shall have the right to appeal to court.

The law shall establish the procedure for compensating material and moral damage inflicted on a person.

Article 31
Every person shall be presumed innocent until proven guilty according to the procedure established by law and until declared guilty by an effective court sentence.

Every indicted person shall have the right to a fair and public hearing by an independent and impartial court. Persons cannot be compelled to give evidence against themselves or against their family members or close relatives.

Punishments may only be administered or applied on the basis of law.

No person may be punished for the same offence twice.

From the moment of arrest or first interrogation, persons suspected or accused of a crime shall be guaranteed the right to defence and legal counsel.

Article 32
Citizens may move and choose their place of residence in Lithuania freely, and may leave Lithuania at their own will.

This right may not be restricted except as provided by law and if it is necessary for the protection of State security or the health of the people, or to administer justice.

A citizen may not be prohibited from returning to Lithuania.

Every Lithuanian person may settle in Lithuania.

Article 33
Citizens shall have the right to participate in the government of their State both directly and through their freely elected representatives, and shall have the equal opportunity to serve in a State office of the Republic of Lithuania.

Each citizen shall be guaranteed the right to criticize the work of State institutions and their officers, and to appeal against their decisions. It shall be prohibited to persecute people for criticism.

Citizens shall be guaranteed the right to petition; the procedure for implementing this right shall be established by law.

Article 34
Citizens who, on the day of election, are 18 years of age or over, shall have the right to vote in the election.

The right to be elected shall be established by the Constitution of the Republic of Lithuania and by the election laws.

Citizens who are declared legally incapable by court shall not participate in elections.

Article 35
Citizens shall be guaranteed the right to freely form societies, political parties, and associations, provided that the aims and activities thereof do not contradict the Constitution and laws.

No person may be forced to belong to any society, political party, or association.

The founding and functioning of political parties and other political and public organisation shall be regulated by law.

Article 36
Citizens may not be prohibited or hindered from assembling in unarmed peaceful meetings.

This right may not be subjected to any restrictions except those which are provided by law and are necessary to protect the security of the State or the community, public order, people's health or morals, or the rights and freedoms of other persons.

Article 37
Citizens who belong to ethnic communities shall have the right to foster their language, culture, and customs.

CHAPTER 3
Society and the State

Article 38
The family shall be the basis of society and the State.

Family, motherhood, fatherhood, and childhood shall be under the care and protection of the State.

Marriage shall be entered into upon the free consent of man and woman.

The State shall register marriages, births, and deaths. The State shall also recognise marriages registered in church.

In the family, spouses shall have equal rights.

The right and duty of parents is to bring up their children to be honest individuals and loyal citizens, as well as to support them until they come of age.

The duty of children is to respect their parents, to care for them in old age, and to preserve their heritage.

Article 39
The State shall take care of families bringing up children at home, and shall render them support in the manner established by law.

The law shall provide for paid maternity leave before and after childbirth, as well as for favourable working conditions and other privileges.

Children who are under age shall be protected by law.

Article 40
State and local government establishments of teaching and education shall be secular. At the request of parents, they shall offer classes in religious instruction.

Non-governmental teaching and educational institutions may be established according to the procedure established by law.

Institutions of higher learning shall be granted autonomy.

The State shall supervise the activities of establishments of teaching and education.

Article 41
Education shall be compulsory for persons under the age of 16.

Education at State and local government secondary, vocational, and higher schools shall be free of charge.

Everyone shall have an equal opportunity to attain higher education according to their individual abilities. Citizens who demonstrate suitable academic progress shall be guaranteed education at establishments of higher education free of charge.

Article 42
Culture, science, research and teaching shall be unrestricted.

The State shall support culture and science, and shall be concerned with the protection of Lithuanian history, art, and other cultural monuments and valuables.

The law shall protect and defend the spiritual and material interests of authors which are related to scientific, technical, cultural, and artistic work.

Article 43
The State shall recognise traditional Lithuanian churches and religious organisations, as well as other churches and religious organisations provided that they have a basis in society and their teaching and rituals do not contradict morality or the law.

Churches and religious organisations recognised by the State shall have the rights of legal persons.

Churches and religious organisations shall freely proclaim the teaching of their faith, perform the rituals of their belief, and have houses of prayer, charity institutions, and educational institutions for the training of priests of their faith.

Churches and religious organisations shall function freely according to their canons and statutes.

The status of churches and other religious organisations in the State shall be established by agreement or by law.

The teachings proclaimed by churches and other religious organisations, other religious activities, and houses of prayer may not be used for purposes which contradict the Constitution and the law.

There shall not be a State religion in Lithuania.

Article 44
Censorship of mass media shall be prohibited.

The State, political parties, political and public organisations, and other institutions or persons may not monopolise means of mass media.

Article 45
Ethnic communities of citizens shall independently administer the affairs of their ethnic culture, education, organisations, charity, and mutual assistance. The State shall support ethnic communities.

CHAPTER 4
National Economy and Labour

Article 46
Lithuania's economy shall be based on the right to private ownership, freedom of individual economic activity, and initiative.

The State shall support economic efforts and initiative which are useful to the community.

The State shall regulate economic activity so that it serves the general welfare of the people.

The law shall prohibit monopolisation of production and the market, and shall protect freedom of fair competition.

The State shall defend the interests of the consumers.

Article 47
Land, internal waters, forests, and parks may only belong to the citizens and the State of the Republic of Lithuania by the right of ownership.

Plots of land may belong to a foreign state by the right of ownership for the establishment of its diplomatic and consular missions in accordance with the procedure and conditions established by law.

The right of ownership of entrails of the earth, as well as nationally significant internal waters, forests, parks, roads, and historical, archaeological and cultural facilities shall exclusively belong to the Republic of Lithuania

The Republic of Lithuania shall have the exclusive ownership right to the air-space over its territory, its continental shelf, and the economic zone in the Baltic Sea.

Article 48
Every person may freely choose an occupation or business, and shall have the right to adequate, safe and healthy working conditions, adequate compensation for work, and social security in the event of unemployment.

The employment of foreigners in the Republic of Lithuania shall be regulated by law.

Forced labour shall be prohibited.

Military service or alternative service, as well as labour which is executed during war, natural calamity, epidemic, or other urgent circumstances, shall not be deemed as forced labour.

Labour which is performed by convicts in places of confinement and which is regulated by law shall not be deemed as forced labour either.

Article 49
Every person shall have the right to rest and leisure, as well as to annual paid holidays.

Working hours shall be established by law.

Article 50
Trade unions shall be freely established and shall function independently. They shall defend the professional, economic, and social rights and interests of employees.

All trade unions shall have equal rights.

Article 51
Employees shall have the right to strike in order to protect their economic and social interests.

The restrictions of this right, and the conditions and procedures for the implementation thereof shall be established by law.

Article 52
The State shall guarantee the right of citizens to old age and disability pension, as well as to social assistance in the event of unemployment, sickness, widowhood, loss of breadwinner, and other cases provided by law.

Article 53
The State shall take care of people's health and shall guarantee medical aid and services in the event of sickness. The procedure for providing medical aid to citizens free of charge at State medical facilities shall be established by law.

The State shall promote physical culture of the society and shall support sports.

The State and each individual must protect the environment from harmful influences.

Article 54
The State shall concern itself with the protection of the natural environment, its fauna and flora, separate objects of nature and particularly valuable districts, and shall supervise the moderate utilization of natural resources as well as their restoration and augmentation.

The exhaustion of land and entrails of the earth, the polution of waters and air, the production of radioactive impact, as well as the impoverishment of fauna and flora, shall be prohibited by law.

CHAPTER 5
The Seimas

Article 55
The Seimas shall consist of representatives of the People. 141 Seimas members who shall be elected for a four-year term on the basis of universal, equal, and direct suffrage by secret ballot.

The Seimas shall be deemed elected when at least three-fifths of the Seimas members have been elected.

The electoral procedure shall be established by law.

Article 56
Any citizen of the Republic of Lithuania who is not bound by an oath or pledge to a foreign state, and who, on the election day, is 25 years of age or over and has permanently been residing in Lithuania, may be elected a Seimas member.

Persons who have not served their court-imposed sentence, as well as persons declared legally incapable by court, may not be elected members of the Seimas.

Article 57
Regular elections to the Seimas shall be held no earlier than 2 months, and no later than 1 month, prior to the expiration of the powers of the Seimas members.

Article 58
Pre-term elections to the Seimas may be held on the decision of the Seimas adopted by three-fifths majority vote of all the Seimas members.

The President of the Republic of Lithuania may also announce pre-term elections to the Seimas:

1) if the Seimas fails to adopt a decision on the new programme of the Government within 30 days of its presentation, or if the Seimas twice in succession disapproves of the Government program within 60 days of its initial presentation; or
2) on the proposal of the Government, if the Seimas expresses direct non-confidence in the Government.

The President of the Republic may not announce pre-term elections to the Seimas if the term of office of the President of the Republic expires within less than six months, or if six months have not passed since the pre-term elections to the Seimas.

The day of elections to the new Seimas shall be specified in the resolution of the Seimas or in the decree of the President of the Republic concerning the pre-term elections to the Seimas. The election to the new Seimas must be organised within three months from the adoption of the decision on the pre-term elections.

Article 59
The term of office of Seimas members shall commence from the day that the newly-elected Seimas convenes for the first sitting. The powers of the previously elected Seimas members shall expire as from the opening of the sitting.

Newly-elected Seimas members shall acquire all the rights of a People's representative only after swearing in the Seimas to be loyal to the Republic of Lithuania.

Seimas members who either do not take an oath in the manner prescribed by law, or who take a conditional oath, shall lose the mandate of a Seimas member. The Seimas shall adopt a corresponding resolution thereon.

In office, Seimas members shall act in accordance with the Constitution of the Republic of Lithuania, the interests of the State, as well as their own consciences, and may not be restricted by any mandates.

Article 60
The duties of Seimas members, with the exception of their duties in the Seimas, shall be incompatible with any other duties in State institutions or organisations, as well as with work in

trade, commercial and other private institutions or enterprises. For term of office, Seimas members shall be exempt from the duty to perform national defence service.

A Seimas member may be appointed only as Prime Minister or Minister.

The service of a Seimas member shall be remunerated, and all expenses incurred from parliamentary activities shall be reimbursed with funds from the State budget. A Seimas member may not receive any other salary, with the exception of payment for creative activities.

The duties, rights and guarantees of the activities of Seimas members shall be established by law.

Article 61

Seimas members shall have the right to submit inquiries to the Prime Minister, the individual Ministers, and the heads of other State institutions formed or elected by the Seimas. Said persons or bodies must respond orally or in writing at the Seirmas session in the manner established by the Seimas.

At sessions of the Seimas, a group of no less than one-fifth of the Seimas members may interpellate the Prime Minister or a Minister.

Upon considering the response of the Prime Minister or Minister to the interpellation, the Seimas may decide that the response is not satisfactory, and, by a majority vote of half of all the Seimas members, express non-confidence in the Prime Minister or a Minister.

The voting procedure shall be established by law.

Article 62

The person of a Seimas member shall be inviolable.

Seimas members may not be found criminally responsible, may not be arrested, and may not be subjected to any other restriction of personal freedom without the consent of the Seimas.

Seimas members may not be persecuted for voting or speeches in the Seimas. However, legal actions may be instituted against Seimas members according to the general procedure if they are guilty of personal insult or slander.

Article 63

The powers of a Seimas member shall be terminated:

1) on the expiration of the term of his or her powers, or when the Seimas, elected in pre-term elections, convenes for the first sitting;

2) upon his or her death;

3) upon his or her resignation;

4) when he or she is declared legally incapable by the court;

5) when the Seimas revokes his or her mandate in accordance with impeachment proceedings;

6) when the election is recognised as invalid, or if the law on election is grossly violated;

7) if he or she takes up, or does not resign from, employment which is incompatible with the duties of a Seimas member; and

8) if he or she loses citizenship of the Republic of Lithuania.

Article 64

Every year, the Seimas shall convene for two regular sessions - one in spring and one in fall. The spring session shall commence on March 10th and shall end on June 30th. The fall session shall commence on September 10th and shall end on December 23rd. The Seimas may resolve to prolong a session.

Extraordinary sessions shall be convened by the Seimas Chairperson upon the proposal of at least one-third of all the Seimas members, and, in cases provided for in the Constitution, by the President of the Republic.

Article 65
The President of the Republic shall convene the first sitting of the newly-elected Seimas which must be held within 15 days of the Seimas election. If the President of the Republic fails to convene the sitting of the Seimas, the members of the Seimas shall assemble the day following the expiration of the 15-day period.

Article 66
The Chairperson or Assistant Chairperson of the Seimas shall preside over sittings of the Seimas.

The sitting directly following elections of the Seimas shall be opened by the eldest member of the Seimas.

Article 67
The Seimas shall:

1) consider and enact amendments to the Constitution;
2) enact laws;
3) adopt resolutions for the organisation of referendums;
4) announce presidential elections of the Republic of Lithuania;
5) form State institutions provided by law, and shall appoint and dismiss their chief officers;
6) approve or reject the candidature of the Prime Minister proposed by the President of the Republic;
7) consider the programme of the Government submitted by the Prime Minister, and decide whether to approve it or not;
8) upon the recommendation of the Government, establish or abolish ministries of the Republic of Lithuania;
9) supervise the activities of the Government, and may express non-confidence in the Prime Minister or individual Ministers;
10) appoint judges to, and Chairpersons of, the Constitutional Court and the Supreme Court;
11) appoint to, and dismiss from, office the State Controller as well as the Chairperson of the Board of the Bank of Lithuania;
12) announce local government Council election;
13) form the Central Electoral Committee and change its composition;
14) approve the State budget and supervise the implementation thereof;
15) establish State taxes and other obligatory payments;
16) ratify or denounce international treaties whereto the Republic of Lithuania is a party, and consider other issues of foreign policy;
17) establish administrative divisions of the Republic;
18) establish State awards of the Republic of Lithuania;
19) issue acts of amnesty; and
20) impose direct administration and martial law, declare states of emergency, announce mobilisation, and adopt decisions to use the armed forces.

Article 68
The right of legislative initiative in the Seimas shall belong to the members of the Seimas, the President of the Republic, and the Government.

Citizens of the Republic of Lithuania shall also have the right of legislative initiative. A draft law may be submitted to the Seimas by 50,000 citizens of the Republic of Lithuania who have the right to vote. The Seimas must consider this draft law.

Article 69
Laws shall be enacted in the Seimas in accordance with the proceduue established by law.

Laws shall be deemed adopted if the majority of the Seimas members participating in the sitting vote in favour thereof.

Constitutional laws of the Republic of Lithuania shall be deemed adopted if more than half of all the members of the Seimas vote in the affirmative. Constitutional laws shall be amended by at least a three-fifths majority vote of all the Seimas members. The Seimas shall establish a list of constitutional laws by a three-fifths majority vote of the Seimas members.

Provisions of the laws of the Republic of Lithuania may also be adopted by referendum.

Article 70
The laws enacted by the Seimas shall be enforced after the signing and official promulgation thereof by the President of the Republic, unless the laws themselves establish a later enforcement date.

Other acts adopted by the Seimas and the Statute of the Seimas shall be signed by the Chairperson of the Seimas. Said acts shall become effective the day following the promulgation thereof, unless the acts themselves provide for another procedure of enforcement.

Article 71
Within ten days of receiving a law passed by the Seimas, the President of the Republic shall either sign and officially promulgate said law, or shall refer it back to the Seimas together with relevant reasons for reconsideration.

In the event that the law enacted by the Seimas is not referred back or signed by the President of the Republic within the established period, the law shall become effective upon the signing and official promulgation thereof by the Chairperson of the Seimas.

The President of the Republic must, within five days, sign and officially promulgate laws and other acts adopted by referendum.

In the event that the President of the Republic does not sign and promulgate such laws within the established period. said laws shall become effective upon being signed and officially promulgated by the Chairperson of the Seimas.

Article 72
The Seimas may reconsider and enact laws which have been referred back by the President of the Republic.

After reconsideration by the Seimas, a law shall be deemed enacted if the amendments and supplements submitted by the President of the Republic were adopted, or if more than half of all the Seimas members vote in the affirmative, and if it is a constitutional law - if at least three-fifths of all the Seimas members vote in the affirmative.

The President of the Republic must, within three days, sign and forthwith officially promulgate laws re-enacted by the Seimas.

Article 73
Seimas controllers shall examine complaints of citizens concerning the abuse of powers by, and bureaucracy of, State and local government officers (with the exception of judges). Controllers shall have the right to submit proposals to the court to dismiss guilty officers from their posts.

The powers of the Seimas controllers shall be established by law.

As necessary, the Seimas shall also establish other institutions of control. The system and powers of said institutions shall be established by law.

Article 74
For gross violation of the Constitution, breach of oath, or upon the disclosure of the commitment of felony, the Seimas may, by three-fifths majority vote of all the Seimas members, remove from office the President of the Republic, the Chairperson and judges of the Constitutional Court, the

Chairperson and judges of the Supreme Court, the Chairperson and judges of the Court of Appeals, as well as Seimas members, or may revoke their mandate of a Seimas member. Such actions shall be carried out in accordance with impeachment proceedings which shall be established by the Statute of the Seimas.

Article 75
Officers appointed or chosen by the Seimas (with the exception of persons specified in Article 74) shall be removed from office when the Seimas, by majority vote of all the members, expresses non-confidence in the officer in question.

Article 76
The structure and procedure of activities of the Seimas shall be determined by the Statute of the Seimas. The Statute of the Seimas shall have the power of law.

CHAPTER 6
The President of the Republic

Article 77
The President of the Republic is the head of State.

The President shall represent the State of Lithuania and shall perform all the duties which he or she is charged with by the Constitution and laws.

Article 78
Any person who is a citizen of the Republic of Lithuania by birth, who has lived in Lithuania for at least the past three years, who has reached the age of 40 prior to the election day, and who is eligible for election to a Seimas member may be elected President of the Republic.

The President of the Republic shall be elected by the citizens of the Republic of Lithuania on the basis of universal, equal, and direct suffrage by secret ballot for a term of five years.

The same person may not be elected President of the Republic of Lithuania for more than two consecutive terms.

Article 79
Any citizen who meets the requirements set forth in part 1 of Article 78 and has collected the signatures of at least 20,000 voters shall be registered as a presidential candidate.

The number of presidential candidates shall not be limited.

Article 80
Regular presidential elections shall be held on the last Sunday two months before the expiration of the term of office of the President of the Republic.

Article 81
The candidate for the post of President of the Republic who, during the first election round in which at least a half of the voters participate, receives the votes of more than half of all the voters who voted in the election, shall be deemed the elected candidate. If less than a half of the registered voters participate in the election, the candidate who receives the greatest number of votes, but no less than one-third of votes of all the voters, shall be deemed the elected candidate. If, during the first election round, no single candidate gets the requisite number of votes, a repeat election shall be organised after two weeks between the two candidates who received the greatest number of votes. The candidate who receives more votes thereafter shall be deemed elected.

If no more than two candidates take part in the first election *round, and* not one of them receives the requisite number of votes, a repeat election shall be held.

Article 82
The elected President of the Republic shall begin his duties on the day following the expiration of the term of office of the President of the Republic, after, in Vilnius and in the presence of the representatives of the People - members of the Seimas, taking an oath to the People, swearing to be loyal to the Republic of Lithuania and the Constitution, to conscientiously fulfill the duties of President, and to be equally just to all. The President of the Republic, upon being re-elected, shall take the oath as well.

The act of oath of the President of the Republic shall be signed by the President and by the Chairperson of the Constitutional Court, or, in the absence of the Chairperson, by a judge of the Constitutional Court.

Article 83
The President of the Republic may not be a member of the Seimas or hold any other office, and may not receive any remuneration other than the salary established for the President as well as compensation for creative activities.

A person elected President of the Republic must suspend his or her activities in political parties and political organisations until a new presidential election campaign begins.

Article 84
The President of the Republic shall:

1) settle basic foreign policy issues and, together with the Government, implement foreign policy;

2) sign international treaties of the Republic of Lithuania and submit them to the Seimas for ratification;

3) appoint or recall, upon the recommendation of the Government, diplomatic representatives of the Republic of Lithuania in foreign states and international organisations; receive letters of credence and recall of diplomatic representatives of foreign states; confer highest diplomatic ranks and special titles;

4) appoint, upon approval of the Seimas, the Prime Minister, charge him or her to form the Government, and approve its composition;

5) remove, upon approval of the Seimas, the Prime Minister from office;

6) accept the powers returned by the Government upon the election of a new Seimas, and charge it to continue exercising its functions until a new Government is formed;

7) accept resignations of the Government and, as necessary, charge it to continue exercising its functions or charge one of the Ministers to exercise the functions of the Prime Minister until a new Government is formed; accept resignations of individual Ministers and commission them to continue in office until a new Minister is appointed;

8) submit to the Seimas, upon the resignation of the Government or after it returns its powers and no later than within 15 days, the candidature of a new Prime Minister for consideration;

9) appoint or dismiss individual Ministers upon the recommendation of the Prime Minister;

10) appoint or dismiss, according to the established procedure, state officers provided by law;

11) propose Supreme Court judge candidates to the Seimas, and, upon the appointment of all the Supreme Court judges, recommend from among them a Supreme Court Chairperson to the Seimas; appoint, with the approval of the Seimas, Court of Appeal judges, and from among them - the Court of Appeal Chairperson; appoint judges and chairpersons of district and local district courts, and change their places of office; in cases provided by Law, propose the dismissal of judges to the Seimas;

12) propose to the Seimas the candidatures of three Constitutional Court judges, and, upon appointing all the judges of the Constitutional Court, propose, from among them, a candidate for Constitutional Court Chairperson to the Seimas;

13) propose to the Seimas candidates for State Controller and Chairperson of the Board of the Bank of Lithuania; if necessary, propose to the Seimas to express non-confidence in said officials;
14) appoint or dismiss, upon the approval of the Seimas, the chief commander of the Army and the head of the Security Service;
15) confer highest military ranks;
16) adopt, in the event of an armed attack which threatens State sovereignty or territonal integrity, decisions concerning defence against such armed aggression, the imposition of martial law, and mobilisation, and submit these decisions to the next sitting of the Seimas for approval;
17) declare states of emergency according to the procedures and situations established by law, and submit these decisions to the next sitting of the Seimas for approval;
18) make annual reports in the Seimas about the situation in Lithuania and the domestic and foreign policies of the Republic of Lithuania;
19) call, in cases provided in the Constitution, extraordinary sessions of the Seimas;
20) announce regular elections to the Seimas, and, in cases set forth in part 2 of Article 58 of the Constitution, announce pre-term elections to the Seimas;
21) grant citizenship of the Republic of Lithuania according to the procedure established by law;
22) confer State awards;
23) grant pardons to sentenced persons; and
24) sign and promulgate laws enacted by the Seimas or refer them back to the Seimas according to the procedure provided for in Article 71 of the Constitution.

Article 85
The President of the Republic, implementing the powers vested in him or her, shall issue acts-decrees. Decrees of the President, specified in items 3, 15, 17, and 21 of Article 84 of the Constitution, shall be valid only if they bear the signature of the Prime Minister or an appropriate Minister. Responsibility for such decrees shall lie with the Prime Minister or the Minister who signed it.

Article 86
The person of the President of the Republic shall be inviolable: while in office, the President may neither be arrested nor charged with criminal or administrative proceedings.

The President of the Republic may be prematurely removed from office only for gross violation of the Constitution, breach of the oath of office, or conviction of an offence. The Seimas shall resolve issues concerning the dismissal of the President of the Republic from office according to impeachment proceedings.

Article 87
When, in cases specified in part 2 of Article 58 of the Constitution, the President of the Republic announces pre-term elections to the Seimas, the newly-elected Seimas may, by three-fifths majority vote of all the Seimas members and within 30 days of the first sitting, announce a pre-term election of the President of the Republic.

If the President of the Republic wishes to compete in the election, he or she shall immediately be registered as a candidate.

If the President of the Republic is re-elected in such an election, he or she shall be deemed elected for a second term, provided that more than three years of the first term had expired prior to the election. If the expired period of the first term is less than three years, the President of the Republic shall only be elected for the remainder of the first term, which shall not be considered a second term.

If a pre-term election for the President of the Republic is announced during the President's second term, the current President of the Republic may only be elected for the remainder of the second term.

Article 88
The powers of the President of the Republic shall be terminated:

1) upon the expiration of the term of office;
2) upon holding a pre-term presidential election;
3) upon resignation from office;
4) upon the death of the President of the Republic;
5) when the Seimas removes the President from office according to impeachment proceedings; and
6) when the Seimas, taking into consideration the conclusion of the Constitutional Court and by three-fifths majority vote of all the Seimas members, adopts a resolution stating that the President of the Republic is unable to fulfill the duties of office for reasons of health.

Article 89
In the event that the President dies or is removed from office according to impeachment proceedings, or if the Seimas resolves that the President of the Republic is unable to fulfill the duties of office for reasons of health, the duties of President shall temporarily be passed over to the Seimas Chairperson. In such a case, the Chairperson of the Seimas shall lose his or her powers in the Seimas, and at the behest of the Seimas, the duties of Chairperson shall temporarily be carried out by the Assistant Chairperson. In said cases, the Seimas shall announce, within 10 days, an election for the President of the Republic which must be held within two months. If the Seimas cannot convene and announce the election for the President of the Republic, the election shall be announced by the Government.

The Chairperson of the Seimas shall act for the the President of the Republic when the President is temporarily absent beyond the boundaries of the country or has fallen ill and by reason thereof is temporarily unable to fulfill the duties of office.

While temporarily acting for the President of the Republic, the Chairperson of the Seimas may neither announce pre-term elections of the Seimas nor dismiss or appoint Ministers without the agreement of the Seimas. During the said period, the Seimas may not consider the issue of lack of confidence in the Chairperson of the Seimas.

The powers of the President of the Republic may not be executed in any other cases, or by any other persons or institutions.

Article 90
The President of the Republic shall have residence. The financing of the President of the Republic and of the President's residence shall be established by law.

CHAPTER 7
The Government of the Republic of Lithuania

Article 91
The Government of the Republic of Lithuania shall consist of the Prime Minister and Ministers.

Article 92
The Prime Minister shall, with the approval of the Seimas, be appointed or dismissed by the President of the Republic. The Ministers shall be appointed by the President of the Republic on the nomination of the Prime Minister.

The Prime Minister, within 15 days of being appointed, shall present the Government which he or she has formed and which has been approved by the President of the Republic to the Seimas and shall submit the programme of its activities to the Seimas for consideration.

The Government shall return its powers to the President of the Republic after the Seimas elections or upon electing the President of the Republic.

A new Government shall be empowered to act after the Seimas approves its programme by majority vote of the Seimas members participating in the sitting.

Article 93

On entering upon their duties, the Prime Minister and the individual Ministers shall, in the Seimas, take an oath to be loyal to the Republic of Lithuania and to observe the Constitution and laws. The text of the oath shall be established by the Law on the Government.

Article 94

The Government of the Republic of Lithuania shall:

1) administer the affairs of the country, protect the inviolability of the territory of the Republic of Lithuania, and ensure State security and public order;

2) implement laws and resolutions of the Seimas concerning the implementation of laws, as well as the decrees of the President;

3) coordinate the activities of the ministries and other governmental institutions;

4) prepare the draft budget of the State and submit it to the Seimas; execute the State Budget and report on the fulfillment of the budget to the Seimas;

5) draft bills and submit them to the Seimas for consideration;

6) establish diplomatic relations and maintain relations with foreign countries and international organisations; and

7) discharge other duties prescribed to the Government by the Constitution and other laws.

Article 95

The Government of the Republic of Lithuania shall resolve the affairs of State administration at its sittings by issuing directives which must be passed by a majority vote of all members of the Government. The State Controller may also participate in the sittings of the Government.

Government directives shall be signed by the Prime Minister and the appropriate Minister.

Article 96

The Government of the Republic of Lithuania shall be jointly responsible to the Seimas for the general activities of the Government.

The Ministers, in directing the spheres of administration entrusted to them, shall be responsible to the Seimas, the President of the Republic, and directly subordinate to the Prime Minister.

Article 97

The Prime Minister shall represent the Government of the Republic of Lithuania and shall direct its activities.

In the absence of the Prime Minister, or when the Prime Minister is unable to fulfill his or her duties, the President of the Republic of Lithuania, upon the recommendation of the Prime Minister, shall charge one of the Ministers to substitute for the Prime Minister during a period not exceeding 60 days; when there is no recommendation, the President of the Republic shall charge one of the Ministers to substitute for the Prime Minister.

Article 98
Ministers shall head their respective ministries, shall resolve issues assigned to the competence of their ministries, and shall also discharge other functions prescribed by laws.

A Minister may be temporarily substituted only by another member of the Government appointed by the Prime Minister.

Article 99
The Prime Minister and Ministers may not hold any other office subject to nomination or election, may not be employed in business, commercial or other private institutions or companies, and may not receive any remuneration other than the salary established for their respective Government offices and compensation for creative activities.

Article 100
The Prime Minister and Ministers may not be prosecuted, arrested or have their freedoms restricted in any other way without the preliminary consent of the Seimas, or, if the Seimas is not in session, of the President of the Republic.

Article 101
Upon the request of the Seimas, the Government or individual Ministers must give an account of their activities to the Seimas.

When more than half of the Ministers are changed, the Government must be re-invested with authority by the Seimas. Otherwise, the Government must resign.

The Government must also resign if:

1) the Seimas disapproves two times in succession of the programme of the newly-formed Government;

2) the majorty of all the Seimas deputies express a lack of confidence in the Government or in the Prime Minister in a secret ballot vote;

3) the Prime Minister resigns or dies; or

4) after Seimas elections, when a new Government is formed.

A Minister must resign if more than a half of all the Seimas members express, in a secret ballot vote, a lack of confidence in him or her.

The President of the Republic shall accept resignations of the Government or individual Ministers.

CHAPTER 8
The Constitutional Courts

Article 102
The Constitutional Court shall decide whether the laws and other legal acts adopted by the Seimas are in conformity with the Constitution and legal acts adopted by the President and the Government, do not violate the Constitution or laws.

The status of the Constitutional Court and the procedure for the execution of powers thereof shall be established by the Law on the Constitutional Court of the Republic of Lithuania.

Article 103
The Constitutional Court shall consist of 9 judges appointed for an unrenewable term of 9 years. Every three years, one-third of the Constitutional Court shall be reconstituted. The Seimas shall choose 3 candidates for Constitutional Court judges from the candidates nominated by the President of the Republic of Lithuania, 3 candidates from those nominated by the Chairperson of

the Seimas, and 3 candidates from those nominated by the Chairperson of the Supreme Court; the Seimas shall appoint the candidates that they choose as judges.

The Seimas shall appoint the Chairperson of the Constitutional Court from among the judges thereof and on the nomination of the President of the Republic of Lithuania.

Citizens of the Republic of Lithuania who have an impeccable reputation, who are trained in law, and who have served, for at least 10 years, in the legal profession or in an area of education related to his or her qualifications as a lawyer, shall be eligible for appointment as judges of the Constitutional Court.

Article 104

In fulfilling their duties, judges of the Constitutional Court shall act independently of any other State institution, person or organisation and shall observe only the Constitution of the Republic of Lithuania.

Before entering office, judges of the Constitutional Court shall, in the Seimas, swear to be faithful to the Republic of Lithuania and the Constitution.

The restrictions on work and political activities which are imposed on court judges shall also apply to judges of the Constitutional Court.

Judges of the Constitutional Court shall have the same rights concerning the inviolability of their person as shall members of the Seimas.

Article 105

The Constitutional Court shall consider and adopt decisions concerning the conformity of laws of the Republic of Lithuania and legal acts adopted by the Seimas with the Constitution of the Republic of Lithuania.

The Constitutional Court shall also consider the conformity with the Constitution of:

1) legal acts of the President; and

2) legal acts of the Government.

The Constitutional Court shall present conclusions concerning:

1) the violation of election laws during presidential elections or elections to the Seimas;

2) whether the President of the Republic of Lithuania's health is not limiting his or her capacity to continue in office;

3) the conformity of international agreements of the Republic of Lithuania with the Constitution; and

4) the compliance with the Constitution of concrete actions of Seimas members or other State officers against whom impeachment proceedings have been instituted.

Article 106

The Government, no less than 1/5 of the members of the Seimas, and the courts shall have the right to address the Consitutional Court concerning legal acts specified in part 1 of Article 105.

No less than 1/5 of the members of the Seimas and the courts shall have the right to address the Constitutional Court concerning the conformity of acts of the President with the Constitution and the laws.

No less than 1/5 of the members of the Seimas, the courts, and the President of the Republic of Lithuania shall have the right to address the Constitutional Court concerning the conformity of an act of the Government with the Constitution and the laws.

Upon the proposal of the President or the decision of the Seimas to investigate the conformity of an act with the Constitution, the applicability of the act shall be suspended.

The Seimas may request a conclusion from the Constitutional Court, and in cases concerning Seimas elections and international agreements, the President of the Republic of Lithuania may also request a conclusion.

The Constitutional Court shall have the right to refuse to accept cases for investigation or to prepare conclusions if the appeal is not based on legal motives.

Article 107
Laws (or parts thereof) of the Republic of Lithuania or any other acts (or parts thereof) of the Seimas, acts of the President of the Republic of Lithuania, and acts (or parts thereof) of the Government may not be applied from the day of official promulgation of the decision of the Constitutional Court that the act in question (or part thereof) is inconsistent with the Constitution of the Republic of Lithuania.

The decisions of the Constitutional Court on issues assigned to its jurisdiction by the Constitution shall be final and may not be appealed.

On the basis of the conclusions of the Constitutional Court, the Seimas shall have a final decision on the issues set forth in part 3 of Article 105 of the Constitution.

Article 108
The powers of a judge of the Constitutional Court shall be terminated:

1) on the expiration of the term of office;
2) upon the death of the judge;
3) upon voluntary resignation;
4) when the judge is incapable to fulfill his or her duties for health reasons; and
5) upon being removed from office by the Seimas according to the impeachment proceedings.

CHAPTER 9
The Court

Article 109
In the Republic of Lithuania, the courts shall have the exclusive right to administer justice.

While administering justice, judges and courts shall be independent.

While investigating cases, judges shall obey only the law.

The court shall adopt decisions on behalf of the Republic of Lithuania.

Article 110
Judges may not apply laws which contradict the Constitution.

In cases, when there are grounds to believe that the law or other legal act applicable in a certain case contradicts the Constitution, the judge shall suspend the investigation and shall appeal to the Constitutional Court to decide whether the law or other legal act in question complies with the Constitution.

Article 111
The court system of the Republic of Lithuania shall consist of the Supreme Court, the Court of Appeal, district courts, and local courts.

For the investigation of administrative, labour, family and other litigations, specialised courts may be established pursuant to law.

Courts with special powers may not be established in the Republic of Lithuania in times of peace.

The formation and competence of courts shall be determined by the Law on Courts of the Republic of Lithuania.

Article 112
In Lithuania only citizens of the Republic of Lithuania may be judges.

Supreme Court judges, as well as the Chairperson of the Supreme Court, who shall be chosen from among them, shall be appointed and dismissed by the Seimas upon the recommendation of the President of the Republic of Lithuania.

Judges of the Court of Appeals, as well as the Chairperson, who shall be chosen from among them, shall be appointed by the President of the Republic of Lithuania upon the approval of the Seimas.

Judges and chairpersons of district courts, local courts, and other specialised courts shall be appointed, and if necessary, transferred to other places of office, by the President of the Republic of Lithuania.

A special institution of judges provided by law shall submit recommendations to the President concerning the appointment of judges, as well as their promotion, transference, or dismissal from office.

A person appointed as judge shall swear, according to the procedure established by law, to be faithful to the Republic of Lithuania and to administer justice only pursuant to law.

Article 113

Judges may not hold any other elected or appointed posts, and may not be employed in any business, commercial, or other private institution or company. They are also not permitted to receive any remuneration other than the salary established for judges as well as payments for educational, scientific, or creative activities.

Judges may not participate in the activities of political parties and other political organisations.

Article 114

Institutions of State power and administration, members of the Seimas and other officers, political parties, public organisations, and citizens shall be prohibited from interfering with the activities of a judge or the court, and violation of this shall incur liability.

Judges may not have legal actions instituted against them, nor may they be arrested or restricted of personal freedom without the consent of the Seimas, or in the period between sessions of the Seimas, of the President of the Republic of Lithuania.

Article 115

Court judges of the Republic of Lithuania shall be dismissed from office according to the procedure established by law in the following cases:

1) at their own will;
2) upon expiration of their powers or upon reaching pensionable age as determined by law;
3) for reasons of health;
4) upon appointment to another office or upon voluntary transference to another place of office;
5) if their behaviour discredits their position as judge; and
6) when judgment imposed on them by court comes into force.

Article 116

If the Chairperson or judges of the Supreme Court or of the Court of Appeals grossly violate the Constitution, break their oath, or are found guilty of an offence, the Seimas may remove them from office according to impeachment proceedings.

Article 117

In all courts the investigation of cases shall be open to the public. Closed court sittings may be held in order to protect the secrecy of a citizen's or the citizen's family's private life, or to prevent the disclosure of State, professional, or commercial secrets.

In the Republic of Lithuania court trials shall be conducted in the State language.

Persons who do not speak Lithuanian shall be guaranteed the right to participate in investigation and court proceedings through an interpreter.

Article 118
Public prosecutors shall prosecute criminal cases on behalf of the State, shall carry out criminal prosecutions, and shall supervise the activities of the interrogative bodies.

Pretrial interrogation shall be carried out by investigators.

The procedure for the appointment of public prosecutors and judges and their status shall be established by law.

CHAPTER 10
Local Governments and Administration

Article 119
Administrative units provided by law on State territory shall be entitled to the right of self-government. This right shall be implemented through local government Councils.

Members of local government Councils shall be elected for a two-year term on the basis of universal, equal and direct suffrage by secret ballot by the residents of their administrative unit who are citizens of the Republic of Lithuania.

The procedure for the organisation and activities of self-government institutions shall be established by law.

Local government Councils shall form executive bodies which are accountable to them for the direct implementation of the laws of the Republic of Lithuania and the decisions of the Government and the local government Council.

Article 120
The State shall support local governments.

Local governments shall act freely and independently within the limits of their competence which shall be established by the Constitution and laws.

Article 121
Local governments shall draft and approve their own budget.

Local government Councils shall have the right within the established limits and according to the procedure provided by law to establish local dues, and to provide for the leverage of taxes and duties at the expense of their own budget.

Article 122
Local government Councils shall have the right to appeal to court regarding the violation of their rights.

Article 123
In higher level administrative units, the administration shall be organised by the Government according to the procedure established by law.

Representatives shall be appointed by the Government to supervise that the Constitution and the laws are observed, and that the decisions of the Government are implemented.

The powers of Government representatives and the procedures of their implementation shall be established by law.

In cases and according to procedures provided by law, the Seimas may introduce direct administration on local government territory.

Article 124
Deeds and actions of local government Councils as well as of their executive bodies and officers which violate the rights of citizens and organisations may be appealed against in court.

CHAPTER 11
Finances, the State Budget

Article 125
In the Republic of Lithuania the central bank shall be the Bank of Lithuania, which is owned by the State.

The Bank of Lithuania shall have the exclusive right to issue bank notes.

The procedures for the organisation and activities of the Bank of Lithuania as well as its powers shall be established by law.

Article 126
The Bank of Lithuania shall be directed by the Bank Board, which shall consist of the Board Chairperson, the deputies to the Chairperson, and the Board members.

The Board Chairperson of the Bank of Lithuania shall be appointed for a five-year term by the Seimas on the nomination of the President of the Republic of Lithuania.

Article 127
The budgetary system of the Republic of Lithuania shall consist of the independent State budget of the Republic of Lithuania and the independent local governments budgets.

State budget revenues shall be accrued from taxes, compulsory payments, dues, receipts from State property, and other income.

Taxes, other budgetary payments, and dues shall be established by the laws of the Republic of Lithuania.

Article 128
Decisions concerning State loans and other basic property liabilities of the State shall be adopted by the Seimas on the recommendation of the Government.

Procedures concerning the management, utilisation, and disposal of State property shall be established by law.

Article 129
The budget year shall begin on the first of January and shall end on the thirty-first of December.

Article 130
The Government of the Republic of Lithuania shall prepare a draft budget of the State, and shall submit it to the Seimas no later than 75 days before the end of the budget year.

Article 131
The draft budget of the State shall be considered by the Seimas, and shall be approved by law by the beginning of the new budget year.

Upon considering the draft budget, the Seimas may only increase expenditures upon specifying financial sources for said expenditures. Expenditures established by law may not be reduced as long as said laws are not amended.

Article 132
If the State Budget is not approved by the prescribed date, monthly budget expenditures at the beginning of the budget year may not exceed one-twelfth of the State Budget expenditures of the previous budget year.

During the budget year the Seimas may change the budget. It shall be changed according to the same procedure by which it was drafted, adopted and approved. As necessary, the Seimas may approve an additional budget.

CHAPTER 12
Control of the State

Article 133
The system and powers of State Control shall be established by law.

State control shall be directed by the State Controller who shall be appointed for a five-year term by the Seimas upon the nomination of the President of the Republic of Lithuania.

Before taking office, the State Controller shall take an oath. The oath shall be established by law.

Article 134
State control shall supervise the legality of the management and utilisation of State property and the realisation of the State budget.

The State Controller shall give an account to the Seimas on the annual execution of the State budget.

CHAPTER 13
Foreign Policy and National Defence

Article 135
In conducting foreign policy, the Republic of Lithuania shall pursue the universally recognized principles and norms of international law, shall strive to safeguard national security and independence as well as the basic rights, freedoms and welfare of its citizens, and shall take part in the creation of sound international order based on law and justice.

In the Republic of Lithuania, war propaganda shall be prohibited.

Article 136
The Republic of Lithuania shall participate in international organisations provided that they do not contradict the interests and independence of the State.

Article 137
Weapons of mass destruction and foreign military bases may not be stationed on the territory of the Republic of Lithuania.

Article 138
The Seimas shall either ratify or denounce international treaties of the Republic of Lithuania which concern:

1) the realignment of the State borders of the Republic of Lithuania;
2) political cooperation with foreign countries, mutual assistance, or treaties related to national defence;
3) the renunciation of the utilisation of, or threatening by, force, as well as peace treaties;
4) the stationing and status of the armed forces of the Republic of Lithuania on the territory of a foreign state;

5) the participation of Lithuania in universal or regional international organisations; and
6) multilateral or long-term economic agreements.

Laws and international treaties may provide for other cases in which the Seimas shall ratify international treaties of the Republic of Lithuania.

International agreements which are ratified by the Seimas of the Republic of Lithuania shall be the constituent part of the legal system of the Republic of Lithuania.

Article 139
The defence of the state of Lithuania from foreign armed attack shall be the right and duty of every citizen of the Republic of Lithuania.

Citizens of the Republic of Lithuania are obliged to serve in the national defence service or to perform alternative service in the manner established by law.

The organisation of national defence shall be established by laws.

Article 140
The main issues of national defence shall be considered and coordinated by the State Defence Council which consists of the President of the Republic of Lithuania, the Prime Minister, the Seimas Chairperson, the Minister of National Defence, and the Chief Commander of the Army. The State Defence Council shall be headed by the President of the Republic of Lithuania. Procedures for its formation, activities and powers shall be established by law.

The Chief Commander of the armed forces shall be the President of the Republic of Lithuania.

The Government, the Minister of National Defence, and the Chief Commander of the Army shall be responsible to the Seimas for the provision and command of State armed forces. The Minister of National Defence may not be a serviceman who has not yet retired from active service.

Article 141
Soldiers in active military service or alternative service, officers of the national defence, the police and the internal service, non-commissioned officers, re-enlistees who have not retired from service, and other paid officers of military and security services may not be members of the Seimas or of local government Councils. They may not hold elected or appointed posts in State civil service, and may not take part in the activities of political parties and political organisations.

Article 142
The Seimas shall impose martial law, shall announce mobilisation or demobilisation, and shall adopt decisions to use the armed forces in defence of the homeland or for the fulfillment of the international obligations of Lithuania.

In the event of an armed attack which threatens the sovereignty of the State or territorial integrity, the President of the Republic of Lithuania shall immediately pass a decision concerning defence against such armed aggression, shall impose martial law throughout the country or in separate parts thereof, shall declare mobilisation, and shall submit these decisions to the next sitting of the Seimas; in the period between sessions, the President shall immediately convene an unscheduled session of the Seimas. The Seimas shall approve or abolish the decision of the President of the Republic of Lithuania.

Article 143
In the event that a regular election must be held in time of military actions, either the Seimas or the President shall adopt a decision to extend the terms of the Seimas, the President, and local government Councils. In such cases, elections must be held within three months of the end of the war.

Article 144
In the event that the constitutional system or public order of the State is threatened, the Seimas may declare a state of emergency throughout the country, or in separate parts thereof, for a period not exceeding six months.

In the event of emergency, and if the Seimas is not in session, the President of the Republic shall have the right to pass such a decision, and shall, at the same time, convene an unscheduled session of the Seimas for the consideration of this issue. The Seimas shall approve or abolish the decision of the President of the Republic of Lithuania.

States of emergency shall be regulated by law.

Article 145
During martial law or a state of emergency, the rights and freedoms specified in Articles 22, 24, 25, 32, 35, and 36 of the Constitution may be temporarily restricted.

Article 146
The State shall provide and care for soldiers whose health is damaged during military service, as well as for the families of soldiers who lose their lives during military service.

The State shall also provide for citizens whose health is damaged while defending the homeland, and for the families of citizens who lose their lives in defence of the State.

CHAPTER 14
Amending the Constitution

Article 147
In order to amend or append the Constitution of the Republic of Lithuania, a proposal must be submitted to the Seimas by either no less than one-fourth of the members of the Seimas, or by at least 300,000 voters.

During a state of emergency or martial law, amendments to the Constitution may not be made.

Article 148
The provision of Article 1 of the Constitution that the State of Lithuania is an independent democratic republic may only be amended by a referendum in which at least three-fourths of the electorate of Lithuania vote in favour thereof.

The provisions of Chapter 1 ("The State of Lithuania") and Chapter 14 ("Amending the Constitution") may be amended only by referendum.

Amendments of other chapters of the Constitution must be considered and voted upon in the Seimas twice. There must be a lapse of at least three months between each vote. Bills for constitutional amendments shall be deemed adopted by the Seimas if, in each of the votes, at least two-thirds of all the members of the Seimas vote in favour of the enactment.

An amendment to the Constitution which is rejected by the Seimas may not be submitted to the Seimas for reconsideration for the period of one year.

Article 149
The adopted law on an amendment to the Constitution shall be signed by the President of the Republic of Lithuania and officially promulgated within 5 days.

If the President of the Republic of Lithuania does not sign and promulgate such a law in due time, this law shall become effective when the Chairperson of the Seimas signs and promulgates it.

The law on an amendment to the Constitution shall become effective no earlier than one month after the adoption thereof.

ANNEX 1

FINAL PROVISIONS

Article 150
The constituent parts of the Constitution of the Republic of Lithuania shall be:

The 11 February 1991 Constitutional Law "On the State of Lithuania";

The 8 June 1992 Constitutional Act "On the Non-Alignment of the Republic of Lithuania with Post-Soviet Eastern Alliances".

Article 151
This Constitution of the Republic of Lithuania shall become effective the day following the official promulgation of the results of the Referendum, provided that in the Referendum more than half of the electorate of Lithuania voted in favour thereof.

Article 152
The procedure for the enforcement of this Constitution and separate provisions thereof shall be regulated by Law of the Republic of Lithuania "On the Procedure for the Enforcement of the Constitution of the Republic of Lithuania", which, together with this Constitution of the Republic of Lithuania, shall be adopted by referendum.

Article 153
Upon the adoption of this Constitution in the Referendum, the Seimas of the Republic of Lithuania may, by 25 october 1993, amend by three-fifths majority vote of all the Seimas members the provisions of the Constitution of the Republic of Lithuania set forth in Articles 47, 55, 56, in item 2 of the second part of Article 58, in Articles 65, 68, 69, in items 11 and 12 of Article 84, in the first part of Article 87, in Articles 96, 103, 118 and in the fourth part of Article 119.

Article 154
Upon their adoption by referendum, the Constitution of the Republic of Lithuania and the Law of the Republic of Lithuania "On the Procedure for the Enforcement of the Constitution of the Republic of Lithuania" shall be signed and promulgated within 15 days by the President of the Supreme Council of the Republic of Lithuania.

ANNEX 2

LAW
ON THE PROCEDURE FOR THE ENFORCEMENT OF THE CONSTITUTION OF THE REPUBLIC OF LITHUANIA

Article 1
Upon the enforcement of the Constitution of the Republic of Lithuania, the Provisional Basic Law of the Republic of Lithuania shall become null and void.

Article 2
Laws, other legal acts, or parts thereof which were in effect on the territory of the Republic of Lithuania prior to the adoption of the Constitution of the Republic of Lithuania, shall be effective provided that they do not contradict the Constitution and this law, and shall remain effective until they are either declared null and void or coordinated with the provisions of the Constitution.

Article 3
Provisions of the laws of the Republic of Lithuania which determine the status of the supreme institutions of State power and administration of the Republic of Lithuania as well as the status of deputies and local governments shall be effective until the elected Seimas decides otherwise.

Article 4
The powers of the Supreme Council and its deputies shall be terminated when the elected Seimas of the Republic of Lithuania convenes into its first sitting.
The members of the Seimas of the Republic of Lithuania shall convene in a sitting on the third working day after the announcement of the Central Electoral Committee, following both election rounds, that at least 3/5 of all the members of the Seimas have been elected.

Article 5
The following text shall be the established oath of members of the Seimas of the Republic of Lithuania:

"I (full name),
Swear to be faithful to the Republic of Lithuania;
Swear to respect and observe its Constitution and laws and to protect the integrity of its territories;
Swear to strengthen, to the best of my ability, the independence of Lithuania, and to conscientiously serve my Homeland, Democracy, and the well-being of the people of Lithuania. So help me God."

The oath may also be taken omitting the last sentence.

Article 6
The legal situation during the period that there is no President of the Republic shall be equivalent to the situation which is provided for in Article 89 of the Constitution of the Republic of Lithuania.

As necessary, the Seimas, by a majority vote of more than half of all the members of the Seimas, may prolong the term provided in Article 89 for a period not exceeding four months.

Article 7
Judges of the Constitutional Court of the Republic of Lithuania including the Chairperson of the Constitutional Court, must be appointed not later than one month after the President of the Republic is elected.

Upon the initial appointment of Constitutional Court judges, three of them shall be appointed for a three-year term, three for a six-year term, and three for a nine-year term.

The President of the Republic, the Chairperson of the Seimas, and the Chairperson of the Supreme Court shall indicate in their proposals to appoint Constitutional Court judges which of them shall be appointed for three years, which for six, and which for nine.

The judges of the Constitutional Court who are appointed for three or six-year terms may hold the same office for one more term after an interval of at least three years.

Article 8
The provisions of part 3 of Article 20 of the Constitution of the Republic of Lithuania shall become applicable once the laws on the criminal procedure of the Republic or Lithuania are coordinated with this Constitution.

Vilnius
6 November 1992

VYTAUTAS LANDSBERGIS
President
Supreme Council
Republic of Lithuania

ANNEX 3

LAW
ON INTERNATIONAL TREATIES
OF THE REPUBLIC OF LITHUANIA

The Supreme Council of the Republic of Lithuania proceeding from the universally recognised principles and norms of international law regulating the conclusion and execution of international treaties, and which were consolidated in the 23 May 1969 Vienna Convention on the Law of International Treaty, the 14 March 1975 Vienna Convention on the Representation of States in their Relations with International organisations, and in the 21 March 1986 Vienna Convention on the Law of Agreements between States and International organisations, or between International organisations, expressing its allegiance to the principle of scrupulous fulfillment of international obligations, adopts this law.

CHAPTER 1
General Provisions

Article 1. Under this law an international treaty of the Republic of Lithuania shall mean an agreement which the Republic of Lithuania concludes in writing with foreign states or international organisations, regardless of the title of said treaty.

Article 2. This law shall establish procedure for the conclusion and execution of all international treaties of the Republic of Lithuania, regardless of which institution or official negotiated and signed, according to established procedure, any international treaty of the Republic of Lithuania.

CHAPTER 2
The Conclusion of International Treaties of the Republic of Lithuania

Article 3. Recommendations concerning conclusion of international treaties of the Republic of Lithuania shall be submitted to the Government of the Republic of Lithuania by the standing committees of the Supreme Council or by Ministries of the Republic of Lithuania upon coordination, or jointly, with the Ministry of Foreign Affairs according to procedure established by the Government of the Republic of Lithuania.

If the proposed international treaties establish norms other than those established by valid laws of the Republic of Lithuania, recommendations concerning these treaties shall be coordinated with the Ministry of Justice of the Republic of Lithuania and shall be submitted together with expert assessment of the discrepancies.

Article 4. Decisions concerning the preparation and negotiation of international treaties of the Republic of Lithuania shall be made by the Government of the Republic of Lithuania or, on its behalf, the Ministry of Foreign Affairs, except decisions concerning the international treaties of the Republic of Lithuania specified in Paragraph 2 of Article 7 of this law. Decisions concerning them shall be made by the Supreme Council of the Republic of Lithuania.

Article 5. The President of the Supreme Council of the Republic of Lithuania, the Prime Minister of the Republic of Lithuania, and the Minister of Foreign Affairs of the Republic of Lithuania shall have the right to negotiate the conclusion of international treaties of the Republic of Lithuania, to adopt their texts or sign them without special authorisation, in accordance with the provisions set forth in Article 4.

A head of a diplomatic mission of the Republic of Lithuania or a representative of the Republic of Lithuania to an international conference, international organisation, or to one of its bodies shall have the right to negotiate the conclusion of an international treaty of the Republic of Lithuania and to adopt its text either with the state wherein the diplomatic mission is located, or at an international conference, international organisation or at one of its bodies, respectively.

Other persons may negotiate the conclusion of an international treaty of the Republic of Lithuania, to adopt its text or sign it only if he has been provided powers set forth in Article 6 of this law.

Article 6. The powers to negotiate and sign international treaties of the Republic of Lithuania shall be conferred by the Government of the Republic of Lithuania and signed by the Prime Minister of the Republic of Lithuania and the Minister of Foreign Affairs of the Republic of Lithuania, except powers to negotiate and sign treaties on behalf of the Republic of Lithuania set forth in Paragraph 2 of Article 7 of this law. Powers to negotiate and sign the international treaties of the Republic of Lithuania specified in Paragraph 2, Article 7 of this law shall be conferred by the Supreme Council of the Republic of Lithuania and signed by the President of the Supreme Council and the Minister of Foreign Affairs of the Republic of Lithuania. Such powers must define the object of negotiations and specify other actions which the negotiator is authorised to perform.

Article 7. International treaties of the Republic of Lithuania shall be ratified by the Supreme Council of the Republic of Lithuania.

Subject to ratification shall be the following international treaties of the Republic of Lithuania:

1) on political cooperation with foreign states;
2) on mutual assistance;
3) peace treaties;
4) on the refusal to use or threaten to use force;
5) on the presence and status of armed forces of the Republic of Lithuania on the territory of foreign states;
6) on the presence and status of armed forces or foreign states on the territory of the Republic of Lithuania;
7) on the borders of the Republic of Lithuania;
8) on the participation of the Republic of Lithuania in both universal and regional international organisations;
9) multilateral and long-term economic agreements;
10) treaties establishing norms differing from those provided for by the laws of the Republic of Lithuania;
11) defence treaties.

Also ratified must be those international treaties which include provision for ratification. The Government of the Republic of Lithuania shall submit by its own decision international treaties of the Republic of Lithuania to the Supreme Council of the Republic of Lithuania for ratification.

Article 8. The Supreme Council of the Republic of Lithuania, having considered an international treaty of the Republic of Lithuania submitted for ratification, shall adopt a relevant decree.

Instruments of ratification shall be issued pursuant to Supreme Council of the Republic of Lithuania decrees.

Article 9. At the behest of the Government of the Republic of Lithuania, the Ministry of Foreign Affairs of the Republic of Lithuania, a diplomatic mission of the Republic of Lithuania in a corresponding foreign state, or a mission of the Republic of Lithuania to an international organisation shall exchange instruments of ratification, and deposit documents of accession to international treaties with the depositary.

Article 10. International treaties of the Republic of Lithuania which are not subject to ratification but for which confirmation procedure is stipulated, shall be confirmed by the Government of the Republic of Lithuania or, at its behest, the Ministry of Foreign Affairs of the Republic of Lithuania according to procedure determined by the Government.

Article 11. A decision to accede to an international treaty shall be made by the Government of the Republic of Lithuania or, at its behest, by the Ministry of Foreign Affairs, except treaties specified in Paragraph 2 of Article 7 of this law, decisions concerning which shall be made by the Supreme Council of the Republic of Lithuania.

CHAPTER 3
The Fulfilment of International Treaties of the Republic of Lithuania

Article 12. International treaties of the Republic of Lithuania shall have the force of law on the territory of the Republic of Lithuania.

Article 13. The Government of the Republic of Lithuania shall fulfil obligations assumed in international treaties of the Republic of Lithuania.

Article 14. Decisions to suspend or terminate international treaties of the Republic of Lithuania according to universally recognised norms of international law shall be made by the Government of the Republic of Lithuania, except treaties specified in Paragraph 2 of Article 7 of this law, decisions concerning which shall be made by the Supreme Council of the Republic of Lithuania.

CHAPTER 4
Final Provisions

Article 15. All international treaties of the Republic of Lithuania shall be registered in the register of international treaties of the Republic of Lithuania with the Ministry of Foreign Affairs.

Article 16. Ratified and confirmed international treaties of the Republic of Lithuania as well as treaties to which the Republic of Lithuania has acceded according to the procedure established by this law, upon recommendation of the Ministry of Foreign Affairs, shall be published in the *Supreme Council and Government of the Republic of Lithuania News*, and in the *Lietuvos aidas*, *Echo Litvy*, and *Kurier Wilenski* newspapers.

Article 17. The Ministry of Foreign Affairs of the Republic of Lithuania shall file the international treaties of the Republic of Lithuania which are in force with the Secretary General of the United Nations Organisation for registration, deposition, and publication.

Vilnius
21 May 1991
No I-1344

VYTAUTAS LANDSBERGIS
President
Supreme Council
Republic of Lithuania

ANNEX 4

LAW
ON THE RATIFICATION OF THE EUROPEAN CONVENTION FOR THE PROTECTION OF HUMAN RIGHTS AND FUNDAMENTAL FREEDOMS, AND THE FOURTH, SEVENTH, AND ELEVENTH PROTOCOLS TO THE CONVENTION

(Official translation)

1. On the basis of Article 138 of the Constitution of the Republic of Lithuania, the Seimas of the Republic of Lithuania ratifies, subject to the below reservations and declarations, the European Convention for the Protection of Human Rights and Fundamental Freedoms, signed on 14 May 1993 and the Fourth, Seventh and Eleventh Protocols to the Convention.

2. Pursuant to Article 64 of the European Convention for the Protection of Human Rights and Fundamental Freedoms, the following reservations are made in respect of Par. 3 of Article 5 of the above-mentioned Convention:

1) The Republic of Lithuania make a reservation that under Article 104 of the Code of Criminal Procedure of the Republic of Lithuania, the right to sanction arrest of persons on suspicion of having committed an offence shall also be vested in the prosecutor. The reservation shall remain in effect for one year after the coming into force of the above Convention in the Republic of Lithuania.

2) The Republic of Lithuania makes a reservation that the provisions of Article 5 of the above Convention shall not apply to national defence servicemen in the cases when disciplinary penalty - arrest - is applied to them in accordance with the Disciplinary Regulations.

3. Pursuant to Article 25 and 46 of the European Convention for the Protection of Human Rights and Fundamental Freedoms, the following declarations have been made:

In respect of Article 25 of the Convention: The Republic of Lithuania declares that it recognises for a three-year period the competence of the European Commission of Human Rights to receive petitions from any natural person.

In respect of Article 46 of the Convention: The Republic of Lithuania declares that it recognises for a three-year period as compulsory the jurisdiction of the European Court of Human Rights in all matters concerning the interpretation and application of the present Convention.

The declarations of the Republic of Lithuania in respect of Articles 25 and 46 of the Convention shall also apply to the Fourth and Seventh Protocols.

I promulgate this Law passed by the Seimas of the Republic of Lithuania.

Vilnius, 27 april 1995
No. I-865

Algirdas Brazauskas
President of the Republic

5. INCORPORATION AND IMPLEMENTATION OF HUMAN RIGHTS IN ICELAND

by Stefán M. Stefánsson, University of Iceland &
Ragnar Aðalsteinsson, Advocate to the Supreme Court

1. THE LEGAL STATUS OF INTERNATIONAL AGREEMENTS IN ICELANDIC LAW

1.1 Monism and Dualism. Broadly speaking, it can be said that in states following the monistic doctrine, international agreements become part of national law automatically. In states adhering to the dualistic doctrine, international law and national law constitute distinct legal systems. Thus, international law generally has no influence on the legal standing of individuals in regions where dualistic systems apply. There is no doubt that Iceland's constitutional structure is based on the dualistic doctrine. Admittedly, it is difficult to point to a clear legal provision in the Icelandic Constitution in support of this assertion, but it may be mentioned that under Article 2 of the Icelandic Constitution, the *Althing* (parliament) and the President exercise legislative authority.[1] The Icelandic Constitution contains further provisions on how the legislature enacts legislation. Furthermore, Article 61 of the Icelandic Constitution states that in the course of their official duties, judges are to judge only in accordance with the law. These legal provisions, together with decades of constitutional and judicial precedent, make it possible to state unequivocally the general principle that international agreements, including human rights conventions, do not automatically acquire legal force in Iceland.

---

[1] For particulars, see Stefánsson in Skýrsla umboðsmanns Alþingis 1988, Fylgiskjal I, and in Evrópuréttur, pp. 30-32. See also Alþingistíðindi 1992-1993, pp. 5879-5880.

M. Scheinin (ed.), International Human Rights Norms in the Nordic and Baltic Countries, 169–202.

1.2 Interpretation of International Law. Although international agreements do not automatically acquire legal force in Iceland, it is nevertheless regarded as a general principle, based on judicial precedent, that the state, the courts and the executive should, at all times, seek to interpret the statutory provisions in harmony with international law, and not in opposition to it. Moreover, in Icelandic law, international law is a specific source of law, though it is subordinate to certain other sources of law, in the same way as the nature of a case or general legal principles may be subordinate to statutes. This has two implications. Firstly, it implies that international law must be used as an aid of interpretation when statutory legislation in a particular field needs to be interpreted. Secondly, it implies that international law is subordinate in the sense that it yields to statutory legislation if these two sources of law contain conflicting rules regarding the same point of law. Consequently, the general rule in Icelandic law is that national law must be interpreted in accordance with the rules of international law as far as possible, but in cases where these two sources of law conflict, international law must yield to the provisions of enacted Icelandic legislation with which it is incompatible.[2]

Theoretically, it is possible to ask what the status of an international agreement would be if there were no enacted legislation in a field covered by the agreement and the agreement had not been incorporated into national legislation. A similar situation arises if legislation in the area in question is seriously imperfect. Naturally, in such cases it is relatively easy to interpret national legislation in accordance with international law. Thus, it is possible to argue that international law is given an enhanced status in such cases, and actually comes close to acquiring binding legal effect in the same way as enacted legislation would.

1.3 Premises for International Agreements. International agreements can be said to be based on the premise that the national law of the contracting state conforms, or must be drawn up to conform with the international agreement. This premise is often an essential condition if the contracting state is to be able to honour the obligation which it

[2] See Stefánsson in Skýrsla umboðsmanns Alþingis 1988, Fylgiskjal I, pp. 4-5.

undertakes when becoming party to the international agreement. In other words, this condition is essential in order to prevent the non-fulfilment by the state of its international legal undertakings.

As described above, a clear judicial tradition has therefore developed in Iceland by which the courts and executive authorities seek to interpret current national law in accordance with international agreements as far as possible.[3] This equally applies to legislation which comes into existence after the relevant international agreement. One of the reasons for this rule is that it is likely that the legislature had the valid international agreement in mind when it enacted the rules on the matters covered by the international agreement, and also that it did not intentionally enact legislation opposed to the agreement.

All in all, it can probably be said that Icelandic law applies both the interpretative rule and the rule of presumption described above in relation to international law. In addition, the executive authorities are always obliged, when issuing executive orders, to take international law into consideration when they are not clearly bound by statutory provisions to act in other ways.

1.4 Direct Effect. International agreements can sometimes have direct effect. Broadly, direct effect means that it is possible to apply the text of the international agreement in the same way as national legislation. Normally, this is based on the content of the agreements being such that individuals and legal persons are able to invoke the provisions in order to protect their rights either before the executive authorities or in the courts in the member states. When invoking such provisions with respect of the government or its institutions one may speak of vertical direct effect. An example: A German manufacturer of building materials considers that goods which he exports to Iceland are subjected to an unlawful countervailing duty which infringes the Agreement on the European Economic Area. The German exporter may base his claim on the provisions of the EEA Agreement, assuming that the provisions of the Agreement have direct effect, irrespective of whether he chooses to bring the case before a court in Iceland or to seek redress through administrative channels.[4]

---

[3] This approach may be classified under the rule of presumption.

[4] For particulars, see Stefánsson in Evrópuréttur, pp. 33-36.

Moreover, direct effect applies if an individual or a legal person in one of the states which are parties to an international agreement is able to invoke a provision of the agreement when bringing a legal action against an individual or a legal person in another member state or even in the same member state (horizontal direct effect). An example: A person who claims that a private enterprise has infringed his or her rights under Article 119 of the Treaty of Rome on equal remuneration between the sexes is able to invoke this article against the enterprise (Drittwirkung).[5]

1.5 When Do International Agreements Have Direct Effect? It is mainly the text of international agreements which determines whether they are able to have direct effect. The main condition is that the text is both clear and unconditional, and also that it is possible to interpret the agreement (or the relevant provision) as if it was intended to have direct effect. This means that the wording or aim must be such that it confers rights on individuals and legal persons, or places obligations on them.

Some international agreements include general declarations or other material which is not generally comparable with normal legal texts, and therefore do not involve direct legal obligations. Other international agreements are not intended to have an effect on the legal system and legal rules which are in force. Finally, some international agreements are intended precisely to play the same role as an ordinary legal text; often, they are intended to confer rights on, or place direct obligations on, a third party, even though he cannot be a party to the international agreement. Such international agreements are intended to have the force of law with the result that courts, executive authorities, individuals and legal persons in the state are obliged to comply with them and may invoke them just like ordinary statutes.

An international agreement is normally made between two or more contracting states or international organizations. It is scarcely possible to argue, *a priori,* that these parties intend to confer rights on individuals or place obligations on them unless it is clearly stated in the agreement. However, this view may change if the international agreement is incorporated into national law. By incorporating an

[5] See Thorarensen in Afmælisrit Gaukur Jörundsson, sextugur, pp. 85-88.

agreement, the legislature in the relevant state makes it an ordinary statute in that state. Then it is no longer necessary to regard the text of the agreement solely as an agreement between two parties; it may also be regarded as an ordinary statute. This makes it possible to examine the rights and duties of individuals and legal persons under such statutes in the same way as traditional legislation.[6]

From the above, it is clear that the various types of international agreements are not all equally well designed to acquire direct effect. Thus, various parts of the EEA Agreement and most of the Agreement on the European Surveillance Authority are not designed to have direct effect, and many other examples could be cited as well. Human rights conventions, on the other hand, are normally intended specifically to have direct effect.

1.6 When Do International Agreements Acquire Direct Effect under National Law? The doctrine according to which international agreements have direct effect is relatively new, and perhaps it has greater validity in those countries which subscribe to the monistic doctrine regarding international and national law. In countries adhering to the dualistic doctrine, the question of the extent to which an international agreement is able to acquire direct effect depends on how the agreement is implemented into national law, or how national law is brought into line with the agreement. Firstly, the agreement may be incorporated, either in its entirety or in part. Secondly, a state is able to adapt its national law to accommodate the international legal undertakings involved in the international agreement. In such cases, national legislation is amended in order to bring it into line with the international agreement (transformation). Thirdly, it may happen that a state considers it does not need to amend its national law in any way, as its laws already meet the international obligations undertaken (passive transformation).

In the first two cases, the international agreement acquires legal force and may also acquire direct effect (admittedly, however, in an indirect way, since its contents must always be implemented specifically in order to achieve this effect) to the extent to which it is

[6] See for further particulars Stefánsson, Evrópuréttur, pp. 33-34 and Thorarensen in Afmælisrit Gaukur Jörundsson, sextugur, pp. 88-93.

incorporated or transformed in law. Where it is important to establish the extent to which a third party is able to invoke such legal rules, this also depends entirely on the implementing legislation. In the third case, it is rather a question of whether national law can be interpreted in accordance with international obligations.

1.7 Precedence of International Agreements Incorporated in National Law. The Icelandic Constitution does not permit international agreements implemented in national law to prevail over other enacted legislation. Nor is it possible to provide for such precedence in enacted legislation without amending the Icelandic Constitution. On the other hand, it must be remembered that international agreements do not lose their character as such simply by being incorporated or transformed into Icelandic law. Consequently, such domestic legislation must be interpreted in conformity with the relevant international agreements so that the provisions of other statutes which may be incompatible with them are made to yield to them as far as possible. An example of this is that after the incorporation of the provisions of the European Convention on Human Rights into Icelandic law, it is likely that other provisions in Icelandic statutes which conflict with the provisions of the Convention will have to yield. This applies irrespective of whether such legislation predates or post-dates the domestic incorporation act and whether or not the latter includes special provisions concerning domestic legislation. However, precedence does not apply if the clear intention of the statutes involved is different, which is probably not the case very often. The conclusion is therefore that under Icelandic law, international agreements which have been incorporated or implemented into domestic law almost prevail over other domestic legislation.[7]

1.8 Legal Effect. International agreements may have a certain legal effect, even though they are not intended to be directly applicable. This effect may be both conditional and unconditional.[8]

---

[7] For further details, see Aðalsteinsson in Tímarit lögfræðinga 1990, pp. 17-20 and Stefánsson in Skýrsla umboðsmanns Alþingis 1988, Fylgiskjal I, pp. 4-5.

[8] See for particulars Stefánsson in Evrópuréttur, pp. 36-38.

It is conditional if the international agreement, or any of its provisions, take the form of declarations or other non-specific texts. In fact, many examples of this type may be found in both national law and international agreements. All such texts have legal effect, but this effect is nevertheless conditional because of the non-specific and conditional nature of the texts. The main significance of such a text is that it plays an important role in the formation and interpretation of other legal rules, both domestic and foreign, which are more specific and less qualified by conditions.

On the other hand, the effect is unconditional when the text of a particular international agreement is, in itself, clear and unconditional. Nevertheless, individuals and legal persons are not necessarily able to invoke the agreement in connection with the protection of their rights. However, the agreement may still have legal effect. For example, often the text of international agreements stipulates that only the contracting states may be involved in a possible violation. The same can be said of all the provisions of international agreements which provide for the organization and management of international institutions. If the text is sufficiently clear and un-conditional, it may be regarded as having unconditional effect. In fact, the same can be said of domestic legislation. Some legal provisions may stipulate that no specific person is able to invoke them in support of his rights. Frequently, for example, no particular person is able to invoke a provision in law because it is not considered that sufficient legal interest is at stake for him personally. An example: Under Article 10 of the Primary Schools Act, No. 63 of 1974, Iceland is divided into educational regions. In most cases, it is unlikely that individuals or legal persons are able to invoke this provision if they are dissatisfied with the aforementioned division. On the other hand, the provision has legal effect in that the government is obliged to comply with it.

Clearly the provisions of international agreements which have unconditional legal effect without having direct effect may have an effect on the interpretation of Icelandic law if they are considered relevant. In general, there is no reason to implement agreements of this type, or any of their provisions, in law, since they are not intended to have an effect on Icelandic law. On the other hand, if this is done, the Icelandic courts and executive authorities may be legally obliged to take such provisions into account when it is deemed relevant.

2. THE APPLICATION OF PROVISIONS OF THE EUROPEAN CONVENTION ON HUMAN RIGHTS BY ICELANDIC COURTS

In the following, some judgments by the Icelandic Supreme Court and one District Court judgment which confirm the general principles referred to above will be discussed, i.e. how international law is not, as such, part of national law, and how national law is interpreted in accordance with international law.[9]

Judgment by the Reykjavík District Court in Case No. 968/1959: As far as can be established, this was the first time the effect of the European Convention on Human Rights was put to test in Iceland. One of the parties to the case based his arguments partly on the view that the rules on high-bracket property tax in Act No. 44 of 1957 violated certain provisions of the Convention. After stating that the *Althing* had authorized the government to ratify the European Convention on Human Rights by Parliamentary Resolution of 19 December 1952 and that the ratification document had been submitted by Iceland on 29 June 1953, the summing-up of the Court continued: "On the other hand, this Convention has never been incorporated into Icelandic law, neither as an ordinary statute nor as a constitutional law. Therefore, the plaintiff is unable to argue in Court that the aforementioned Convention grants him any right of exemption from the tax provisions of Act No. 44 of 1957, to which, as has been described above, he is not entitled under the provisions of the Icelandic Constitution."

Supreme Court Judgment 1975.601: The Supreme Court judgment resolved a case in which it was demanded that the Court should recognize the illegality of the refusal by the Reykjavík City authorities to allow a person to keep a dog. The Supreme Court regarded the refusal as permissible under specific provisions in statutes, regulations and by-laws; the summing-up of the Court included the following comment: "Finally, the Court can not agree ... that the aforementioned rules violate Article 66 of the Constitution of the Republic of Iceland ... or that they should be disregarded because they are opposed to Article 8 of the European Convention on Human Rights. ... The ECHR has not

[9] These judgments are referred to in the report following the draft to the law on the incorporation of the ECHR, see Alþingistíðindi 1992-1993, pp. 5882-5889. Some of the following judgments are also discussed by Aðalsteinsson in Tímarit lögfræðinga 1990, pp. 17-22.

acquired legal force in Iceland, in addition to which the prohibition of keeping dogs does not infringe the aforementioned provisions of the ECHR."

Supreme Court Judgment 1985.1290: This judgment addressed a situation in which a man had been convicted of a traffic offence in a judgment delivered in a district Court, in which the deputy judge was also the representative of the commissioner of police in the same administrative region. Thus, he was the superior of the police officers who had originally investigated the offence committed by the convicted person. In the Supreme Court, the defendant requested the invalidation of the district court judgment on the grounds that the judgment had not been delivered by an impartial judge. The fact that the same person had dealt with the case both as the commissioner of police and as a judge violated the basic principles of Articles 2 and 61 of the Icelandic Constitution and Article 6 of the European Convention on Human Rights. Regarding this claim, the Supreme Court summing-up said: "Under the Icelandic judicial structure, judicial power at the lower-court level outside Reykjavík is in the hands of the town magistrates and district commissioners, who are also the heads of the police. In the opinion of the Court, the judgment of the District Court can not be declared invalid on the grounds that the representative of the Akureyri Town Magistrate was in charge of this case. Moreover, no special points have been demonstrated to establish the incompetence of the Town Magistrate or this deputy of his." A similar claim was resolved by Supreme Court Case 1987.356.

Supreme Court Judgment 1988.1532: This judgment resolved the question of whether it was lawful to impose as a condition for having a licence to drive a taxi the requirement that the licensee had to be a member of a particular taxi drivers' union. It was argued that such compulsory membership of a union was, *inter alia.,* opposed to the provisions of Article 73 of the Icelandic Constitution and Article 11 of the European Convention on Human Rights. In its judgment, the Supreme Court rejected the view that this obligatory membership was opposed to the aforementioned provisions of the Icelandic Constitution. The summing-up furthermore stated: "The appellant has not demonstrated that there is a discrepancy between Article 73 of the Icelandic Constitution and the provisions of the international conventions to which he refers and which are discussed in the district court judgment, which in any case would not automatically invalidate enacted provisions of the Constitution."

These judgments tested the argument that Icelandic national law was not compatible with the provisions of the European Convention on Human Rights. The Supreme Court either overturned this argument on the grounds that no such incompatibility existed, or rejected the claims based on the grounds that even though Icelandic national law and the provisions of the Convention were incompatible, this would not alter the validity of the enacted statutes, or, as appropriate, the Constitution, in Iceland.

In recent years, however, a considerable change has taken place in judicial practice in this area, as the following examples demonstrate:

Supreme Court Judgment 1990.2: This case again addressed a situation in which the Court was presented with a demand for the invalidation of a district court judgment in a criminal case on the grounds that the president of the district court where the case had been resolved was also the commissioner of police in the same administrative region, and was thus the superior of the police officers who had investigated the case at the initial stages. As in the former cases, the claim for invalidation was based, *inter alia,* on the argument that this arrangement violated the rights of the individual under Article 6 of the European Convention on Human Rights guaranteeing the right to have one's case tried by an impartial judge. In its judgment, the Supreme Court referred to the above-mentioned cases from 1985 and 1987, in which the view had been taken that Article 2 of the Icelandic Constitution did not prevent one and the same person from both executing judicial functions and exercising control of the police. Though, the Court stated that this did not conform with the view in states which were in other respects based on a concept of law similar to the Icelandic. Next, it cited the provisions of paragraph 1 of Article 6 of the ECHR and the fact that Iceland had ratified the ECHR, so undertaking to comply with its rules. It was pointed out that, at the time of ratification, the Government had regarded Icelandic law to be in conformity with the ECHR, but since then, many of the provisions under the ECHR had been interpreted in greater detail by the European Commission on Human Rights and the European Court of Human Rights. Among other things, the persons who had been convicted in the aforementioned cases from 1985 and 1987 had brought cases against the Icelandic state for violations of Article 6 of the ECHR, and in one of these cases, the Commission had ruled unanimously that such a violation had taken place. The European Commission on Human Rights had referred the case to the European Court of Human Rights, following which the Icelandic state made a friendly settlement with the appellant, referring to the fact that the state had rectified the situation on which the action was based by passing the Separation of Powers Act, No. 92 of 1989 (the Act on the Separation of Judicial and Executive Power at the District Court Level). The Court said that the European Court of Human Rights was expected to take a stance on whether it recognized that the case was concluded by this settlement. The Supreme Court summing-up then stated that the Icelandic Constitution was based on the distinction between the three branches of government; and that the historical and geographical reasons which accounted for the same persons, for the most part, being entrusted with both judicial and executive power outside Reykjavík, were now no longer as important as previously; that an act had been introduced effecting the separation of the judiciary from the executive at the district court level; that the Icelandic state had entered into a commitment in international law to uphold the European Convention on Human Rights; and that the European Commission on Human Rights had resolved in the aforementioned case that Iceland had violated this undertaking, but that the case was to be concluded by a friendly settlement. The summing-up also referred to the fact that under the then applicable laws on judicial procedure, the judge ought to have stepped down in a case if there was a risk that he could not assess the facts of the case impartially. The Court conceded that there was nothing to indicate that the deputy judge who resolved the case in the district court had shown partiality in assessing the facts of the case, but the Court concurred with the European Commission on Human Rights that in general, there was not a sufficient guarantee of impartiality in the functions of a court in criminal cases if the judge was, at the same time, involved in the administration of the police, as was the case in this instance. Finally, the Supreme Court summing-up stated: "With regard to the foregoing discussion, the Court takes the view that the aforementioned provisions in law must now be interpreted as meaning that the District Commissioner of the County of Árnessýsla and his deputy, who delivered the district court judgment, ought to have stepped down from their seats in this case". The judgment was annulled on these grounds. It should be mentioned that following this, judgments have been delivered in many comparable cases before the Supreme Court, in which a similar conclusion has been reached.[10]

Supreme Court Judgment 1990.92: During the handling of this case at the lower levels, a person had been remanded in custody during the investigation of a criminal case under a provision in the Code of Criminal Procedure which was valid at the time, and which permitted such a deprivation of freedom in instances where it was considered that there was reason to believe that the suspect had committed a criminal offence and that his offence was punishable with at least two years' imprisonment. Subsequently, a criminal action was brought against the person, and the judge to whom the case was assigned for judgment was the same person who had previously resolved the demand that the person be remanded in custody. The Supreme Court summing-up refers to the fact that the Icelandic state had, in 1953, ratified the European Convention on Human Rights, so undertaking according to international law to ensure that a person accused of a criminal offence receive a fair trial by an impartial judge. The summing-up refers to a judgment by the European Court of Human Rights delivered on 24 May 1989 against Denmark (*Hauschildt v. Denmark*, ECHR, A 154), in which it was not considered that the guarantees under Article 6 of the ECHR of the impartiality of the judge had been met in a case in which one and the same judge delivered a ruling in the case after having previously given several orders for the remand of the accused person in custody in the initial stages of the case, this being done under the same sort of rule in Danish law as had been applied as the basis for remanding the person in custody in this case. The Supreme Court summing-up then mentions that its judgment referred to in the last example above was based on the view that Icelandic legal provisions on the competence of judges should be interpreted with reference to the European Convention on Human Rights and that the conclusion had been that the district court judge should have stepped down due to his involvement in the early stages of the case, described above. It should be mentioned that a ruling of the same type can be found in Supreme Court Judgment 1990.266.

---

[10] See *Annex 1*.

Supreme Court Judgment 1992.174: This judgment resolved a criminal charge against a person who was not capable of expressing himself in Icelandic, and had therefore made use of the aid of a court interpreter during the trial. Under the rules of the Code of Criminal Procedure which was in force at the time, No. 74 of 1974, expenses in connection with the use of a court interpreter were explicitly counted among prosecution expenses, and would therefore be charged to the accused if convicted. The Supreme Court judgment upheld the conclusion of the district court regarding conviction, but stated that Act No. 74 of 1974 was to be interpreted in accordance with item *e* of paragraph 3 of Article 6 of the European Convention on Human Rights and that the expenses for the use of a court interpreter were therefore to be charged to the Treasury, while other prosecution expenses were charged to the accused.

3. REFERENCES TO SOURCES OF INTERNATIONAL LAW OTHER THAN TREATIES

It must be remembered that a survey of such references must here be restricted to published judgments and rulings, and only the judgments of the Supreme Court, with the relevant district court judgments, are published. The conclusions and comments of the Parliamentary Ombudsman are published. Only a limited number of executive decisions are published.

There are probably no examples to be found in which the courts, the executive authorities, the Parliamentary Ombudsman or other such bodies have based their conclusions on non-binding international human rights instruments and made direct reference to them. On the other hand, it is common that lawyers base claims before the courts and the executive authorities on direct references to such instruments. Thus, they have an unequivocal effect, and it can often be seen from the premises on which judgments and decisions are based that references by lawyers to such instruments have influenced judges and decision-takers, even though they do not refer directly to the instruments in question.

The same point of view applies in connection with references to customary international law or general principles of international law in the sphere of human rights and the use of international or foreign case law on human rights in the reasoning of courts and administrative bodies. Only in exceptional cases, do the courts refer to judgments by the European Court of Human Rights, even though lawyers who argue cases before the courts make extensive references to such judgments.

4. ASSESSMENT OF LAW AND PRACTICE

In July 1992, the Minister of Justice appointed a committee to investigate whether the time had come to incorporate the European Convention on Human Rights into domestic law in Iceland. The committee presented its report in April 1993, recommending that the ECHR with protocols should be incorporated in its entirety.[11] The minority in the committee recommended that only the substantive provisions of the ECHR and the protocols should be incorporated into domestic law. The European Convention on Human Rights was subsequently incorporated by the *Althing* under the European Convention on Human Rights Act No. 62 of 1994, which came into force on 30 May 1994.[12]

In its report, the committee said, *inter alia*, that when Iceland ratified the ECHR, it had been assumed that the provisions of Icelandic law were in conformity with it. Subsequently, according to the report, it had come to light that Icelandic law and the ECHR were not always in harmony. The report said the rulings of Icelandic courts and of the European Commission on Human Rights and the European Court of Human Rights in matters concerning Iceland showed that Icelandic legislation did not provide complete guarantees according to the European Convention on Human Rights. The report said that as incompatibility between the two had become more and more evident, support had grown for the view that the ECHR should be incorporated.

The committee considered that the main arguments in favour of incorporating the ECHR were as follows:

- the rights of the individual would be additionally protected;
- security under the law would be increased;

[11] See "Frumvarp til laga um mannréttindasáttmála Evrópu", pp. 66-94.

[12] See *Annex* 2.

- some provisions of the ECHR were more detailed than those in Icelandic legislation, and in some cases they filled gaps in Icelandic legislation;
- parties to judicial cases would be able to invoke provisions of the ECHR as direct legal authorities;
- incorporation would facilitate judicial rulings and decisions by the executive authorities;
- following incorporation, individuals would be able to secure judicial rulings in Iceland on various matters which otherwise would have to be referred to the institutions in Strasbourg;
- incorporation would involve an increased awareness of, and respect for, human rights among the general public, the judiciary, lawyers, executive employees and those involved in the preparation of legislation;
- incorporation would be in line with the general trend in Europe and would bring Icelandic legislation into line with that of countries with which Iceland has most contact; this would lead to increased international trust in the respect for human rights shown by the Icelandic government; and
- an indirect effect of incorporation would be a strong tendency to apply a broader interpretation of the Icelandic Constitution in accordance with the rules of the ECHR, where appropriate.

The dissenting opinion of the minority of the committee expressed the opinion that judgments by the Supreme Court in the immediately preceding years indicated that the court found that it had the authority to determine in each individual instance the extent to which Icelandic citizens enjoyed the protection of the substantive provisions of the European Convention on Human Rights. The minority took the view that the incorporation of the substantive provisions would eliminate this element of uncertainty and ensure that Icelandic citizens could invoke the provisions of the ECHR just like any other provisions of national law.

The committee's report stated that attempts had been made to a certain extent to transform national law to bring it into line with the provisions of the European Convention on Human Rights, but at the same time it said that this had not been effected successfully. The committee therefore considered that incorporation would be a more fruitful alternative than transformation. Furthermore, the committee referred to the fact that the ECHR had been incorporated into domestic law in Denmark and Finland, and that proposals on incorporation had been made in Norway and Sweden.

Even though only a year has passed since the ECHR was incorporated in Iceland at least one highly important judgment has been passed by the Supreme Court of Iceland. This was a decision in a criminal case dated 18 May 1995. In the district court the decision was made by a deputy judge as has been common procedure in Iceland for a long time. The terms of employment of the deputy judges are similar to the terms of ordinary civil servants in Iceland and the deputy judges do not enjoy the same protection of law as the ordinary judges who are appointed for life. The counsel for the defence demanded that the district court decision be invalidated on the grounds that an organization of the judiciary entrusting associate judges with the passing of judgments did not conform with Article 2 of the Icelandic Constitution and was in breach of Article 6 (1) of the European Convention on Human Rights which had been incorporated into Icelandic law by Act No. 62/1994. In the premises of the judgment, the Supreme Court compared the conditions in Iceland, as regards the position of deputy judges, with the rights an indicted person may expect to enjoy under the provisions of the Icelandic Constitution and the European Convention on Human Rights. The Court concluded that the position of deputy judges as described in the premises did not meet the basic requirements of the principles of the Constitution on the independence of the judiciary, as these are to be interpreted in conformity with the provisions of Article 6 (1) of the European Convention on Human Rights on independent and impartial judges, in order for the deputy judges to make judicial decisions in their own name and responsibility.

This decision indicates that the effect of the incorporation of the European Convention on Human Rights on judicial practice will be even more far-reaching than foreseen by the committee preparing the legislative bill on the incorporation.

5. RECENT DEVELOPMENTS AND REFORM

On 17 June 1994, the 50th anniversary of the foundation of the Icelandic Republic, the *Althing* resolved to work towards completing the revision of the human rights section of the Icelandic Constitution of 1944 before the next regular general election which was held in the spring of 1995. The resolution states that steps are to be taken towards bringing the provisions in the section into line with international human rights conventions to which Iceland is a party. Furthermore, the recommendations submitted on 5 April 1994 by the Committee on the Icelandic Constitution are to be taken into account in the course of the review.

The explanatory notes accompanying the proposal for the resolution state that the reference to international human rights conventions refers mainly to the European Convention on Human Rights, the European Social Charter, the International Covenant on Civil and Political Rights and the International Covenant on Economic, Social and Cultural Rights.

The proposals of the Committee on the Icelandic Constitution accompanied the Parliamentary Resolution. The proposal for a new section on human rights consisted of 14 articles, 11 of which dealt with civil rights and three with economic, social and cultural rights. The three last mentioned articles cover the right to assistance in connection with illness, disability, old age and unemployment, the right to education and instruction and the right to employment and to vacation from employment. In all cases, it is stated that these rights are subject to further provisions in law. No allowance is made for any form of direct reference to international conventions in the text of the human rights section of the Icelandic Constitution.

This proposal for a Parliamentary Resolution, together with the recommendations of the Committee on the Icelandic Constitution did not, at that time, give rise to any appreciable discussion, neither among the legal profession nor among the general public. No move was made by the Government to publicize the proposals or to stimulate public discussion of them.

In the autumn of 1994, a committee consisting of parliamentarians from the five political parties represented in the *Althing* was established in order to draft a final proposal for a new human rights section in the Icelandic Constitution. The committee presented a bill amending the Icelandic Constitution in December 1994 and the Constitutional Bill was debated in the *Althing* for the first time on 19

December 1994, a few days after it had been presented.[13] The Parliamentary Constitutional Committee publicly requested interested parties to file comments on the Constitutional Bill within three to four weeks, but until then drafts of the final Bill had not been made public. A lively and even sharp debate started in the media and various parties filed their comments on the Bill. Among organizations that filed opinions and comments were the Icelandic Section of Amnesty International, the Icelandic Red Cross, Church Aid, Save the Children, the Bishop of Iceland, UNIFEM, the Icelandic Bar Association and the Icelandic Human Rights Center. These contributions were quite important in the parliamentary debates which resulted in 14 proposed amendments to the Constitutional Bill all of which were passed.[14] Parliamentary elections were held in Iceland in June 1995 and the newly elected Parliament must also pass the Constitutional Bill in order for it to become effective. The final passage of the Constitutional Bill was made on 15 June 1995 and it entered into force on 5 July 1995.

The amendments to the Icelandic Constitution deal with freedom of religion; equality before the law; the equal rights of men and women in all respects; freedom of movement; personal liberty; protection against torture, inhuman or degrading treatment; the principle of legality; the prohibition of capital punishment; the right to a fair trial; freedom from interference with privacy, home and family life; the right to private ownership; the right to freedom of opinion and belief; freedom of expression; freedom of association for any lawful purpose including the forming of political associations and trade unions; freedom to pursue an occupation of one's own choosing; the right to negotiate terms of employment; a guarantee of necessary assistance in case of sickness, invalidity, infirmity by reason of old age, unemployment and similar circumstances; a guarantee of a suitable general education and teaching; and a guarantee for children for the protection and care for their welfare demands.

As far as is known, the Government has no plans regarding the incorporation into domestic law of international human rights conventions other than the European Convention on Human Rights. In its comments on Iceland's report on the implementation of the

---

[13] See *Annex 3.*

[14] See *Annex 4.*

International Covenant on Civil and Political Rights, the UN Human Rights Committee said, *inter alia*, that it found it unfortunate that more importance was attached to the European Convention on Human Rights than to the International Covenant on Civil and Political Rights, both in Icelandic domestic law as well as in legal doctrine and jurisprudence. The committee recommended that Iceland take the appropriate measures to incorporate the provisions of the International Covenant on Civil and Political Rights into Icelandic law and to ensure that it is not accorded less importance than regional human rights conventions. It is not yet clear what the response to this recommendation will be.

The UN Human Rights Committee also recommended that the Icelandic Government paid attention to the amendment to the Icelandic Constitution with a view to making it reflect adequately the provisions of the International Covenant on Civil and Political Rights and other international conventions which Iceland has ratified. Preparations for such amendments had begun long before this recommendation was made.

6. PRACTICAL ASPECTS OF IMPLEMENTATION

Access to documentation in the field of human rights in Iceland is rather restricted. The only library in the field is to be found at the offices of the Parliamentary Ombudsman, where, at least, lawyers have been extremely well received and provided with all available information, especially as regards the Strasbourg organs. The Ministry of Foreign Affairs has endeavoured to provide UN documents on request. These solutions are not satisfactory, and better solution must be found.

On 17 June 1994, the Icelandic Human Rights Center was established. The Centre is a non-governmental organization, the founders being nine associations. The Centre plans to organize a library and a database in the field of human rights.

International human rights conventions ratified by Iceland are published in the official languages and in Icelandic in Division C of the Law Gazette, which is by no means a widely accessible publication. The European Convention on Human Rights is to be found in the most recent edition of the Collection of Statutes (1990). The Universal

Declaration of Human Rights is not easily available to the public. As this lack of easy access to the most important human rights instruments was felt in many places, and as the government authorities seemed to show no interest in the publication and dissemination of the instruments, a private law firm published the most important ones in book form in 1992, presenting a considerable part of the print-run to the Ministry of Education for distribution in schools, and to the Ministry of Justice for distribution in prisons, police stations, etc.[15]

The Icelandic Red Cross engaged Ágúst Þór Árnason to write a book on human rights for pupils aged 12-14. It was published in early 1994 and was presented to pupils in this age group in Icelandic schools. The publication was financed mainly by the Icelandic Red Cross.

The Law Faculty of the University of Iceland has, in co-operation with the Association of Icelandic Judges and the Icelandic Bar Association, established a research institute in the field under the title of the Human Rights Institute of the University of Iceland. For several years, the Law Faculty has offered law students a course in international human rights.

In the aforementioned comments by the UN Human Rights Committee, the Government was urged to take further measures to ensure that the provisions of the International Covenant on Civil and Political Rights are more widely disseminated, particularly among the legal profession and members of the judiciary. The Icelandic Bar Association reacted by organizing an intensive three-day seminar that was held in October 1994, featuring lecturers of international standing.

REFERENCES

Alþingistíðindi (Parliamentary Report of Iceland) 23. hefti 1992-1993, þingskjal 1160.

Aðalsteinsson, Ragnar: Alþjóðlegir mannréttindasáttmálar og íslenskur landsréttur (International Human Rights Conventions and Icelandic Domestic Law). *Tímarit Lögfræðinga*, 1. hefti 1990, bls. 3-27.

Alþjóðlegir mannréttindasáttmálar. [Edited by Ragnar Aðalsteinsson et al.]. Reykjavík, 1992.

---

15 Alþjóðlegir mannréttindasáttmálar. Reykjavík, 1992.

Frumvarp til laga um mannréttindasáttmála Evrópu (Lagt fyrir Alþingi á 117. löggjafarþingi 1993). 1993.

Stefánsson, Stefán Már: *Er þörf á lögfestingu þjóðréttarsamninga* (Is there a Need for an Incorporation of International Conventions), skýrsla umboðsmanns Alþingis fyrir árið 1988, Fylgiskjal I, pp. 1-17.

Stefánsson, Stefán Már: *Evrópuréttur, réttarreglur og stofnanir Evrópubandalagsins* (The European Law, Rules and Institutions of the European Community, Textbook). Reykjavík, 1990.

Thorarensen, Björg: *Einkaréttaráhrif Mannréttindasáttmála Evrópu og skyldur ríkja til athafna samkvæmt sáttmálanum* (Civil Effect of the European Human Rights Convention and Obligation of the States to Act According to the Convention), in Afmælisrit Gaukur Jörundsson, sextugur, 1994, pp. 83-121.

Þórhallsson, Páll: Lögfesting Mannréttindasáttmála Evrópu (The Incorporation of the Human Rights Convention) in *Úlfljótur*, 2. tbl. 1994, pp. 157-171.

ANNEXES

1. Supreme Court Judgment No. 120/1989: The Public Prosecutor vs. Guðmundur Breiðfjörð Ægisson.
2. The European Human Rights Convention Act.
3. 389th Constitutional Bill amending the Constitution of the Republic of Iceland, No. 33/1944, as later amended.
4. Amendment Proposal to the Bill amending the Constitution of the Republic of Iceland, No. 33/1944, as later amended.

ANNEX 1

(Translation from Icelandic)

THE PUBLIC PROSECUTOR
VS.
GUÐMUNDUR BREIÐFJÖRÐ ÆGISSON

in the year 1990, Tuesday, January 9, the Supreme Court
in case No. 120/1989

rendered the following

JUDGMENT:

This case is adjudged by the Supreme Court Judges Guðmundur Jónsson, Benedikt Blöndal, Bjarni K. Bjarnason, Guðrún Erlendsdóttir, Haraldur Henrysson, Hrafn Bragason, and Þór Vilhjálmsson.

The Public Prosecutor appealed the district court judgment to the Supreme Court by a summons dated 7 March 1989 at the request of the defendant, and also on behalf of the Public Prosecutor for conviction according to the indictment and an increased sentence. Furthermore, a claim is made for confirmation of the district court judgment's provision relating to damages.

The defense claims, primarily, that the judgment appealed against should be invalidated and the case remanded to the district court for renewed adjudication, or, secondly, that the sentence imposed be as light as the law allows, and made conditional.

I

The deputy who pronounced the judgment appealed serves on the responsibility of the county magistrate of Árnessýsla, and, in a letter dated 12 December 1989 Mr. Andrés Valdimarsson, county magistrate, described his duties as follows:

"I hereby confirm that Mr. Þorgeir Ingi Njálsson, lawyer, came to serve with this office on 1 June 1987. His commission for the position of judge's deputy is dated 12 June 1987.

His duties, from the time stated and until 16 September, last, were the following: Civil court, i.e., filing of cases, endorsements, and default judgments; magistrate's court every second month; police cases; criminal court (settlements and indictments); chattel auctions; and, as needed, auction court decisions generally.

His duties in the field of police cases have, i.a., been assisting the police in the investigation of criminal cases and providing instructions relating to the conduct of investigations. He has been responsible for the office's complaints file, determined fines imposed by the chief of police, written letters accompanying cases sent to the Public Prosecutor, and sent cases to to other jurisdictions for further investigation, to mention some of his functions."

According to the case documents the case was investigated by the police of Árnessýsla. The documents contain no indication that Mr. Njálsson was involved in the investigation, apart from sending the case to the Public Prosecutor for instructions with a letter dated 6 July 1988.

II

For a long time administrative and judicial functions in Iceland have been discharged locally under an arrangement similar to that described in the letter of the county magistrate of Árnessýsla; however, this has not been the case in Reykjavík for a considerable period of time, and some change has been effected in a few other localities. In Supreme Court Reports 1985 p. 1290 and 1987 p. 356 this Court held that such an arrangement was not prevented by Article 2 of the Icelandic Constitution, no. 33/1944, viewing the fact that its Article 61 assumes that judges may hold administrative offices. Owing to historical and geographical conditions judicial as well as administrative functions have, in this country, been discharged by the same persons. This is not in harmony with the views prevailing in states whose legal conceptions are in other respects similar to those of Iceland.

III

In 1953 the Council of Europe Convention on Human Rights and Fundamental Freedoms was ratified on behalf of Iceland, cf., Announcement no. 11/1954. The Convention is commonly referred to as the European Human Rights Convention. Article 6 para. 1 of the Convention reads, i.a., as follows:

"In the determination of his civil rights and obligations or of any criminal charge against him, everyone is entitled to a fair and public hearing within a reasonable time by an independent and impartial tribunal established by law."

The Government originally sought the approval of the *Althing* to become a party to the European Human Rights Convention on behalf of Iceland in the autumn of 1951, but debate on the matter was not completed during that session. A reading took place, however, but only one Member spoke, who was Mr. Bjarni Benediktsson, Minister of Justice at the time. Among other words, he said:

"As regards the rights enumerated here one can say briefly that in all aspects of any significance they are already expressly granted the citizens in Icelandic statute law and to some extent in the Icelandic Constitution itself, or that they are rights of such basic nature that they are deemed to be included in Icelandic general legal principles, even if they are not expressly stated. Therefore it can be said that Chapter 1 of the Convention is no novelty in Iceland, since it enumerates the rights which are already enjoyed by the citizenry and regarded as an obvious part of the protection of Icelandic citizens against the might of the State or against aggression by others." (Reports of the *Althing* 1951, D 239-240).

This indicates that when the Human Rights Convention was ratified the Government considered that Icelandic legal principles were in conformity with it as it was interpreted at the time. Since then many of its provisions have been subject to further interpretation in case practice with the European Commission of Human Rights and the European Court of Human Rights.

According to international law Iceland, by ratifying the ECHR, undertook the obligation to comply with its provisions.

With Act no. 92/1989 on Separation of District Judicial and Administrative Powers the policy was adopted that these two branches of state authority should not be wielded by the same persons. The Act enters into effect 1 July 1992.

IV

The persons found guilty by the two Supreme Court judgments mentioned have sent an application to the European Commission of Human Rights as permitted in the ECHR. As regards the case of Jón Kristinsson, which was adjudged by the Supreme Court by the judgment in Reports 1985 p. 1290, the Human Rights Commission prepared a report which was completed 8 March 1989. The Commission summarizes its conclusion in the following words:

"The Commission concludes unanimously that there has been a violation of Article 6 para. 1 of the ECHR, in that the District court of Akureyri, when convicting and sentencing the applicant, was not an impartial tribunal."

The Commission referred the case of Jón Kristinsson to the European Court of Human Rights, and it is scheduled for a hearing in February 1990. The following document has been submitted to the Supreme Court:

"The undersigned, the Government of Iceland and Mr. Jón Kristinsson, residing at Byggðavegur 95, Akureyri, Iceland, have today agreed to ask the European Court of Human Rights to dismiss, with the approval of the European Commission of Human Rights, the Commission's case against the Government of Iceland, as we now have concluded the following

SETTLEMENT

On 27 December 1984 Mr. Jón Kristinsson was sentenced by the criminal court of Akureyri to pay a fine of Icel. Kr. 3.000 to the Icelandic State Treasury on account of violations of the Traffic Act allegedly committed 20 and 26 June that year, and was also ordered to pay all costs due to the prosecution of the case against him. The judgment was appealed to the Supreme Court of Iceland on his request, and was in part upheld by a Supreme Court judgment pronounced 25 November 1985, whereby a fine of Icel. Kr. 1.500 was imposed and he was ordered to pay all costs of the case in district as well as Supreme Court. On 5 February 1986 Mr. Kristinsson paid in accordance with the judgment a fine of Icel. Kr. 1.500, and costs of the case, Icel. Kr. 25.150, to the Icelandic State Treasury, or a total of Icel. Kr. 26.650. On 12 May 1986 Mr. Kristinsson submitted an application to the European Commission of Human Rights alleging that the Government of Iceland, by Act no. 74 of 27 April 1972 on District Judicial Organization, Police and Customs Administration, etc., had violated Article 6 para. 1 of the European Convention for the Protection of Human Rights and Fundamental Freedoms, which was ratified by the President of Iceland on 19 June 1953. Mr. Kristinsson considered that this violation had taken place by the fact that on the basis of the act mentioned his case had been investigated by the director of police of Akureyri and adjudged by the same official as the criminal court judge of Akureyri, and that therefore he had not been afforded a fair hearing by an independent and impartial tribunal. The European Commission of Human Rights decided on 13 October 1987 that Mr. Kristinsson's petition was admissible. The Commission furthermore, on 10 April 1989 (sic), expressed its unanimous opinion that the government of Iceland had in the above manner violated the said Article 6 para. 1 of the Convention for the Protection of Human Rights and Fundamental Freedoms, and therefore decided to refer the case against the Government of Iceland to the European Court of Human Rights. On 19 May 1989 the *Althing* enacted a Bill in respect of Separation of District Judicial and Administrative Powers, which was approved by the President 1 June 1989. This enactment, Act no. 92/1989, which will enter into effect 1 July 1992, provides that police administration will as from that time be in the hands of district executive agents titled magistrates, and that district court judges, independent and separate from the executive branch of government, resolve issues relating to criminal charges.

Owing to the enactment of Act no. 92/1989 on Separation of District Judicial and Administrative Powers, and to the stand taken by the European Commission of Human Rights as described above, the Government of Iceland and Mr. Jón Kristinsson are in agreement to settle their dispute on the following terms:

1. That the Government of Iceland reimburse Mr. Jón Kristinsson for his fine and costs of the case he has paid, Icel. Kr. 26.650, with interest as from 12 May 1986, Icel. Kr. 53.353, or a total of Icel. Kr. 80.003.
2. That the Government of Iceland pay Mr. Jón Kristinsson the costs incurred by him for legal assistance on account of his application to the European Commission of Human Right,

totalling Icel. Kr. 461.130 when the financial assistance received by Mr. Kristinsson from the European Commission of Human Rights has been taken into account.

3. That Mr. Jón Kristinsson undertake, following the payment of the above amounts and without receiving damages or any further payments from the Icelandic State Treasury, not to prosecute the case now before the European Court of Human Rights any further, and not to take any other legal action against the Government of Iceland before Icelandic or international courts on account of the facts described above.
4. That Mr. Kristinsson accept that the Icelandic State Treasury pay the above payments immediately, provided the European Court of Human Rights agrees to strike the case of the European Commission of Human Rights against the Government of Iceland out of its list in accordance with Article 48 para. 2 of its Rules.
5. That the Icelandic Minister of Justice will request the Public Prosecutor of Iceland to have a comment entered into the State Criminal Registry relating to Mr. Jón Kristinsson, stating that the Government of Iceland has today, on account of the stand taken by the European Commission of Human Rights with regard to his application, concluded a settlement with him providing for refund of the amounts he was ordered to pay to the Icelandic State Treasury by the judgment of the Supreme Court of Iceland pronounced 25 November 1985.
6. That the obligations here undertaken by the Government of Iceland on one hand, and Mr. Jón Kristinsson on the other, be automatically cancelled in case the European Court of Human Rights withholds its approval as referred to under (4) above.

Done at Reykjavík, 18 December 1989.

On behalf of the Government
of Iceland:
Mr. Óli Þ. Guðbjartsson
Minister of Justice
In accordance with a decision
of the Government of Iceland
24 November 1989.

On behalf of
Mr. Jón Kristinsson:
Mr. Eiríkur Tómasson
Supreme Court Advocate
In accordance with a power of
attorney
dated 17 November 1989.

Information on the action taken until now by the European Commission of Human Rights with regard to the application of Mr. Einar Sverrisson, who was sentenced by Supreme Court Judgment in Reports 1987 p. 356, has not been submitted. A settlement has been concluded between Mr. Sverrisson and the Government, similar in substance to the settlement made with Mr. Jón Kristinsson.

V

In this case, the following is to be considered:

The Constitution of the Republic is based on the main principle that state authority is divided into three branches, and that judicial powers are exercised separately by judges.

The particular historical and geographical conditions underlying the arrangement of frequently committing both administrative and judicial duties to the same persons outside Reykjavík are now of less significance than previously, i.a. on account of better communications than in the past.

The *Althing* has passed an Act relating to separation of district administrative and judicial powers, which shall enter into effect 1 July 1992.

Iceland has undertaken the obligation according to international law to honour the European Human Rights Convention.

The European Human Rights Commission has unanimously concluded that the procedure described above in the case of Mr. Jón Kristinsson was not in conformity with Article 6 para. 1 of the Human Rights Convention.

The Icelandic Government has, after the above matter was referred to the European Court of Human Rights, concluded a settlement with Mr. Jón Kristinsson in the manner described, and also with another person who has submitted a petition relating to a similar matter.

Article 36 para. 7 of the Code of Civil Procedure, no. 85/1936, provides, i.a., that a judge shall yield his seat if there is a danger "that he may not be able to view the case impartially." According to Article 15 para. 2 of the Code of Criminal Procedure, no. 74/1974, this provision is also to be applied to criminal cases.

In this case no evidence has been submitted to indicate that the judge's deputy who rendered the district court judgment held partial views. Nevertheless this Court must concur with the opinion of the European Commission on Human Rights that impartiality in the performance of judicial functions is not adequately secured when a person performs such functions while also administering police matters.

With regard to the above the legal provisions quoted shall now be construed as having the effect that the county magistrate of Árnessýsla and his deputy, who rendered the district court judgment, should have yielded their seat in this case. The judgment appealed from shall therefore be invalidated and the case remanded to the district court for renewed procedure and adjudication.

The accrued costs of the case shall be borne by the State Treasury, including defense counsel's fees as stated in the conclusion. The amount specified does not include sales tax or value added tax.

C O N C L U S I O N :

The judgment appealed against, and all procedure in the case before the criminal court of Árnessýsla, is invalidated. The case is remanded to the district court for lawful procedure and adjudication.

All accrued costs of the case shall be borne by the State Treasury, including the fees of the defendant's appointed counsel, Stefán Pálsson, Supreme Court Advocate, kr. 50.000,00.

Certified a true transcript
Fee kr. 1100,-
Paid:

The Supreme Court of Iceland [seal]
Erla Jónsdóttir [signature]

ANNEX 2

(Translation from Icelandic)

THE EUROPEAN HUMAN RIGHTS CONVENTION ACT NO. 62 - 19 MAY, 1994

The Representatives of the President of Iceland

according to Article 8 of the Icelandic Constitution

the Prime Minister, the Speaker of the united *Althing*, and the President of the Supreme Court,

make known: The *Althing* has passed this Law, and we have confirmed it by our approval:

SECTION 1

The European Human Rights Convention, comprising the following agreements, shall have the force of law in Iceland:

1. Convention of 4 November 1950 for the Protection of Human Rights and Fundamental Freedoms, as amended by the following Protocols:
   a. Protocol No. 3 of 6 May 1963 amending Article 29 of the Convention.
   b. Protocol No. 5 of 20 January 1966 amending Articles 22 and 40 of the Convention.
   c. Protocol No. 8 of 19 March 1985 amending Articles 20, 21, 23, 28, 29, 30, 31, 34, 40, 41 and 43 of the Convention.
2. Protocol of 20 March 1952 to the Convention for the Protection of Human Rights and Fundamental Freedoms (the First Protocol).
3. Second Protocol, of 6 May 1963, to the Convention for the Protection of Human Rights and Fundamental Freedoms, conferring upon the European Court of Human Rights competence to give advisory opinions.
4. Fourth Protocol, of 16 September 1963, to the Convention for the Protection of Human Rights and Fundamental Freedoms, securing certain rights and freedoms other than those already included in the convention and in the first protocol thereto.
5. Sixth Protocol, of 28 April 1983, to the Convention for the Protection of Human Rights and Fundamental Freedoms, concerning the abolition of the death penalty.
6. Seventh Protocol, of 22 November 1984, to the Convention for the Protection of Human Rights and Fundamental Freedoms.

The Convention for the Protection of Human Rights and Fundamental Freedoms, as amended, and the First, Second, Fourth, Sixth and Seventh Protocols, are published as an Appendix to this Law.

SECTION 2

Resolutions of the European Commission of Human Rights, the European Court of Human Rights and the Committee of Ministers of the Council of Europe do not have a binding effect under Icelandic national law.

SECTION 3

This Law shall enter into effect immediately.

ANNEX 3

(Translation from Icelandic)

389TH CONSTITUTIONAL BILL
AMENDING THE CONSTITUTION OF THE REPUBLIC OF ICELAND NO. 33/1944, AS LATER AMENDED

1994. - 1064 Years from the Institution of the *Althing*
118th Legislative Assembly - Matter No. 297

Brought up by Geir H. Haarde, Finnur Ingólfsson,
Sigurbjörn Gunnarsson, Ragnar Arnalds and Kristín Ástgeirsdóttir

Article 1

Article 63 shall read as follows:
The people are entitled to form religious associations and to practice their religion in conformity with their individual convictions. Nothing may however be preached or practised which is immoral or prejudicial to public order.

Article 2

Article 64 shall read as follows:
No one may lose any of his civil or national rights on account of his religion, nor may anyone refuse to perform any civic obligation on religious grounds.
Everyone shall be free to remain outside religious associations. No one shall be obliged to pay any personal dues to any religious association of which he is not a member.
A person who is not a member of any religious association shall pay to the University of Iceland the dues which he would have had to pay to such an association, if he had been a member. This may be amended by law.

Article 3

Article 65, which shall become the first Article of Chapter VII, shall read as follows:
Everyone shall be equal before the law, irrespective of sex, religion, opinion, ethnic origin, race, colour, property, or birth or other status.

Article 4

Article 66 shall read as follows:
No one may be deprived of Icelandic citizenship. Loss of citizenship may however be provided for by law, in case a person accepts citizenship in another State. An alien can only be granted Icelandic citizenship by law.
An Icelandic citizen can not be barred from entering Iceland nor expelled from Iceland. The right of aliens to enter Iceland and stay there, and the reasons for which they may be expelled, shall be laid down by law.

No one can be barred from leaving Iceland except by judicial decision. A person may however be prevented from leaving Iceland by lawful arrest.

Every person lawfully staying in Iceland shall be free to choose his residence and shall enjoy freedom of travel subject to any limitations laid down by law.

Article 5

Article 67 shall read as follows:

No one may be deprived of his liberty except as permitted by law.

Any person deprived of his liberty shall be entitled to be informed promptly of the reasons for this measure.

Any person arrested by reason of suspicion of criminal conduct shall be brought before a judge without undue delay. If he is not released at once the judge shall, within 24 hours, give a reasoned decision on wether he shall be imprisoned on remand. Imprisonment on remand may only be ordered on account of a charge subject to heavier sanctions than fines or punitive custody. The right of a person imprisoned on remand to refer the decision on his remand to a superior court shall be guaranteed by law. A person shall never be imprisoned on remand for longer than necessary; if the judge deems that he may be released on bail the amount of bail shall be determined by a judicial order.

Any person deprived of his liberty for other reasons shall be entitled to have the legality of the measure reviewed by a court as soon as possible. If his deprivation of liberty proves to have been unlawful he shall be released forthwith.

Any person deprived of his liberty without valid reasons shall have a right to compensation.

Article 6

Article 68 shall read as follows:

No one may be subjected to inhuman or degrading treatment or punishment.

No one shall be required to perform compulsory labour.

Article 7

Article 69 shall read as follows:

No one may be subjected to punishment unless found guilty of conduct that was punishable at the time of its commission or is totally analoguous to such conduct. The sanctions may not be more severe than the law permitted at the time of commission.

Capital punishment may never be stipulated by law.

Article 8

Article 70 shall read as follows:

For the determination of his rights and obligations, or in the event of a criminal charge against him, everyone shall be entitled to the resolution of an independent and impartial court of law within a reasonable time. A hearing by a court of law shall take place in public, except if the judge decides otherwise as provided for by law in the interest of morals, public order, the security of the State or the interests of the parties.

Everyone charged with criminal conduct shall be presumed innocent until proved guilty.

Article 9

Article 71 shall read as follows:

Everyone shall enjoy freedom from interference with privacy, home, and family life.

Bodily or personal search or a search of a person's premises or possessions may only be conducted in accordance with a judicial decision or a statute law provision. This shall also apply to the examination of documents and mail, and to any other comparable interference with a person's right to privacy.

Notwithstanding the provisions of the first Paragraph above, freedom from interference with privacy, home or family life may be limited by statute provisions if this is necessary for the protection of the rights of others.

Article 10

Article 72 shall read as follows:

The right of private ownership shall be inviolate. No one may be obliged to surrender his property unless required by public need. Such a measure shall be provided for by law, and full compensation shall be paid.

The right of persons who are not Icelandic citizens to become owners of real property interests or shares in business enterprises in Iceland may be limited by law.

Article 11

Article 73 shall read as follows:

Everyone has the right to freedom of opinion and belief.

Everyone shall be free to express his thoughts, but shall also be liable to answer for them in court. The law may never provide for censorship or other similar limitations to freedom of expression.

The above provisions shall not prevent restriction of the freedom of expression by law in the interests of public order or the security of the State, for the protection of health or morals, or for the protection of the rights or reputation of others.

Article 12

Article 74 shall read as follows:

Associations may be formed for any lawful purpose; in this respect a licence granted in advance shall not be required. An association may not be dissolved by administrative decision. The activities of an association considered to aim for unlawful objectives may however be banned, in which case legal action shall be brought without undue delay for a judgment dissolving the association.

No one may be obliged to be a member of any association. Membership of an association may however be made obligatory by law if this is necessary in order to enable an association to discharge its functions in the public interest or on account of the rights of others.

People are free to assemble unarmed. Public gatherings may be attended by police. Public gatherings in the open may be banned if it is feared that riots may ensue.

Article 13

Article 75 shall read as follows:

Everyone is free to pursue the occupation of his choosing. This right may however be restricted by law, if such restriction is necessary with a view to the public interest.

Labour-related rights and vacation rights shall be regulated by law.

Article 14

Article 76 shall read as follows:

Everyone shall be entitled to the necessary assistance in case of sickness, invalidity, infirmity by reason of old age, unemployment and similar circumstances, as further laid down by law.

Everyone shall be entitled to suitable general education and teaching as further laid down by law.

For children, the law shall guarantee the protection and care which their welfare demands.

Article 15

Article 77 shall read as follows:

Matters concerning taxes shall be regulated by law. The power to decide whether to levy a tax, change a tax or abolish a tax may not be committed to administrative authorities.

No tax may be levied unless the levy was permitted by law at the time when the facts occurred on which the tax liability is based.

Article 16

Article 78 shall read as follows:

The right of municipalities to manage their affairs independently under the supervision of State authorities shall be regulated by law.

Municipal sources of income shall be provided for by law.

Article 17

This Law shall enter into effect immediately.

ANNEX 4

(Translation from Icelandic)

759. AMENDMENT PROPOSAL
TO THE BILL AMENDING THE CONSTITUTION OF THE REPUBLIC OF ICELAND NO. 33/1944, AS LATER AMENDED

1994. - 1064 Years from the Institution of the *Althing*
118th Legislative Assembly - Matter No. 297

From the Committee on the Constitution

1. To Article 1. The first sentence to read as follows: All persons have the right to form religious associations and to practice their religion in conformity with their individual convictions.
2. To Article 2: The first paragraph to read as follows: No one may lose any of his civil or national rights on account of his religion, nor may anyone refuse to perform any generally applicable civil duty on religious grounds.
3. To Article 3. Two paragraphs to take the place of the present paragraph, reading as follows:
   Everyone shall be equal before the law and enjoy human rights irrespective of sex, religion, opinion, ethnic origin, race, colour, property, or birth or other status.
   Men and women shall enjoy equal rights in all respects.
4. To Article 6. The first sentence to read as follows:
   No one may be subjected to torture or any other inhuman or degrading treatment or punishment.
5. To Article 7. The first sentence of the first paragraph to read as follows: No one may be subjected to punishment unless found guilty of conduct that was punishable according to law at the time of its commission, or is totally analogous to such conduct.
6. To Article 8. The first sentence of the first paragraph to read as follows: Everyone shall, for the determination of his rights and obligations or in the event of a criminal charge against him, be entitled, following a fair trial and within a reasonable time, to the resolution of an independent and impartial court of law.
7. To Article 9.
   a. The second sentence of the second paragraph to read as follows: This shall also apply to the examination of documents and mail, communications by telephone and other means, and to any other comparable interference with a person's right to privacy.
   b. The third paragraph to read as follows:
      Notwithstanding the provisions of the first paragraph above, freedom from interference with privacy, home or family life may be otherwise limited by statute provisions if this is urgently necessary for the protection of the rights of others.
8. To Article 10. The second paragraph to read as follows:
   The right of foreign parties to own real property interests or shares in business enterprises in Iceland may be limited by law.
9. To Article 11. Paragraph 3 to read as follows:

Freedom of expression may only be restricted by law in the interests of public order or the security of the State, for the protection of health or morals, or for the protection of the rights or reputation of others, if such restrictions are deemed necessary and in agreement with democratic traditions.

10. To Article 12. The first sentence of the first paragraph to read as follows: Associations may be formed for any lawful purpose, including political associations and trade associations; in this respect a licence granted in advance shall not be required.
11. To Article 13. The second paragraph to read as follows: The right of people to negotiate the terms of employment and other labour-related matters shall be regulated by law.
12. To Article 14.
    a. The first paragraph to read as follows:

       The law shall guarantee for everyone the necessary assistance in case of sickness, invalidity, infirmity by reason of old age, unemployment and similar circumstances.
    b. The second paragraph to read as follows:

       The law shall guarantee for everyone a suitable general education and teaching.
13. To Article 16.

    Article 78 to read as follows:

    The municipalities shall manage their affairs independently as laid down by law.

    The income sources of the municipalities, and the right of the municipalities to decide whether and how to use their sources of income, shall be regulated by law.

6. INCORPORATION AND IMPLEMENTATION OF HUMAN RIGHTS IN NORWAY

by Kyrre Eggen,
University of Oslo

1. INTRODUCTION - HUMAN RIGHTS IN NORWEGIAN LAW

The subject "The status of Human Rights Treaties in Norway" has been thoroughly discussed in Norwegian legal theory during the last decades,[1] and it is not the purpose of this report to contribute to this debate. My intention is merely to present a summary of the status of human rights treaties in Norway, and to refer to recent developments.

In 1993, a public committee ("*Menneskerettighetslovutvalget*" hereinafter called "the Committee") submitted a report and proposals for reform of the status of human rights treaties in Norway (NOU 1993:18). My report is based on the contents of this report. Parts of the English Summary of the Committee's report are reproduced as *Annex 1*.

The Committee proposed a constitutional provision and an Act of Parliament on the status of human rights in Norway. On 15 July 1994, the Committee's proposal for a constitutional provision on human rights treaties was adopted by Parliament (Sec. 110 of the Norwegian Constitution, hereafter cited as grl.). The impact of this provision will be commented below under section 5. As for the second part of the

---

[1] See inter alia Castberg, Frede, *Den europeiske konvensjon om menneskerettighetene*, Oslo 1971; Dolva, Trond, *Internasjonale menneskerettighetskonvensjoner og intern norsk rett*, TfR. 1990 pp. 121–133; Eckhoff, Torstein, *Rettskildelære*, 3. ed., Oslo 1993 pp. 260–265; Fleischer, Carl A., *Folkerett*, 6. ed., Oslo 1994, Sec. 26; Helgesen, Jan, *Teorier om folkerettens stilling i norsk rett*, Oslo 1982; Jensen, Søren Stenderup, *The European Convention on Human Rights in Scandinavian Law*, København 1992; Ryssdal, Rolv, *The Relation between the Judiciary and the Legislative and Executive Branches of the Government in Norway*, North Dakota Law Review 1981 s. 534. and Carsten og Lucy Smith, *Norsk rett og folkeretten*, 2. ed., Oslo 1982.

M. Scheinin (ed.), International Human Rights Norms in the Nordic and Baltic Countries, 203–225.

Committee's proposal, a bill will probably be submitted to Parliament in 1995.

As an introduction, I shall give a brief outline of the general status of human rights under Norwegian law. The natural starting point is the constitutional protection of individual rights and freedoms (individets grunnlovsvern). These provisions, to a certain degree, protect traditional basic freedoms such as freedom of speech (grl. Sec. 100), freedom of religion (grl. Sec. 2) and protection of property (grl. Sec. 105), and contain provisions to protect the liberty and security of individuals. Furthermore, our Constitution contains certain political rights, *inter alia* the right to vote, and the right to be elected to political posts. Apart from this, human rights are almost invisible in Norwegian law, but they still appear in a somewhat silent way. In this context, the *principle of legality* is of great importance. The principle of legality – which is unwritten law of constitutional status – dictates that any legal decision or factual measure taken by the authorities involving an infringement of an individual must be prescribed by an Act of Parliament (formal law), or have other sufficient legal ground.[2] The principle of legality can be seen as an element of the "rule of law" principle. Several basic rights and liberties are also positively provided, confirmed and enacted by statutory provisions, even though they are not expressly referred to as human rights, *inter alia,* protection of privacy and family life, guarantees of a fair and impartial trial, and numerous economic, cultural and social rights which usually exist in a welfare state. Lastly – turning to the subject of this report – an important aspect of human rights is the status of human rights treaties in Norwegian law. Regardless of the traditional "dualistic" starting point, according to which Norwegian law and international law are considered to be two separate legal systems, human rights treaties are seen as a very important source of Norwegian law.

---

[2] See *inter alia* Andenæs, Johs., *Statsforfatningen i Norge,* 7 ed., Oslo 1990 pp. 210–219 and Eckhoff, Torstein, *Forvaltningsrett,* 5. ed. by Eivind Smith, Oslo 1994, pp. 136–164.

2. STATUS OF HUMAN RIGHTS TREATIES IN NORWAY – GENERAL CONSIDERATIONS

In this section, I shall give an outline of the status of human rights treaties under Norwegian law.

2.1 The Traditional Starting Point – Norway as a Dualistic State. Usually, one distinguishes between monistic and dualistic states. In monistic states, treaties which bind the state are deemed to take immediate effect as internal rules of law. In dualistic states, a special act of implementation is, in principle, required for the treaty to be applicable as part of internal law.

In *traditional* Norwegian legal theory, it is presupposed that the Norwegian legal system is based on a dualistic principle.[3] However, human rights treaties are undoubtedly "part of" Norwegian law. I shall try to illustrate this in the following sections. Firstly, I will briefly comment on the status given to human rights treaties in Norwegian law. Secondly, I will show how human rights treaties are regarded as sources of law when Norwegian courts interpret national law. Lastly, I will discuss the question of which rule is considered to have priority in the event of a conflict between Norwegian law and human rights treaties.

2.2 Human Rights Treaties and Norwegian Legislation. Neither the Norwegian Constitution – apart from the new grl. Section 110 C, see section 5 below – nor general legislation contains any general rules concerning the status of human rights treaties in Norwegian law. One does, however, find sporadic provisions in the body of legislation that give effect to treaties within their own area of applicability. Some of these are of importance to human rights treaties.

The most practical provision – in the sphere of human rights – is Section 4 of the Criminal Procedures Act (*straffeprosessloven* av 22. mai 1981). In legal theory commenting on this provision it is explained that the provision means that, in the event of a conflict between the two, the treaties will prevail over the Criminal Procedures Act.[4] The

---

[3] See *inter alia* Andenæs, Johs., *Statsforfatningen i Norge*, 7 ed., Oslo 1990 pp. 4–10.

[4] Andenæs, Johs., Norsk straffeprosess, 2. ed., Oslo 1994, vol. I pp. 10–11 and vol. II p. 145.

Norwegian Supreme Court has in its rulings chosen to use more moderate wordings, *e.g.* in the case Rt. (Norsk Retstidende) 1991 p. 777, where it is stated that "Section 183 of the Criminal Procedures Act must be interpreted so that it does not conflict with article 5 of the European Convention on Human Rights." However, in Rt. 1994 p. 610, it is stated that Norwegian courts must interpret the Criminal Procedures Act in accordance with treaty commitments, and that it is possible to set aside Norwegian rules in the event of a conflict with treaty provisions. The requirement for doing so is that the treaty provision is sufficiently clear and unambiguous.

Other examples of such legislation are Section 36a of the Civil Procedures Act (*Tvistemålsloven* av 13. aug. 1915), Sections 1-4 of the Enforcement of Obligations Act (*Tvangsfullbyrdelsesloven* av 26 juni 1992 nr. 86), and Section 4 of the Foreign Citizens Act (*Utlendingsloven* av 24 juni 1988).

Next, I shall in the following comment on how the Norwegian legislature usually implements human rights treaties.

In Norway, the methods for implementing treaties in national law are usually called "transformation", "incorporation" and "ascertainment of legal harmony". Transformation means reproduction of treaty commitments in Norwegian legislation, in the form of a translation with necessary adaptations. Incorporation means the legal enactment of a treaty as part of national law in its original form and language. Ascertainment of normative harmony means ascertaining that national law is in accordance with the convention in question.

The last mentioned method has been used most frequently when implementing treaties – also human right treaties – in Norway.[5] Only in rare cases, have statutes been passed in connection with the ratification of such treaties.

2.3 Human Rights Treaties as Sources of Law in the Courts' Interpretation of Norwegian Law – The Principle of Presumption. The *principle of presumption* dictates that if domestic law provides for more than one interpretation, the interpretation that complies best with

[5] NOU 1993:18 pp. 47–51.

international law is to be given preference.[6] It also implies that domestic law is presumed to be compatible with international law. This means that the law enforcing authorities may act on the presumption that the legislature did not intend to legislate contrary to any international obligations undertaken. Due to the principle of presumption human rights treaties are undoubtedly *relevant* sources of Norwegian law.[7]

Possibly, one must make a reservation on the relevance of human rights treaties when they are applied to impose *duties* on the individual. Due to the principle of legality, public authorities may only impose duties on the individual when such action is prescribed by an Act of Parliament (formal law).[8] However, since human rights treaties seldom impose duties *directly* on the individual,[9] this reservation is of little practical importance.

The practically important question, when it comes to human rights treaties as sources of Norwegian law, is what *weight* they are given in the courts' interpretation of Norwegian law.

In this context, an important statement of principle can be found in Rt. 1984 p. 1175, where the Supreme Court stresses that "... Norwegian law must, as far as possible, be presumed to be in accordance with treaties by which Norway is bound..." By using the words "as far as possible" the Supreme Court indicates that it is willing to go lengths in order to avoid a conflict between Norwegian and international law, by means of harmonizing the interpretation of Norwegian law.

In NOU 1993:18 (pp. 77–78) the Committee gives the following summary on the weight of human rights treaties in Norwegian law:

> "There is no doubt that human rights treaties are relevant sources of law of considerable weight in the application of Norwegian law. There is no precedent as to their actual weight,

---

[6] Eckhoff, Torstein, *Rettskildelære*, 3. ed., Oslo 1993, pp. 261–263 and Andenæs, Johs., *Statsforfatningen i Norge*, 7 ed., Oslo 1990 p. 7.

[7] Eckhoff, Torstein, *Rettskildelære*, 3. ed., Oslo 1993, p. 262 and Helgesen, Jan, *Teorier om folkerettens stilling i norsk rett*, Oslo 1982, p. 86.

[8] Helgesen, Jan, *Teorier om folkerettens stilling i norsk rett*, Oslo 1982, p. 85 and Jensen, Søren Stenderup, *The European Convention on Human Rights in Scandinavian Law*, København 1992, pp. 177–180.

[9] Another matter is that human rights treaties may imply that *states* are required to take positive measures to secure human rights, even in relations between individuals (*Drittwirkung*).

> but the Supreme Court has ruled that Norwegian law shall, as far as possible, be interpreted in accordance with our obligations under treaties. The exact meaning of this will presumably depend on the individual case. There is, however, reason to believe that the Supreme Court will go to some lengths in order to avoid rulings that are in conflict with treaties."

2.4 The Question of Conflict between Norwegian Law and Human Rights Treaties: Which Is the Lex Superior? The Norwegian Supreme Court has never acknowledged any conflict between Norwegian law and a human rights convention, and has therefore not come to any decision as to which rule takes priority in the event of a conflict.[10]

Different opinions exist in legal theory regarding as to which rule shall be given preference in the event of conflict. The traditional view has been that Norwegian law will be given preference.[11] However, the tendency seems to be that more and more writers accept the possibility that the Supreme Court will accord precedence to human rights conventions.[12]

It is therefore not possible to answer the legal question of how to solve a conflict between Norwegian law and human rights treaties with certainty.

2.5 Summary. Today, there is no doubt that human rights conventions are relevant sources of law of considerable importance for those engaged in applying Norwegian law. There is reason to believe that the Supreme Court will go to considerable lengths to avoid making decisions that are in conflict with treaties on human rights. This is also reflected in the way Norwegian courts enforce human rights treaties in Norwegian law by way of harmonizing interpretation. Finally – it is impossible to give certain answers to the question of which rule will prevail in the event of a conflict. The tendency in legal theory is, however, to regard human rights conventions as having priority.

---

[10] NOU 1993:18 p. 68.

[11] Andenæs, Johs., *Statsforfatningen i Norge*, 7 ed., Oslo 1990 p. 7. and Castberg, Frede, *Den europeiske konvensjon om menneskerettighetene*, Oslo 1971 p. 24.

[12] See *inter alia* Helgesen, Jan, *Teorier om folkerettens stilling i norsk rett*, Oslo 1982 pp. 107–108; Carsten og Lucy Smith, *Norsk rett og folkeretten*, 2. ed., Oslo 1982 pp. 207–224 and Ryssdal, Rolv, *The Relation between the Judiciary and the Legislative and Executive Branches of the Government in Norway*, North Dakota Law Review 1981 p. 534.

3. SURVEY OF EXISTING CASE LAW BY DOMESTIC COURTS

A thorough survey of existing Norwegian case law regarding human rights treaties is given in NOU 1993:18 pp. 51–68. My purpose is not to give an extensive list of Norwegian cases regarding human rights. I shall limit myself to presenting some cases illustrating how Norwegian courts apply human rights treaties in national law.

Most Norwegian cases involving human rights treaties concern the European Convention on Human Rights.

The first case explicitly involving the European Convention on Human Rights is the *Iversen Case* in Rt. 1961 p. 1350, concerning the question of whether a provisional act on compulsory civilian service for dentists violated Article 4 of the Convention. The Supreme Court held that Article 4 of the Convention did not prohibit "... brief, well paid work in one's own profession in immediate connection with completed professional training." Accordingly, the Supreme Court held that there was no contradiction between the Convention and the Norwegian act in question, and that there was no need to enter into the question of which rule would prevail in the event of a conflict.[13]

An important case appears in Rt. 1984 s. 1175. The question was whether a person who had been committed to a mental hospital under Section 39 (1) e of the Norwegian Penal Code could invoke the provision under section 9 a of the Mentally Ill Persons Act and, on this basis, claim judicial review of the compulsory means employed. The Supreme Court first observed that neither the wording of the Mentally Ill Persons Act, or the preparatory works gave any direct guidance as to whether persons committed to a mental hospital on the basis of a judgment would also be entitled to judicial review. Then the court stated that the decision in the case had to be based, *inter alia,* on the consideration that "... Norwegian law must, as far as possible, be presumed to be in accordance with treaties by which Norway is bound – in this case the European Convention on Human Rights of 4 November 1950." The Supreme Court found that the harmony with Article 5 of the Convention would best be achieved if also individuals committed to a mental hospital on the basis of a judgment were

[13] The case was brought before the European Commission of Human Rights which declared it inadmissible as manifestly ill-founded in accordance with Art. 27 (Application No. 1468/62).

entitled to judicial review. The Supreme Court made reference to Strasbourg case law, namely the *Winterwerp Case, X Case* and the Commission's findings in the case *Y v. the United Kingdom*.[14]

The Supreme Court has in a number of other cases made reference to Strasbourg case law, and I shall briefly mention some of them below.

The case in Rt. 1990 p. 257 concerned defamation. A politician had brought action against the editor of a newspaper. The editor invoked, *inter alia*, Article 10 of the European Convention on Human Rights. The Supreme Court acquitted the editor of the claim for punishment and damages, *inter alia* with reference to the *Lingens case*.[15] In Rt. 1990 p. 312 and Rt. 1990 p. 319, the Supreme Court found that the reading of evidence in the form of police reports containing interrogations of two witnesses was in accordance with Articles 6 (1) and (3) (d) of the European Convention on Human Rights. In both cases, the Supreme Court discussed in detail how the judgments in the *Unterpertinger Case*[16] and the *Kostovski Case*[17] should be interpreted. Rt. 1990 p. 1221 also concerned the reading aloud of statements given by witnesses to the police, and the Supreme Court discussed the *Unterpertinger Case* thoroughly. In these cases, it seems as if the Supreme Court took for granted that Norwegian law should be interpreted in conformity with the Convention, as the Convention had been interpreted by the European Court in Strasbourg. However, one must keep in mind the important reservation, made by the Supreme Court in Rt. 1994 s. 610, that the requirement for setting aside Norwegian rules in the event of a conflict with treaty provisions is that the treaty provision must be sufficiently clear and unambiguous.

The Supreme Court has not used human rights treaties on economic, social and cultural rights on many occassions. However, the case Rt. 1988 p. 476 is an example of exactly this. A contract of employment had been terminated. The crucial question was whether this was to be regarded as a termination under the Labour Act, which

---

[14] European Court of Human Rights, *Winterwerp Case*, Series A Vol. 33, European Court of Human Rights, *Case of X v. the United Kingdom*, Series A Vol. 46 and Application No. 6870/75.

[15] European Court of Human Rights, *Lingens Case*, Series A Vol. 103.

[16] European Court of Human Rights, *Unterpertinger Case*, Series A Vol. 110.

[17] European Court of Human Rights, *Kostovski Case*, Series A Vol. 166.

would provide for the bringing of the case before a Norwegian Labour Court. The appealing party was an American citizen who, under his contract of employment with an American oil company, was subject to an extensive obligation to move abroad upon company orders. Although he, after being stationed in Norway, automatcally entered into a contract of employment with the Norwegian subsidiary of the American parent company, the obligation to move was unchanged. In the proceedings, it was argued that foreign nationals should not be guaranteed less protection than Norwegian employees and reference was made to the European Social Charter, article 19, in support of this claim. The Supreme Court Interlocutory Appeals Committee concluded that the Court of Appeals' interpretation of the law could not be seen to imply any discrimination against foreign citizens, as far as the decisive factor was the nature of the contract of employment, not the nationality of the employee.

The Supreme Court also seldomly makes reference to non-binding rules of international law. However, in Rt. 1983 p. 1566 the Supreme Court Interlocutory Appeals Committee made reference to a resolution by the Committee of Ministers in the Council of Europe on the principles of remand in custody (Res. (65) 11 of 9 April 1965). The question in the case was whether Norwegian law on the procedure in criminal cases should be interpreted narrowly to be in accordance with the resolution of the Committee of Ministers. The Supreme Court Interlocutory Appeals Committee stated that the resolution was only a recommendation to the Norwegian government, and thus not legally binding on Norwegian legislation. The Interlocutory Appeals Committee therefore concluded that the Court of Appeals had not based its ruling on an incorrect interpretation of the law, when it interpreted Norwegian law on the procedure in criminal cases according to its wording.

In the *Case of E. v. Norway* (Judgment of 29 August 1990, Series A, Vol. 181) the European Court of Human Rights included in its judgment an analysis of the role of the provisions of the European Convention as a source of law in Norway. Excerpts of the judgment are provided as *Annex 2*.

Summary. Case law shows that human rights treaties are relevant sources of domestic law with considerable weight.[18] The Supreme Court has interpreted provisions in the treaties and commented on international case law in this connection. However, the Supreme Court has never found that there has been a conflict between national law and human rights treaties, and therefore never made any ruling on which rule would prevail in the event of a conflict.

Case law also shows that the Norwegian Supreme Court uses the Strasbourg case law as precedent cases when harmonizing Norwegian law and the European Convention on Human Rights. Therefore, it is reasonable to say that the Norwegian courts put great emphasis on the judgments from the European Court of Human Rights, and that they are probably willing to revise their own case law as a consequence of the judgments from the European Court of Human Rights.[19] However, the criterion for doing the latter is, as stated in Rt. 1994 s. 610, that European case law regarding the relevant treaty provisions is sufficiently clear and unambiguous.

There is no explicit indication in Norwegian case law that the courts distinguish between civil and political rights and economic, social and cultural rights. However, case law concerning economic, social and cultural rights is very limited, and therefore it is not possible to draw any conclusions as to whether there is a difference between the status of civil and political rights and economic, social and cultural rights in Norwegian law. There are also sporadic references to non-binding rules of international law in Norwegian case law, but the Supreme Court does not seem to attach decisive importance to such recommendations.

4. ADMINISTRATIVE PRACTICE

4.1 Administrative Practice in General. Any attempt to examine and describe the importance of human rights treaties in administrative practice in Norway today is bound to exceed the limitations of this

[18] NOU 1993:18 p. 67.

[19] See Jensen, Søren Stenderup, *The European Convention on Human Rights in Scandinavian Law*, København 1992, p. 158.

report. I shall therefore merely present some points of particular interest:

The human rights treaties binding on Norway place demands on the legislature, the courts and on the administrative authorities. Therefore, it would constitute a breach of the treaties if the administrative branches were to use their authority contrary to provisions in human rights treaties binding on Norway. It is the responsibility of the civil service to see to it that Norway implements the provisions under international law by which it is bound. This may well be construed in such a way that Government by ratifying a treaty actually orders the civil service to observe the requirements of the treaty. It must therefore be assumed that civil service by merit of its own initiative both can and shall observe the obligations laid down by the human rights treaties – in the process of regulating as well as interpretating or in the use of its margin of discretion in individual cases.

When administrative decisions are tried before the courts, the question arises whether the courts, in the event of a breach of a treaty, can overrule the decision of the administrative authority. The crucial question is whether the courts, in the event that the decision is contrary to international law, can overrule the parts of the decision which fall within the margin of discretion traditionally left to administrative authorities in Norwegian law.

In the *Alta Case*, Rt. 1982 p. 241, the Supreme Court established that Norwegian administrative authorities must exercise their margin of discretion in accordance with, *inter alia*, human rights treaties binding on Norway. Furthermore, it was stated that "... the rules concerning the courts' power to review the validity of administrative acts do not prevent the Court from fully and comprehensively considering whether the expansion works violate rules of international law."

In legal theory, different views exist on how this statement is to be interpreted.[20] The tendency seems to be that the statement implies that Norwegian administrative decisions will be regarded as invalid by the courts if they imply a breach of international law, even if the

[20] See, *inter alia*, Helgesen, Jan, *Teorier om folkerettens stilling i norsk rett*, Oslo 1982 pp. 47–51 and Andenæs, Johs., *Statsforfatningen i Norge*, 7 ed., Oslo 1990 p. 370.

administrative decision is in conformity with Norwegian law. A reservation must, however, be made in the case that the administrative decision is *required* by Norwegian law. The answer to this situation depends on how the question of conflict between Norwegian law and human rights treaties will be solved in general.[21]

4.2 Ombudsmen. The mandate of the Civil Ombudsman encompasses questions that may also be governed by human rights treaties, cf Sections 3, 10 and 11 of the Civil Ombudsman Act. This has also been expressed by the Ombudsman in his annual report of 1990 (pp. 22–23). He points out that the Committee of Ministers in the Council of Europe adopted a recommendation which stated that the institution of an ombudsman is an instrument well fit to promote human rights. He furthermore points out that the Ombudsman should play an important part in the process of directing the civil service into not only respecting but also actively promoting the rules and principles of human rights treaties. He continues that he will, in his work with individual cases presented to him for examination, control that the civil service has taken into due consideration international human rights obligations binding on Norway.

Both the Ombudsman for the Non-Discrimination of Sexes and the Children's Ombudsman have also raised questions concerning human rights treaties (See NOU 1993:18 pp. 69–70).

5. RECENT DEVELOPMENTS AND REFORM

5.1 The New Constitutional Provision – grl. Section 110 C. As mentioned in the introduction, Norway recently got a new constitutional provision on human rights in Norwegian law. The new provision – grl. Section 110 C – reads as follows:

> "Det paaligger Statens Myndigheder at respektere og sikre Menneske-retighederne.
> Nærmere Bestemmelser om Gjennomføresen af Traktater herom fastsettes ved Lov."
>
> (*English translation*)
> "It is incumbent upon the Authorities of the State to respect and ensure Human Rights.

---

21 See, section 2.4 above.

> Further Provisions concerning the Implementation of Treaties thereon shall be laid down by an Act of Parliament."

First, I will give a general comment on the constitutional provision (5.1.1), and secondly, I will comment on some specific points regarding the wording used in the first sentence of the provision (5.1.2).

5.1.1 General Comments. As the text of the provision says, the authorities are obliged to respect and ensure human rights, but the actual decision to incorporate various human rights treaties has to be made by an Act of Parliament. This has not yet been done in Norway, but it is likely that a bill based on the Committee's proposal for legislation will be sent to Parliament in 1995. I shall comment on this proposal in the next section.

The reason for combining a constitutional provision and ordinary legislation is partly that the constitutional provision will be of a strong symbolic value, without highlighting some conventions in the constitution on the expense of others, and partly that the need for a certain legislative flexibility will be accommodated.[22]

However, the constitutional provision is not only a statement of principle, it is also of legal importance.[23]

The first sentence in the constitutional provision will be of legal importance in several ways. *Firstly,* the sentence will be binding on public authorities. In practice, this means that authorities will not be legally permitted to adopt measures in contradiction to the provision. The consequences of what will happen if the public authorities violate the provision has not been established yet. However, a violation may theoretically lead to constitutional liability, as well as to political and parliamentary responsibility.[24] *Secondly,* the principle in the first sentence will be an important factor when other legal rules are to be interpreted.[25] The expression "Human Rights" refers, *inter alia,* to human rights treaties which are already of considerable importance in the application of Norwegian law. *Thirdly,* the principle will be a

---

[22] NOU 1993:18 p. 157.

[23] NOU 1993:18 p. 159.

[24] NOU 1993:18 p. 159.

[25] NOU 1993:18 p. 159.

restriction on the margin of discretion left by Norwegian law to public authorities.[26] But as mentioned earlier, this was probably the legal situation already before the constitutional provision was enacted (see Rt. 1982 p. 241). The second and the third point mentioned above mainly operate as codifications of the principle of presumption.

The second sentence does not specify which treaties are to be incorporated, but it prescribes that the selection of treaties shall be done by Act of Parliament. The provision also leaves it to the discretion of the legislature to decide on how many conventions are to be incorporated. This means that the legislature is free to decide if and when implementation legislation is necessary in respect of a certain convention.[27] Furthermore, the legislature is free to choose the method of implementation – incorporation or transformation.[28] The Committee suggests that incorporation is the preferable method of implementation (see below).

5.1.2 Specific comments on the first sentence of the provision. "*Human Rights*" is a general term, but it must be read in the light of the words "Treaties thereon" in the second sentence of the provision. Conventions regarded as human rights treaties are included, both general and specific conventions. Furthermore, both civil and political rights and economic, social and cultural rights are included.[29]

The words "*respect and ensure*" are the same as in Article 2 of the Covenant on Civil and Political Rights. However, the use of these words does not entail incorporation of this or other international provisions using the same words.[30] The provision is a Norwegian constitutional provision which must be interpreted in the light of Norwegian legal principles. Another matter is that international provisions will be considered as relevant sources of Norwegian law when the constitutional provision is to be interpreted. The words "respect and ensure" means that the Norwegian State has a double

[26] NOU 1993:18 p. 159.

[27] NOU 1993:18 p. 160.

[28] NOU 1993:18 p. 160.

[29] NOU 1993:18 p. 158.

[30] NOU 1993:18 p. 158.

responsibility.[31] Those who represent the state shall not only abstain from violating rights, because it is sometimes necessary to take positive steps to secure non-violation of human rights.

The words "the Authorities of the State" may mean different things in a linguistic sense. In the provision, it is used in the widest sense, which implies that the legislature (*Stortinget*), the Government (*Regjeringen*), other central, regional and local public authorities, and the Courts are covered by the provision.[32] This is in best harmony with international law where the State can also be held responsible for actions on local or regional levels of the State apparatus.

5.2 The Committee Proposal for Legislation on the Status of Human Rights Treaties in Norwegian Law. On the question of which method of implementation should be used, the Committee proposed that human rights conventions that are to be implemented in Norwegian law should be incorporated. Briefly, the reason for this is partly that incorporation is the most faithful method of implementation possible of such conventions, and partly that incorporation is the most widespread method used in countries that are comparable to Norway.

Turning to the question of which conventions should be incorporated, the Committee firstly emphasized some general considerations. It was pointed out that it is neither necessary nor appropriate to incorporate unwritten rules of international law concerning human rights. Furthermore, the Committee prefered that legislation relating to the actual incorporation explicitly mentions which conventions are included in the reform, listing, as opposed to a general clause stipulating incorporation of "human rights conventions".

After this clarification, the Committee then discussed what the criteria for the selection of conventions should be. It was pointed out that a minimum criterion is that Norway is bound by the convention. Then, the Committee discussed its terms of reference, mentioning for instance the inclusion of principal human rights conventions. Even though the Committee found that this criterion was rather ambiguous, it pointed out that some conventions lie in the "core area" of human rights from a Norwegian point of view. Next, the Committee pointed

---

[31] NOU 1993:18 p. 158.

[32] NOU 1993:18 pp. 159-160.

out some other criteria as to precisely which conventions would be suitable for inclusion in Norwegian law. The fact that the provisions in human rights conventions are often very general, is not seen as an obstacle to incorporation. It was also pointed out that whether a convention is suitable for domestic implementation depends on the system of international supervision in connection to the convention. The more comprehensive the practical application by the supervisory body concerned, the greater the guidance will be for those engaged in applying the law nationally. Furthermore, the Committee mentioned that the individual right of complaint is an argument in favour of the convention being suitable for incorporation, because individual cases are of particular help in the clarification of the substance of the rights. In this context, the Committee turned to discuss whether conventions concerning economic, social and cultural rights should be incorporated. It was pointed out that economic, social and cultural rights are partly formulated in terms of objectives, that their realization is, to a great degree, connected with the availability of resources, that many of those rights are vaguely formulated, and that none of the main conventions concerning such rights are enforced internationally by individual complaints. In spite of these counter-arguments, the Committee did not, in principle, rule out that economic, social and cultural rights could be incorporated.

As to the question of which specific human rights treaties should be incorporated, the Committee suggested that self-evidently, the European Convention on Human Rights should be incorporated. It was pointed out that this convention is already of great importance in Norway both in principle and in practice, and that the convention would undoubtedly be suitable for incorporation.

The Committee also found that the Covenant on Civil and Political Rights should be incorporated. It was pointed out that the Covenant, to a great extent, covers the same rights as the European Convention, but provides better protection in some areas, and that if only the European Convention was incorporated, it might leave the impression that the European protection of human rights was overemphasized.

The Committee found it inappropriate to propose that the European Social Charter should be incorporated, partly because it is presently under revision.

As regards the Covenant on Economic, Social and Cultural Rights, it was pointed out that several of its provisions are imprecise and set forth programmatic standards of achievement, and that it does not provide for the individual right of complaint. However, on the basis of an overall assessment, the Committee came to the conclusion that the technical legal doubts should be put aside, so that the Covenant on Economic, Social and Cultural Rights also could be included in the Incorporation Act.

Lastly, turning to the status of incorporated treaties in the Norwegian law hierarchy, the Committee suggested that the incorporated conventions should apply as Acts of Parliament. However, it is stipulated in paragraph 3 of the Incorporation Act that the convention provisions concerning rights and fundamental freedoms shall take precedence over statutory provisions which provides a weaker protection of such rights and freedoms. This provision means that statutory provisions which are in conflict with the incorporated human rights treaties must yield, unless the legislature has clearly stipulated otherwise.[33]

6. PRACTICAL ASPECTS OF IMPLEMENTATION

Incorporation will help ensure that Norwegian law and practice meet the requirements of international human rights conventions and will increase the general knowledge of these conventions. Furthermore, by including them in the national legislation, Norwegian authorities will send a signal and stress that they take human rights seriously.

It is a question whether an incorporation will disturb the balance between the legislature and the judiciary. It will still be the responsibility of the legislature to see to it that legislation is, at all times, in accordance with the requirements of the conventions. All in all, there is little reason to believe that the incorporation of the human rights conventions will in itself disturb the balance between the legislature and the judiciary.

Another aspect to consider is whether implementation will affect the relationship between national authorities and international bodies. Incorporation does not in itself mean that authority is transferred to international bodies. However, it can not be excluded that, in practice,

---

[33] NOU 1993:18 p. 170.

the influence of international convention organs on Norwegian law will increase.

Will the implementation of human rights conventions then affect the work of those engaged in applying Norwegian law? Applying provisions of an international origin may offer special challenges, due to such factors as the formulation of the original texts, the foreign language(s) in which they are drawn up, and the ease of access to sources of law. However, this is not, in principle, a new situation in relation to present circumstances, and further problems in connection with the implementation may be remedied by practical measures, such as increased availability and in-house training. Furthermore, it can be argued that a clarification of the status of human rights treaties in Norwegian law is an advantage for those engaged in the application of the law.

A consequence of incorporating one or more conventions in national law may be that the position of conventions not included will be weakened. However, implementation may be carried out in such a way that this consequence is avoided, *inter alia* by emphasizing, in the preparatory works, that this is not the intention of the incorporation act.

REFERENCES

Andenæs, Johs., Norsk straffeprosess, 2. ed., Oslo 1994.

Andenæs, Johs., *Statsforfatningen i Norge*, 7 ed., Oslo 1990.

Castberg, Frede, *Den europeiske konvensjon om menneskerettighetene*, Oslo 1971.

Dolva, Trond, *Internasjonale menneskerettighetskonvensjoner og intern norsk rett*, TfR. 1990 pp. 121–133.

Eckhoff, Torstein, *Forvaltningsrett*, 5. ed. by Eivind Smith, Oslo 1994.

Eckhoff, Torstein, *Rettskildelære*, 3. ed., Oslo 1993 pp. 260–265.

Fleischer, Carl A., *Folkerett*, 6. ed., Oslo 1994.

Helgesen, Jan, *Teorier om folkerettens stilling i norsk rett*, Oslo 1982.

Jensen, Søren Stenderup, *The European Convention on Human Rights in Scandinavian Law*, København 1992.

Ryssdal, Rolv, *The Relation between the Judiciary and the Legislative and Executive Branches of the Government in Norway*, North Dakota Law Review 1981 p. 534.

Carsten og Lucy Smith, *Norsk rett og folkeretten*, 2. ed., Oslo 1982.

ANNEXES

1. Excerpt of the English Summary of NOU 1993:18.
2. Excerpt of the Jugdment by the European Court of Human Rights in the case of *E. v. Norway* (29 August 1990, Series A, Vol. 181).

ANNEX 1

NOU 1993:18
ENGLISH SUMMARY

(*Excerpt*)

Chapter 11 contains firstly a number of possible formulations of constitutional provisions concerning human rights. Next, an account is given of one proposed test that is unanimously recommended by the Committee. All alternatives have been submitted to the Storting.

The alternative the Committee proposes is that both a constitutional provision and a statute should be enacted. By the constitutional provision the authorities should be obliged to respect and to ensure human rights. The actual decision to incorporate should be made by statute. Such a combination of a constitutional and a statutory provision will be of strong symbolic value, without highlighting some conventions in the constitution at the expense of others. In addition the need for a certain legislative flexibility will be accommodated. The Committee's proposal for a constitutional provision reads as follows:

> "It is incumbent upon the Authorities of the State to respect and to ensure Human Rights.
> Further Provisions concerning the Implementation of Treaties thereon shall be laid down by Statute."

Chapter 12 contains the Committee's legislative proposal and its comments on the individual draft provisions.

The Committee first discusses which human rights conventions should be incorporated by statute, taking as its starting point those conventions that form the foundation stock (*grunnstamme*) of the international protection of human rights: the European Convention on Human Rights (ECHR), the Covenant on Civil and Political Rights (CCPR) and the Covenant on Economic, Social and Cultural Rights (CESCR). These principal conventions deal with a number of rights and may be applicable to practically all fields of Norwegian legal and societal life. Many of the other conventions (here called special conventions) may essentially be said to specify or amplify the rights dealt with in these general conventions. The special conventions are, of course, also important, but if some of them are included in an incorporative statute, it may be difficult to justify why these in particular, and not others, have been included. At the same time both the constitutional provision and the general statutory provision setting forth the objects and purpose of the Act, both of which will contain a general reference to human rights, will emphasize that all human rights conventions shall be regarded as weighty sources in Norwegian law. Nor is there any impediment to incorporating the special conventions at a later stage, either by amending the Incorporation Act or in separate legislation.

Of the principal conventions, the ECHR should be included as a matter of course. In principle and in practice it is already of great significance for Norway, and it is undoubtedly suitable for incorporation. If more that one convention is to be incorporated, the CCPR must be included. To a great extent it coverns the same rights as the ECHR, but it provides better protection in some areas. If only the ECHR is chosen, it may give the impression of over-emphasizing the European protection of human rights. In principle, it is important to maintain that it is a matter of two principal conventions which play their respective roles globally and regionally in the sphere of human rights. The Committee therefore finds that the CCPR should also be incorporated.

The Committee finds it inappropriate to propose that the European Social Charter should be incorporated. It is at present under revision. As regards the CESCR, it is pointed out that several of the convention's provisions are imprecise and set forth programmatic standards of achievement, and that it does not provide an individual right of complaint. Nevertheless the view is gaining ground internationally that there is no justification for maintaining a distinction in principle as regards the implementation of civil and political rights, on the one hand, and economic, social and cultural rights, on the other. Some of the rights in the CESCR, must in the light of convention practice, be regarded as equally suitable for implementation as the rights granted by the CCPR and the ECHR. In striking a balance for or against incorporation weight can be given to two types of argument:

- One option is to start from the fact that traditionally Norway has aimed to avoid inserting manifestos into legislation. Vague human rights provisions provide little guidance for the solution of individual cases and can contribute to obscuring the real legal position. Only conventions that provide practical guidance to those engaged in applying the law should be incorporated. The general constitutional provision proposed by the Committee will take care of the equality in principle of the two groups of rights and the need to give an effective signal that they merit equal respect.
- The other option is to attach decisive importance to equating the rights in principle. Norway has a well-developed body of legislation for economic, social and cultural rights, and incorporation will hardly alter the legal situation palpably. Norwegian legislative practice is not exclusively court-orientated. An essential point about the reform is the effect it will have as a signal. Its value in this regard may diminish concerns about statutes containing manifestos and imprecise provisions.

On the basis of an overall assessment, the Committee has come to the conclusion that the technical legal doubts should be put aside, so that the CESCR should also be included in the Incorporation Act.

The Committee finds it desirable that a single act shold be passed, even if it is decided to incorporate several conventions. The act should contain a provision to the effect that its purpose is to strengthen the position of human rights in Norwegian law (section 1 of the draft bill).

The Committee is of the opinion that it is best to lay it down in the act that the ECHR, the CESCR, and the CCPR, and their protocols shall apply as statutory law in Norway (section 2). The Incorporation Act should also stipulate that the convention provisions concerning rights and fundamental freedoms shall take precedence over statutory provisions which afford such rights and freedoms weaker protection (section 3).

The conventions that are incorporated by statute shall be published in the Norwegian Law Gazette (Norsk Lovtidend) in an original language and in a Norwegian translation (section 4 of the draft bill), thus ensuring that the texts of the conventions are more easily available.

ANNEX 2

CASE OF *E. v. NORWAY* (12/1989/172/228)

The European Court of Human Rights
Strasbourg 29 August 1990

JUDGMENT
(*Excerpt*)

42. When exercising their control over the public authorities, the Norwegian courts will also as far as possible interpret domestic law in such a way as to conform with treaties binding on Norway, such as the Convention, even if these have not been formally incorporated into the Norwegian legal system ("the principle of presumption").

The Norwegian Supreme Court has thus on a number of occasions examined the conformity of its interpretation of domestic law with Norway's obligations under international human rights instruments and in particular under the Convention as interpreted by the Court and the Commission: judgment of 16 December 1961, *Norsk Rettstidende* ("*NRt*") 1961, p. 1350; judgment of 28 March 1966, *NRt* 1966, p. 476, containing a reference to the Commission's decision declaring application no. 1468/62, Iversen v. Norway, inadmissible; judgment of 8.10.1974, *NRt* 1974, p. 935; judgment of 26 February 1982, *NRt* 1982, p. 35; judgment of 23 October 1984, *NRt* 1984, p. 1175, containing references to the European Court's judgments in the Winterwerp case (24 October 1979, Series A no. 33) and in the case of X v. the United Kingdom (5 November 1981, Series A no. 76); judgment of 15 May 1987, *NRt* 1987, p. 612, with reference to the Court's judgment in the case of Klass and Others (6 September 1978, Series A no. 28); the judgment of 16 March 1990 previously cited (see paragraph 33 above); judgment of 16 March 1990 (in case L.nr. 470/1990), with reference to the Court's judgment in the Hauschildt case (24 May 1989, Series A no. 154).

However, there has been no case in which the Supreme Court has been confronted with a clear conflict between the Convention and domestic legislation.

The Convention's status as a relevant source of law was endorsed by the plenary court in the above-mentioned judgment of 26 February 1982, which concerned, *inter alia*, the consequences of water-regulation works on the Alta river. Justice Christiansen stated on behalf of the unanimous court:

> "What I said about the limits of judicial review needs to be qualified. In the present case it has been argued that the Sami people are protected against such interferences with their interests as follow from the regulation of the Alta river by virtue of rules of international law which are binding upon Norway. The rules concerning the courts' power to review the validity of administrative acts do not prevent the Court from fully and comprehensively considering whether the expansion works violate rules of international law [the Convention and the International Covenant on Civil and Political Rights].

The "principle of presumption" was given particularly clear expression in the above-mentioned judgment of 23 October 1984, which dealt with the question of what judicial review should be available where a person already sentenced to security measures is committed to a mental hospital pursuant to Article 39 § 1 (e). The court first observed that neither the wording of the relevant Act nor its drafting history gave any direct indication as to how the problem before the court should be resolved. The judgment went on:

> "The decision to be taken must accordingly take into account all relevant circumstances, in particular the consideration that domestic law must be interpreted, as far as possible, in accordance with those treaties under international law which Norway has ratified, in this instance the [Convention]."

After a comprehensive survey of the relevant case-law of the European Court, the Supreme Court concluded that its interpretation of Norwegian law on the point at issue conformed with the requirements of Article 5 § 4.

The relevance of the principle when examining the scope of judicial review required in respect of detention decisions under Article 39 of the Penal code was also recently mentioned in a concurring opinion in the Supreme Court (judgment of 11 December 1989, *NRt* 1989, p. 1327). One of its members, Justice Smith, found it necessary to disapprove a statement made in a dissenting opinion in the Court of Appeal to the effect that no judicial review would have been possible of the prosecuting authorities' decisions regarding security measures under Article 39 of the Penal Code:

> "In reply (...) it should be pointed out that the Supreme Court has decided [in the above-mentioned case of 23 October 1984], amongst other things on the basis of Article 5 § 4 of the [Convention], as interpreted by the Court and the Commission, that a person subject to security measures and also detained in a mental hospital has the right to obtain a decision at reasonable intervals as to whether continued detention is lawful. I maintain that this right to judicial review which is enshrined in Article 5 § 4 and which the Supreme Court has established for one category of persons subject to security measures, must be applied by the courts also in relation to other persons subject to such measures who are deprived of their liberty in other institutions."

7. Incorporation and Implementation of Human Rights in Denmark

by Birgitte Kofod Olsen,
The Danish Centre for Human Rights

1. STATUS OF HUMAN RIGHTS TREATIES IN DENMARK

1.1 A Monistic or Dualistic Approach to International Law. As to the question whether international law should be applied on a monistic or dualistic basis, Danish legal tradition suggests that a dualistic approach be applied. One of the most prominent legal scholars in the field of international and constitutional law is Alf Ross, who has argued that international law may be considered valid only in the relationship and cooperation among states not within each state.[1]

The dualistic principle, pursuant to which international and national law are viewed as two different systems of law with different sources and different subjects, is characterized by the separation of powers between Goverment and Parliament concerning implementation of treaties in Danish law. Hence, the power to negotiate, prepare and conlude treaties is a prerogative of the Danish Government, cf. Section 19, paragraph 1 of the Danish Constitution. However, the Government cannot ratify any treaties without the consent of the Parliament. This means that Parliament is given the power to decide whether or not a concluded treaty should be ratified by Denmark and, in the affirmative, to hand over the deposit of the ratification instrument to the Government. The power of Parliament also includes, if necessary, incorporation of concluded and ratified treaties. As a result of the above mentioned division of powers, it is generally accepted that

[1] See Ross 1980, p. 397 f. and Ross 1984, Sec. 6.

M. Scheinin (ed.), International Human Rights Norms in the Nordic and Baltic Countries, 227–256.

Danish law does not allow for automatic or quasi-automatic incorporation of international law.

The dualistic principle has also been expressed in Danish case law. In a decision by the Supreme Court from 1986, the court found that the European Convention on Human Rights (ECHR) was not directly applicable in a case concerning dismissal owing to membership of a trade union. Justice Erik Riis underscored this point in an extra-judicial comment on the decision by claiming that the Convention is binding on the Government, but is "however, not transformed by a general statute to being part of the applicable law of this country".[2]

The dualistic viewpoint has been challenged by several authors within the past ten years. Several scholars have argued that international law is part of domestic law, in the sense that international treaties can be used as a legal source by the courts and administrative authorities, even without specific basis in national statutes.

It has thus been stated that, as regards the ECHR, it can be argued that Danish courts will, at least in certain fields of law, have to respect the constraints which can be derived from the Convention. Following the same line of thought, it is assumed that administrative authorities are obliged to exercise their powers of discretion according to international treaties duly entered into.[3]

Other legal scholars depart from the dualistic principle by making the point that international law should be looked upon as "a source of law in the sense that international law is accepted as part of the general factors influencing the judge's formulation of the rule on which he bases his decision".[4]

The legal position is not quite clear but as some legal scholars argue with reference to Danish case law, there are reasons to be open-minded

---

[2] The decision is found in the *Weekly Law Journal* (UfR) 1986, p. 898 f and the comment by Erik Riis in the *Weekly Law Journal* 1987, Sec. B, p. 50ff.

[3] See Niels Eilschou-Holm, *Nordisk Tidsskrift for International Ret* 1981, p. 140 f. For further details concerning the obligations of administrative authorities, see 1.4. below.

[4] See Claus Gulman in the *Nordic Journal of International Law 1983*, p. 48 f. Similar views were introduced by Espersen in 1970 in his dissertation, *Indgåelse og opfyldelse af traktater*. See also Madsen 1986, p. 33ff.

with regard to principles and policies found in international law although they are not expressly implemented into Danish law.[5]

However, it is hardly possible to view this monistic approach to international law as an endorsement to the monistic theories, rather it may be characterized as "practical monism".[6]

Divergent from this semi-monistic approach to international law is the approach to legislation derived from the European Union (EU). The basic treaties of the EU, i.e. the Treaties of the European Community and the Treaty on European Union, have all been made part of domestic law by the amendments to Act No. 447 of November 11, 1972 on Accession to the Treaties of the European Communitites. The same Act incorporates the then existing EU-rules of a directly applicable character. Besides, it lays down that directly applicable EU-regulations, concluded subsequently to the Act of Accession are made part of domestic law by transfering competence to the EU-institutions to issue such regulations. EU-legislation which is not directly applicable, i.e. EU-directives, is made part of Danish law by incorporation. Consequently, Parliament is obliged to respect EU-regulations when adopting new Acts. Similarly, the courts have to apply EU-regulations and EU case law if relevant and the administrative authorities have to consider the EU-aspects of administrative acts and decisions.

It seems that especially the transfer of competence to the EU-institutions to issue legally binding and directly applicable norms is of interest in the context of international law, as the consequences of this procedure may be regarded as a move from both the traditional dualistic and the practical monistic thinking towards a pure monistic approach.

1.2 Methods of Implementation. International treaties are (in general) implemented into Danish law by means of three different methods, which may be characterized as passive transformation, active

---

[5] See Madsen 1986, p. 33 ff. See also Gulmann et al. 1989, p. 95. The analyses of case law and the conclusions made by Niels Madsen have been critized by Frederik Harhoff in *Årsberetning 1986 for Retsvidenskabeligt Institut B ved Københavns Universitet.*

[6] See Zahle 1989, p. 94.

transformation and incorporation, in Danish referred to as "normharmoni", "omskrivning" og "inkorporering ved henvisning".[7]

Once an international treaty is concluded by the Danish Government, the ratification process is initiated by the Parliament. The Parliament will carry out an investigation of the compatibility of existing Danish law with the treaty in question. The aim of this investigation is to ascertain whether amendments to domestic legislation are needed in order to achieve harmony with the treaty provisions. If no amendments are needed the international treaty is implemented by passive transformation (*normharmoni*).

If amendments are needed to achieve compatibility either active transformation or incorporation is applied. The instrument used most frequently is active transformation, whereby the provisions of a treaty are transformed either by reproduction or reformulation into Danish provisions which are included in relevant statutes (*omskrivning).*

Another way of transforming treaty provisions into Danish law is by the so-called continuous fulfilment of obligations contained in international treaties. This method is used to secure that Danish law is compatible with all ratified treaties at all times (*tilpasning ved løbende normopfyldelse).*

Incorporation differs substantially from both passive and active transformation as the treaty becomes part of Danish law in its original form. In effect, a statute incorporating a treaty or part(s) of a treaty is adopted by the Danish Parliament and published together with the treaty in its original language(s) in the Danish Legal Gazette (Lovtidende), Sec. A (*henvisning*).

The predominant method of implementation is transformation, although the use of incorporation as a means of implementation has increased during the past ten years, see for instance the Act on the Convention on Contracts for the International Sale of Goods, Act No. 733 of December 7, 1988.

Similarly, transformation is the preferred method with regard to human rights treaties. This is the case with respect to the major UN-treaties, i.e. the International Covenant on Civil and Political Rights (CCPR) and the International Covenant on Economic, Social and Cultural Rights (CESCR), and for the main part of the conventions

[7] See *Report* (Betænkning) *No. 682/1973.*

concluded by the contracting parties to the Council of Europe. The ECHR modifies this point of departure as this Convention has been incorporated into Danish law by Act No. 285 of April 29, 1992. A translation into English of the incoporation Act is attached hereto as *Annex 1.*

1.3 Hierarchical Status of Human Rights Treaties. With reference to the dualistic principle mentioned in 1.1., it has been stated that a treaty validly concluded but not incorporated can neither be applied by Danish courts and administrative authorities on an equal basis with Danish law nor prevail over Danish law. Consequently, a treaty provision which is incompatible with Danish law will be "overruled" by the domestic rule. Similarly, a treaty provision does not constitute a recognized source of law in the context of the principle of legality, i.e. that any measures by public authorities must have as its basis an accepted source of law. [8]

It has been argued that three principles of construction, i.e. the so-called rule of interpretation, the rule of presumption and the rule of instruction, (for further details, see 1.4) modify this point of departure. These rules are applied by courts and administrative authorities in order to solve concrete cases where an international aspect or even a conflict between Danish law and international treaties, including human rights treaties must be taken into consideration.[9]

This (vague) approval of international law as an interpretative legal source has been contested by some legal scholars who have expanded the view by arguing that international law should be applied as a legal source, irrespective of whether it is incorporated or not and as (almost) equivalent to domestic legal sources.[10]

It is, however, not quite clear how these scolars would solve a conflict between international and domestic law. Merely, it is pointed out that the question of conflict is purely theoretical and would seldom arise in practice. It is added that the courts may contribute to the

---

[8] See Hagel-Sørensen in von Eyben (ed.) 1989, p. 146. See also Claus Gulmann in *Nordic Journal of International Law* 1983, p. 49.

[9] See Niels Eilschou Holm, *Nordic Journal of International Law*, 1981, p. 125; Carl Åge Nørgaard in the *Weekly Law Journal* 1987, Sec. B, p. 74 f.; and Gulmann et al. 1989, p. 90 f.

[10] See Jensen 1992, p. 29 f, and Rehof and Trier 1990, p. 86 ff.

infringement of international treaties if conflicts are solved on the basis of domestic law rather than on international law, and further it is stressed that such a situation is unacceptable from a human rights point of view.[11]

The question of conflicts has been at focus in an analysis based on a constitutional law approach. In this context, it is argued that there is no basis for attaching first priority to international rules. Moreover, it is adduced as to the conflicts of sources that "such conflicts cannot be resolved by referring to simple principles". In case of a conflict between international and domestic rules it is thus suggested that a number of analytical rules are applied in each individual case, including the relevance of the international rule, the clearness of the domestic rule, the international aspect, the acknowledged supremacy of the domestic rule, etc.[12]

The tendency among legal scholars towards the acknowledgment of international rules as legal sources is underscored by an analysis of Danish case law showing an increase in the application of international law by the courts. [13]

Also, in the report by the Committee on the Incorporation of the ECHR, 1991, p. 80 f, it is stated that Danish case law indicates that the ECHR and the relevant case law are used as an acknowledged source of law. As to the decisions from the Supreme Court it is noteworthy that the court refrains from an independent interpretation and only interprets in accordance with case law from the European Court of Human Rights. This attitude is a natural consequence of a Danish legal tradition according to which the courts avoid the so-called "dynamic interpretation". One of the underlying principles in this respect is the principle of predictability and transparency in the legal system which creates the basis for the doctrine of the rule of law. Moreover, it is considered an important element in the maintainance of the balance between the legislative and the executive powers.[14] [15]

---

[11] See Rehof and Trier 1990, p. 94 f.

[12] For further details, see Zahle 1989, pp. 96 and 102 ff.

[13] See Madsen 1986, p. 38 ff.

[14] To this end see *Report No. 1220* on the Incorporation of the European Convention on Human Rights and Fundamental Freedoms, 1991, p. 149 f.

It seems that treaties, including human rights treaties, are generally accepted as sources of law on the same level as domestic statutes.

However, this basis is modified in different ways. Firstly, coordination norms may prevail over international treaties, for instance the principle of *lex posterior*, i.e. a Danish statute may displace an earlier treaty or treaty provision. This is especially important if domestic legislation is passed by Parliament in circumstances where Parliament was aware that a given Act was or would be in conflict with international obligations. In such cases, the administrative authorities and the courts would have to respect the decision made by the Parliament and thus apply domestic law.[16]

Furthermore, it seems appropriate to modify the conclusion with respect to both judicial and administrative decisions placing burdens on the citizen. Thus, it seems to be in accordance with the traditional Scandinavian doctrine of the rule of law to require a positive and publicly accessible basis of law when imposing obligations on citizens. In the context of international law this may imply either incorporation or at least immidiate publication of treaties placing obligations on the individual.The importance of such a requirement is underscored by the fact that international treaties are usually published much later than at the time of ratification or at the time of coming into force. Nevertheless, case law shows an example where the confiscation of accounting materials was claimed on the basis of an international non-incorporated treaty. Such a claim was found not to have any grounds in Danish law.[17]

As regards decisions in favour of citizens based on international rules containing rights pertaining to the individual citizen, no similar considerations seem necessary. This point of view may be the rationale behind an unreported decision from the Copenhagen City Court in 1966 in which translation costs were passed on to a public authority with reference to Article 6 (3) of the ECHR. According to this

---

[15] A study of Danish case law involving the ECHR is made by Professor Eva Smith, see *The Weekly Law Journal* (UfR), 1994, Sec. B, p. 94 ff.

[16] See Claus Gulmann in *Juristen* 1988, p. 290, note 16; Gulmann et al. 1989, p. 95; and Ulf Østergaard-Nielsen in the *Weekly Law Journal*, 1992, Sec. B, p. 59 ff.

[17] The Supreme Court decision is found in the *Weekly Law Journal*, 1972, p. 600. An analysis thereof by Niels Madsen is found in the *Weekly Law Journal*, 1986, Sec. B, p. 38 f.

viewpoint, human rights treaties should be applied by the courts even when there is no legal basis in domestic law and irrespective of incorporation.

Also, it should be mentioned that the influence of EU-law on Danish law may under certain circumstances form a modification to the above-mentioned point of departure concerning the hierarchical status of human rights in Danish law. If the meaning of a provision in an EU-statute can be derived only by using the principles of the ECHR and relevant case law as interpretative instruments, the member states of the EU will have to apply the ECHR provision in question rather than a domestic rule. However, it has been pointed out that the EU member states are not obliged to follow such an interpretation.[18]

1.4 Rules of Construction. When facing a problem concerning the compatibility of Danish law with an international treaty, Danish courts tend to apply two rules of construction in order to avoid setting aside the obligations contained in international treaties.

The *rule of interpretation* is applicable when there is doubt about the interpretation of a Danish statute. In such a case, the rule indicates that Danish law should be interpreted by the Danish courts as being in compliance with international law. The rule of interpretation shows how to avoid a violation of international obligations and is thus only applicable in cases involving a potential conflict between domestic and international law.[19]

However, the scope of application of the rule of interpretation is not very well-defined. Moreover, the rule perhaps also encompasses situations where the question not only relates to a possible violation, but also in the event of doubt about the interpretation of a Danish statute. In a Supreme Court case from 1975 (U 1975.30 H) this was actually the situation. The Supreme Court applied an interpretation which complied with the convention in question. In a comment by Justice Jørgen Trolle, he stated, that "the tendency will naturally be to

[18] See *Report No. 1220* on the Incorporation of the European Convention on Human Rights and Fundamental Freedoms, 1991, s. 141 ff, and Lorenzen et al. 1994, p. 37 ff.

[19] See Gulmann et al.1989, p. 91 f and Niels Eilschou Holm in *Nordisk Tidsskrift for International ret*, 1981, p. 128.

understand that a statute meets our international obligations rather than understand it as being contrary to them".[20]

Said rule of interpretation has been criticized by Professor Henrik Zahle who argues that the rule implies two phases, the first one consists of an interpretation of the Danish legal source, and the second of an interpretation of international law. The second phase is only activated if the Danish statute gives rise to doubt. According to Professor Zahle, this division into interpretative phases does not reflect what is actually done by the courts when they handle cases involving aspects of international law. The doubt may not be attached to the domestic rule as is implied in the rule of interpretation, it may just as well be attached to the international rule which, consequently, both creates the doubt and solves the problem as was the case in U 1975.30 H.[21]

Another principle of construction is the *rule of presumption.* According to this principle, the courts should in cases of divergence between a (ratified, incorporated) treaty provision and a subsequent Danish provision presume that the Danish provision was intended to respect the treaty provision when it was adopted by Parliament. Contrary to the rule of interpretation, the rule of presumption does not imply any doubt about the understanding of Danish law. The presumption should be applied even if the Danish provision is formulated in direct or indirect conflict with the treaty provision, unless Parliament was aware of the incompatibility with international law at the time when the provision was adopted. The rule of presumption applies analoguously to customary law.[22]

The field of application of the rule of presumption is not quite distinct and besides it is not easy to draw the line between this rule and the rule of interpretation. These topics have recently been discussed among Danish scholars. Hence, it has been stated that the rule of presumption is only applicable to international treaties and customary law in force prior to the enactment of the statute in question. If the presumption should reflect reality, the connection

---

[20] See the *Weekly Law Journal*, 1975, Sec. B, p. 112. See also Madsen 1986, p. 37 and the Supreme Court decision in the *Weekly Law Journal*, 1964, p. 624.

[21] See Zahle 1989, p. 97 f.

[22] See Gulmann et al. 1989, p. 92 f.

between domestic law and more recent international law should not be considered encompassed by the rule of presumption.[23]

It has been stated that such a restraint cannot be upheld as Denmark should try to establish compliance between international law and domestic law.[24]

In this connection it should be mentioned that in a decision from 1972, the Supreme Court reached the decision that a treaty from 1931 should be included when applying a statute from 1916. (U 1972.600 H). An unreported decision from the Copenhagen City Court is also rather remarkable as the court by referring to Article 6 (3) of the ECHR imposed on an administrative authority to pay translation costs, even though the Danish Administration of Justice Act, which came into force prior to the ECHR, provides that such costs are to be paid by the convicted person.

Different opinions on this matter have been expressed by several authors, many of whom, however, argue that the rule of presumption is applicable, but only to the extent that the relevant Danish rule is not deprived of its substance.[25]

Also, the Danish administrative authorities are considered to be obliged to exercise their discretionary powers pursuant to statutory provisions in a way which safeguards the observance of Denmark's international obligations. This obligation is now known as the *rule of instruction*. Another aspect of this rule is that rule-making by an administrative authority must comply with the regulation laid down in international treaties, i.e. the responsible minister is obliged to issue rules which make it possible to ensure the continuous fulfilment of obligations contained in international treaties.[26] For further details on this method of implementation, see 1.2.

---

[23] See Ross et al. 1984, p. 75 ff, and Zahle 1989, p. 98.

[24] See Espersen 1970, p. 379 and 388.

[25] See Espersen 1970, p. 388; Claus Gulmann in *Nordisk Tidsskrift for International Ret* 1983, p. 50; Madsen 1986, p. 39; and Nina Holst-Christensen in *Juristen*, 1989, p. 49. See also Jensen 1992, p. 20 ff who also discusses the legal suitability of a distinction between treaties and customary law with regard to the rule of presumption.

[26] The rule of instruction was introduced by Ole Espersen in *Indgåelse og opfyldelse af traktater*, 1970, p. 170 and 381 f and discussed by Claus Gulmann, Denmark, in Jacobs and Roberts, eds., 1987 *The Effect of Treaties in Domestic Law*, p. 35; Henrik Zahle, *Dansk Forfatningsret*, 1989, vol. 2, p. 99; and Hans Gammeltoft-Hansen et al., *Forvaltningsret*, 1994, p. 240 ff.

The application of the rule of instruction presupposes that a treaty which is guiding for the adminstrative exercise of discretionay powers is both reasonably precise and unconditional. Besides, the treaty must protect the citizens against the authorities and not only regulate the relationship among states.[27]

Danish courts have not yet had the opportunity to address the issue of whether or not the obligation contained in the rule of instruction should apply in Danish law, but it seems probable that the courts will eventually accept it.[28]

In his book, The European Convention on Human Rights in Scandinavian Law, 1992, p. 162 ff, Søren Stenderup Jensen argues that a decision by the High Court from 1992 indicates that the rule of instruction is a legal obligation to exercise discretionary powers in accordance with international law. The case concerned refusal to grant residence permit to an Iranian woman whose daughter and two grandsons were living in Denmark based on the family's lack of financial means to undertake the maintainance of the applicant. The City Court concluded that the exercise of discretion in connection with the decision taken by the Directorate of Aliens should include considerations with regard to international law, including Article 8 of the ECHR. Subsequently, the Higt Court upheld the ruling but unlike the City Court, concluded that the decision was unlawful under Danish law, because the family had actually maintained the applicant, and that the international obligations invoked were of no relevance as the Danish practice of requirering family maintainance was compatible with international law. Besides, there was no question of exercising discretionary powers as the practice by the Directorate was deemed to be consequent. The High Court seems to have disregarded the question of discretion and the judgment can thus hardly be said to support the existence of a rule of instruction in Danish law.

The Ministry of Justice mentioned the rule of instruction indirectly in a Danish report to the UN Human Rights Committee concerning the implementation of CCPR Article 26 by declaring that "Danish law on the general effect of a validly concluded treaty on domestic law implies inter alia that administrative acts - whether in the form of decisions or of general regulations - conform to validly contracted international commitments".[29]

As access to administrative acts is - in effect - restricted and as the number of cases in which international law has been dealt with is probably limited, it is not easy to say whether the rule of instruction is applied to its full extent. However, it seems, on the basis of the

---

[27] See Madsen 1986, p. 40.

[28] See Claus Gulmann, Denmark, in Jacobs and Roberts, eds 1987, p. 35.

[29] See *UN-doc. CCPR/C/I Add. 51.*

investigations made by the Ombudsman, that administrative authorities often "forget" the existence of both international and human rights law.

In their book, Menneskeret,[30] Lars Rehof and Tyge Trier introduce a new rule of construction called the *filling in rule*. It is suggested that both courts and administrative authorities should apply international law in cases where domestic law does not cover the subject matter and where there is no doubt about the interpretation of the relevant international rule. Furthermore, the application of the filling in rule presupposes that the principle of legality does not consitute an obstacle for applying the international rule.

2. APPLICATION OF INTERNATIONAL LAW BY THE COURTS AND THE ADMINISTRATIVE AUTHORITIES

2.1 Case law of the Danish Courts. Surveys of decisions and rulings by the Supreme Court, the High Courts and the City Courts in which human rights or other inernational treaties have been invoked and/or applied are found in *Annex 2*.

2.1.1 The Supreme Court. A survey of Supreme Court decisions in the period 1979-1994 involving human rights questions shows a tendency towards an increased application of the ECHR. The number of such cases has increased in the first part of the nineties. Thus, the Supreme Court has tried three cases in 1990, five in 1991, three in 1992, two in 1993 and eight cases in 1994.

In particular U 1990.13 HK og U 1990.181 H are of importance, the former being a provisional ruling (*kendelse*), the latter a decision (*dom*). Both the decision and the ruling were given in accordance with a judgment by the European Court of Human Rights (ECHR, A 154 *Hauschildt v. Denmark*) in which the Court held that Article 6 (1) of the ECHR had been violated. In said case, the applicant, Mr. Hauschildt, claimed that he had not received a hearing by an impartial tribunal as both the trial judge and the appeal judge had made pre-trial decisions in his case. The Court concluded that the Danish system

[30] Rehof and Trier 1990, p. 86.

in itself did not violate Article 6 (1) of the ECHR, but in the circumstances of the concrete case Mr. Hauschildt's fears that the tribunal did not seem impartial towards him were objectively justified. It should be noted that subsequently the Danish Adminstration of Justice Act was amended to reflect the concerns raised by the Hauschildt case.

A recent case (U 1994.988 H)[31] should also be noted. In this case, the Supreme Court referred to a judgment by the European Court of Human Rights (A 298 *Jersild v. Denmark*) and reached the conclusion that a journalist was allowed to trespass the garden of a politician in order to obtain information for a television feature.

The cases seem to concentrate on issues covered by Article 6 of the ECHR. Within this subject it is mainly the procedural protections contained in Article 6 (3) which are in focus.[32]

2.1.2 The High Courts. The trend towards increased application of the ECHR in the period from the late eighties until today may also be illustrated by focusing on the case law by the two Danish High Courts. In particular, it seems as if the High Courts have been more attentive to the Convention after the incorporation of the ECHR in the spring of 1992. In this connection, it is remarkable that in a decision from 1992 concerning documentation of testemonies in a criminal case (U 1992.949 V), the court, *ex officio*, raised the question of compatibility with Article 6 (3) litra d of the ECHR.

As is the case with decisions and rulings of the Supreme Court, the High Court decisions and rulings also concentrate on Article 6 of the ECHR, especially Section 1 and 3 of this Article. 16 out of 27 cases from the period from 1984 to 1994 thus relate to Article 6.

One unreported decision from one of the High Courts (ØLD 1989 185/88) is noteworthy as the CESCR was invoked by the plaintiff. The plaintiff submitted that the Ministry of Taxation should acknowledge that the taxation of persons with an income below the EC poverty line was a violation of the CESCR Article 11 (1). However, the Court did

---

[31] See the *Weekly Law Journal* (UfR) 1994, p. 988.

[32] A collection of summaries of decisions from the Supreme Court until July 1994 is found in *Menneskeret ved domstolene*, Karen Lise Thylstrup and Birgitte Kofod Olsen, 1994.

not apply the CESCR but dismissed the case due to the fact that the plaintiff was not in position to file suit because of lack of any concrete interest in the matter.

It should be noted that the survey contained in *Annex 2* covers both reported and unreported decisions and rulings, of which the latter is, however, an incomplete list.

2.1.3 The City Courts. Decisions and rulings from the Danish City Courts are usually not published, hence the survey in *Annex 2* is developed on the basis of Danish legal litterature and only contains the more important cases.

Against this background, it is hardly possible to draw a picture of the use of international human rigths law by the City Courts.

2.2 *Administrative Practice*. It is difficult to obtain an overview of the application of international treaties in the practice of the Danish administrative authorities as the decisions by these institutions are not published in an easily accessible form. It is neither possible to extract decisions involving international law by electronic means, nor to get physical access to the documents as the administrative authorities do not keep records identifying decisions that involve international law.

In this connection it should be noted that the Danish Ombudsman has been assigned to monitor and control administrative authorities and their exercise of their discretionary powers in compliance with Danish legal adminstrative principles and obligations derived from international obligations, including the ECHR.[33]

A survey of decisions by the Ombudsman shows that cases involving human rights aspects are relatively rare. There seems, however, to be a slight concentration of cases within the past 2 years. It is also remarkable that the main part of the cases concerns the protection of private and family life, cf. Article 8 of the ECHR. One case is of particular interest because the Ombudsman, based on an *ex officio* investigation, points out that obligations contained in international treaties are under certain circumstances of relevance for

[33] See *Folketingets Ombudsmands Beretning 1982,* pp. 9 and 159, and 1985, pp. 10-12.

the exercise of discretionary powers by the administrative authority in question.[34]

2.3 Particular Features of Danish Case Law.

2.3.1 Direct versus Indirect Applicability. As mentioned above, legal theory in general tends to acknowledge international treaties as sources of law at the same level as Danish legal sources. The question is, however whether this is reflected in the decisions where international human rights law is applied. The surveys in *Annex 2* only cover decisions and rulings in which the ECHR has been invoked and the following conclusions are only based on this material.

The surveys show that in the majority of cases heard before both the Supreme Court and the High Courts, the provisions of the ECHR have been invoked as autonomous legal norms.

As to the Supreme Court, the provisions of the ECHR have been invoked as complementing Danish domestic rules in only one third of the cases. The application of the ECHR as an interpretative instrument has been even more limited as regards the High Courts.

2.3.2 Vertical versus Horizontal Effect. As the main part of Danish case law involving human rights aspects concerns the procedural protections within Article 6 of the ECHR, the picture that can be drawn regarding vertical versus horizontal effect of human rights provisions is dominated by cases between individuals and the Danish administrative authorities.

Only in a small number of the cases, in particular the cases concerning the right to assembly, cf. Article 11 of the ECHR and the right to freedom of expression, cf. Article 10 of the ECHR, have the provisions of the ECHR been invoked and applied in disputes between private parties.

2.3.3 Non-Binding International Human Rights Instruments. Non-binding international human rights instruments are rarely invoked before the Danish courts. Among the decisions reported, two examples from one of the High Courts from 1989 illustrate how "soft law" has

---

[34] See *Folketingets Ombudsmands Beretning 1992*, p. 437 f.

been invoked by the parties. In a case concerning reunion of members of a refugee family, a recommendation relating to the Convention to the Status of Refugees of 1951 and the final act to a UN conference held the same year was invoked (apart from Article 8 of the ECHR). The Court applied the invoked Convention but concluded that the human rights instruments were not violated by refusing family reunion.[35]

In another case concerning the imprisonment of an asylum seeker, a conclusion from the UNHCR Executive Committee of 1986 was invoked together with Article 3 and Article 5 of the ECHR. In this case, however, the Court only applied the ECHR and concluded that Article 5 had not been violated by the imprisonment of the asylum seeker.[36]

As regards Danish adminstrative practice, it cannot be confirmed if non-binding human rights instruments are applied on a regular basis. However, it is fair to assume that this is not the case.

One case should be mentioned from the Ombudsman's practice. The case relates to a decision by an administrative authority concerning the allocation and categorization of inmates. After having investigated the case, the Ombudsman concluded that the Standard Minimum Rules for the Treatment of Prisoners adopted by the Council of Europe Committee of Ministers in 1987 were not infringed by the decision.[37]

3. ASSESSMENT OF LAW AND PRACTICE

The ECHR was not incorporated into Danish law until 1992. However, the number of human rights cases has risen in the period from 1990, i.e. starting before the ECHR was incorporated. This can probably be ascribed to a general trend towards an increased focus on human rights matters and a greater alertness with respect to the protection of the rights of individuals. Also, legal scholars have shown more interest in human rights as a legal discipline than was previously the case.

It is probably too early to evaluate whether the incorporation has had significant practical consequences. The ECHR has - so far - been

---

[35] See the *Weekly Law Journal* (UfR), 1989, p. 775.

[36] See the *Weekly Law Journal* (UfR), 1989, p. 302.

[37] See the Ombudsman's decision of July 15, 1993.

applied by the courts more frequently in 1994 than in previous years. Whether this is a coincidence or indeed a trend towards more attention to and acknowledgement of the Convention as a legal source equivalent to domestic sources cannot be determined at this point.

Another issue of interest is whether Denmark's membership of the EU has had an impact on the implementation of human rights treaties in Danish law. The European Court of Justice has in its case law acknowledged the ECHR as an interpretative instrument in connection with the protection of fundamental rights in an EU context. Pursuant to this statement, the ECHR should be applied at the same level as any EU rule when relevant for the interpretation of the EU-rule, i.e. it should prevail over Danish law.[38]

Danish case law only has few examples of cases in which both EU-law and the ECHR have been of relevance. On this basis, it is not possible to establish whether the legal reasoning by the judges has been influenced by the priority given to human rights by the European Court of Justice.

4. RECENT DEVELOPMENT AND REFORM

There are no current plans to introduce constitutional reform concerning fundamental rights. Moreover, Danish courts have proved reluctant to review the compliance of acts of parliament and administrative practice with the fundamental rights set forth in the Danish Constitution and the human rights found in the ECHR.

Furthermore, no plans have been launched so far for the purpose of implementing or incorporating the CCPR and the CESCR. The vague expression of the rights and duties contained in these documents has probably been and is still part of the reason why at least the CESCR and to some extent the CCPR have been ignored. The growing alertness among politicians of human rights and the tendency towards changes in attitudes concerning human rights instruments among legal scholars, judges and to a lesser degree public servants may lead to the

---

[38] The relationship between EU law and human rights has been dealt with by Jørgen Steen Sørensen in the *Weekly Law Journal* (UfR), 1991, Sec. B, p. 102 ff. For further details concerning case law involving human rights aspects from the European Court of Justice, see Rasmussen and Schønberg 1994.

application of the UN Covenants on a more regular and frequent basis. This could mean an effective and perhaps sufficient implementation of the instruments in question. In any case, a step further towards incorpartion of the UN Covenants does not seem to be realistic within the near future.

As it may be of importance for the effectiveness of the ECHR within the EU-institutions, especially the European Court of Justice, it should be mentioned that a project for the purpose of evaluating the consequences of allowing EU to be a member of the Council of Europe is being prepared by the Danish Ministry of Justice.

5. PRACTICAL ASPECTS OF IMPLEMENTATION

Documentation of human rights activities within the UN and the Council of Europe is available in different forms and from different institutions.

The Danish Centre for Human Rights has a library where both physical and electronic access to a number of human rights documents is possible. The library contains books and prints of judgments from the European Court of Human Rights, and decisions and reports from the European Commission on Human Rights. The most recent cases before the Court and the Commission are found in press releases from the Council of Europe and are also available in the library. Also, resolutions, recommendations and declarations from the Committee of Ministers and resolutions, recommendations and opinions from the Parliamentary Assembly of the Council of Europe are found in the library.

Additionally, the Centre library may assist in the search for documentation by electronic means. The inhouse databases give access to decisions by the European Court of Human Rights, decisions and reports by the European Commission of Human Rights, and Danish cases pending before the Strasbourg-institutions. At the UN-level, two databases are of importance, one covering the texts of international human rights treaties, the other covering the state of signatures of international human rights treaties. Access to the databases of the

Council of Europe in Strasbourg can be arranged by the library as well.[39]

In 1994, a new law review was released by the Danish Ministry of Justice. Under the title "EU-ret og Menneskeret" summaries of the judgments by the Court of Human Rights as well as articles on human rights and EU-issues are published every second month.

In order to improve knowledge of human rights instruments, especially the ECHR and the related case law among judges, lawyers, public servants and teachers, a number of training-courses has been established or initiated in 1994 by the Danish Centre for Human Rights, some of these in cooperation with the Danish Ministry of Justice, teacher-training colleges and colleges for social workers.

Hence, access to and dissemination of human rigths documentation seem sufficient, especially if the new law review and the training courses prove successfull.

However, it should be noted that international human rights treaties are not published in the Legal Gazette on a permanent and consistent basis, but are found in two different volumes of the gazette depending on which method of implementation has been chosen by the Parliament.

Concluded and ratified treaties are published in Section C of the Legal Gazette, whereas Danish acts are found in Section A. A subscription to the Legal Gazette does not automatically cover both sections which in many cases means that only Section A is read by the majority of subscribers. The publication of treaties in Section C is often delayed compared to the date of ratification or coming into force. The CCPR and the CESCR were, for instance, published four years after the Danish ratification. The date of coming into force may be more important to both citizens and professionals than the date of ratification. However, human rights treaties tend to be published six months after they have come into force. Both the chosen form of publication and the time of publication thus seem to imply confusion and unpredictability concerning the rights of the citizens and the duties of the state.

---

[39] For further information about searching of sources relevant to the ECHR, see Thylstrup and Olsen 1994, Vol. 1, p. 13.

As regards treaties that have been incorporated into Danish law, such treaties are publicized as annexes to the incorporation Act in Section A of the Legal Gazette. A Danish act does not enter into force until it has been published in Section A. Accordingly, the publication usually follows immidiately after the adoption of the Act by Parliament. This way of publishing international treaties seems to comply with the doctrine of the rule of law to a higher extent than the way adopted for treaties published in Section C of the Legal Gazette.

REFERENCES

Espersen, Ole: *Indgåelse og opfyldelse af traktater*. Copenhagen 1970.

Eyben, W.E. von, ed.: *Juridisk Grundbog*, vol. 2, 4. ed. Denmark, 1989.

Folketingets Ombudsmandsberetning. Denmark 1982, 1985, 1992 and 1993.

Gammeltoft-Hansen, Hans et al.: *Forvaltningsret*. Denmark 1994.

Gulmann, Claus et al.: *Folkeret*. Denmark 1989.

Jacobs, Francis G. and Roberts, Shelley, eds.: *The Effect of Treaties in Domestic Law*. London 1987.

Jensen, Søren Stenderup: *The European Convention on Human Rights in Scandinavian Law*. Copenhagen 1992.

Juristen. Denmark 1988 and 1989.

Lorenzen, Peer et al.: *Den Europæiske Menneskeretskonvention med kommentarer*. Denmark 1994.

Madsen, Niels: *Festskrift til Højesteret*. Copenhagen 1989.

Nordic Journal of International Law. Denmark 1981 and 1983.

Nordisk Tidsskrift for International Ret. Denmark 1981.

Rasmussen, Louise Nan and Schønberg, Søren: *EU-menneskeret - en udfordring til dansk ret*. Copenhagen, 1994.

Rehof, Lars Adam and Trier, Tyge: *Menneskeret*. Copenhagen, 1990.

Report No. 682/1973.

Report No. 1220 on the Incorporation of the European Convention on Human Rights and Fundamental Freedom 1991.

Ross, Alf: *Dansk Statsfortatningsret*. Copenhagen, 1980.

Ross, Alf et al.: *Lærebog i Folkeret*. Copenhagen, 1984.

Thylstrup, Karen Lise and Olsen, Birgitte Kofod: *Menneskeret ved domstolene*. Copenhagen 1994.

UN-doc. CCPR/C/I Add. 51.

Weekly Law Journal (UfR). Denmark 1964, 1972, 1975, 1986, 1987, 1989, 1991, 1992 and 1994.

Zahle, Henrik: *Dansk Forfatningsret, vol. 2*. Copenhagen, 1989.

Årsberetning 1986 for Retsvidenskabeligt Institut B. Copenhagen 1987.

ANNEXES

1. Incorporation Act of the European Convention on Human Rights, Act No. 285 of April 29, 1992. Unauthorized translation.
2. Surveys of decisions and rulings by the Supreme Court, the High Courts and the City Courts

ANNEX 1

ACT NO. 285 OF APRIL 29, 1992
- THE EUROPEAN CONVENTION ON HUMAN RIGHTS

SECTION 1
The following provisions shall be in effect in this country:

Subsection 1.

1) The Convention of November 4, 1950 for the Protection of Human Rights and Fundamental Freedoms, cf. Ministerial Order No. 20 of June 11, 1953, The Legal Gazette C, the procedural rules of which have been changed according to the following protocols:

a) Protocol No. 2 of May 6, 1963 to the Council of Europe Convention for the Protection of Human Rights and Fundamental Freedoms by which the Court of Human Rights is given competence to bring forward advisory opinions, cf. Ministerial Order No. 67 of November 23, 1964, The Legal Gazette C.

b) Protocol No. 3 of May 6, 1963 to the Council of Europe Convention for the Protection of Human Rights and Fundamental Freedoms by which Article 29, 30 and 34 of the Convention have been amended changed, cf. Ministerial Order No. 67 of November 23, 1964, The Legal Gazette C.

c) Protocol No. 5 of January 20, 1966 to the Council of Europe Convention for the Protection of Human Rights and Fundamental Freedoms on amendments to Article 22 and 40 of the Convention, cf. Ministerial Order No. 35 of March 22, 1972, The Legal Gazette C.

d) Protocol No. 8 of March 19, 1985 to the Council of Europe Convention for the Protection of Human Rights and Fundamental Freedoms, cf. Ministerial Order No. 33 of March 15, 1990.

2) Amending Protocol of March 20, 1952 to the Council of Europe Convention for the Protection of Human Rights and Fundamental Freedoms, cf. Ministerial Order No. 20 of June 11, 1953, The Legal Gazette C.

3) Protocol No. 4 of September 16, 1963 to the Council of Europe Convention for the Protection of Human Rights and Fundamental Freedoms, cf. Ministerial Order No. 17 of February 17, 1965, The Legal Gazette C.

4) Amending Protocol No. 6 of april 28, 1983 to the Council of Europe Convention for the Protection of Human Rights and Fundamental Freedoms, cf. Ministerial Order No. 72 of September 20, 1985, The Legal Gazette C.

5) Amending Protocol No. 7 of November 22, 1984 to the Council of Europe Convention for the Protection of Human Rights and Fundamental Freedoms, cf. Ministerial Order No. 41 of April 7, 1989, The Legal Gazette C.

Subsection 2.

A Danish translation of the Convention and the protocols mentioned in *Subsection 1* is annexed to the Act.

SECTION 2

The Government may agree to amend the provisions on the composition and mode of operation of the bodies established by the Convention. Amendments entered into force will be printed in Danish as annexes to the Act.

SECTION 3

This Act does not give rise to amendments of Section 962, *Subsection 2* of the Administration of Justice Act, on the restriction of the possibility to appeal against certain decisions in criminal cases.

SECTION 4

This Act will enter into force on July 1, 1992.

SECTION 5

This Act is not valid in Greenland and the Faroe Islands, but may enter into force for these parts of the country by Royal decree, wholly or partly with due regard, however, to the particular requirements of Greenland and the Faroe Islands.

ANNEX 2

JUDGMENTS AND RULINGS OF THE *SUPREME COURT* IN WHICH THE COURT HAS APPLIED THE EUROPEAN CONVENTION ON HUMAN RIGHTS

No. in the Weekly Law Journal (UfR)	Type of case	Invoked articles of the Convention	Reference to ECHR judgments
U 1994.988 H	Journalist, Freedom of expression.	ECHR Art. 10	A 298
U 1994.804 H	Criminal Code, Expulsion.	Litterature on the ECHR	
U 1994.617 H	Criminal Code, Alien Act, Expulsion.	ECHR Art. 3.	
U 1994.536 H	Criminal Code, The Administration of Justice Act, Capacity.	ECHR Art. 6, (1).	A 11, 43, 80, 84, 86, 155, 132.
U 1994.478 H	Criminal Code, The Administration of Justice Act, Documentation.	ECHR Art. 6, (1) and (2).	
U 1994.419 R	Trial of Impeachment, Documentation.	Principles of the ECHR	
U 1994.404 R	Trial of Impeachment, Impartiality.	ECHR Art. 6.	A 53, 86, 132, 155, 210, 279-A
U 1994.292 H	Journalist, Liability, Fair Trial.	ECHR in general	
U 1993.389 H	Criminal Code, The Administration of Justice Act, Procedural error.	ECHR Art. 6, 10.	
U 1993.384 H	Criminal Code, The Administration of Justice Act.	ECHR Prot. No. 7 Art. 2.	

ANNEX 2

No. in the Weekly Law Journal (UfR)	Type of case	Invoked articles of the Convention	Reference to ECHR judgments
U 1992.879 H	Criminal Code, The Administration of Justice Act, Documentation.	ECHR Art. 6.	A 194-A
U 1992.877 HK	Criminal Code, The Administration of Justice Act, Pre-trial detention.	ECHR Art. 5, (3).	A 207, 218
U 1992.87 H	Criminal Code, The Administration of Justice Act, The production of witnesses.	ECHR Art. 6, (3), litra d.	
U 1991.720 H	Criminal Code, Interpretation.	ECHR Art. 6, (3).	
U 1991.580 H	Criminal Code, The Administration of Justice Act, Documentation.	ECHR Art. 6, (3), litra d.	
U 1991.522 HK	Civil proceedings, Freedom of association.	ECHR Art. 11.	
U 1991.523 HK	Criminal Code, Extradition.	ECHR Art. 8.	
U 1991.255 H	Criminal Code, The Administration of Justice Act, Documentation.	ECHR Art. 6, (3), litra d.	
U 1990.903 H	Criminal Code, The Administration of Justice Act, Procedural error.	ECHR Art. 6, (3), litra d.	
U 1990.181 H	Criminal Code, The Administration of Justice Act, Capacity.	ECHR Art. 6, (2).	A 154
U 1990.13 HK	Criminal Code, The Administration of Justice Act, Capacity.	ECHR Art. 6, (1).	
U 1989.928 H	Civil proceedings, The Social Assistance Act, Displaced children.	Principles of the ECHR	Case law of the Court in general

No. in the Weekly Law Journal (UfR)	Type of case	Invoked articles of the Convention	Reference to ECHR judgments
U 1987.440 HK	Criminal Code, The Administration of Justice Act, Appointment of a counsel for the defence.	ECHR Art. 6, (3), litra c.	
U 1986.898 H	Civil proceedings, Freedom of association.	ECHR Art. 11.	
U 1985.1080 H	Criminal Code, The Administration of Justice Act, Documentation.	ECHR Art. 6, (3), litra d.	
U 1982.179 H	Civil proceedings, Principle of law, Freedom of expression.	ECHR Art. 10.	
U 1979.1011 HK	Criminal Code, The Administration of Justice Act, Solitary confinement.	ECHR Art. 3.	

JUDGMENTS AND RULINGS OF THE *HIGH COURTS* IN WHICH THE COURTS HAVE APPLIED THE EUROPEAN CONVENTION ON HUMAN RIGHTS

No. in the Weekly Law Journal (UfR)	**Type of case**	**Invoked articles of the Convention**	**Reference to ECHR judgments**
U 1994.225 Ø	Criminal Code, The Administration of Justice Act, Capacity.	ECHR Art. 6.	
U 1994.15 Ø	Civil proceedings, The Administration of Justice Act, Searches.	ECHR Art. 8.	
U 1993.512 V	Criminal Code, The Administration of Justice Act, Documentation.	ECHR Art. 6, (3), litra d.	
U 1992.949 V	Criminal Code, Alien Act, The Administration of Justice Act, Documentation.	ECHR Art. 6, (3), litra d. Applied *ex officio*.	

U 1992.948 V	Criminal Code, The Administration of Justice Act, Fingerprint.	ECHR Art. 8.	
U 1992.930 Ø	Criminal Code, The Administration of Justice Act, Documentation.	ECHR Art. 6, (3), litra d.	
U 1991.749	Criminal Code, The Administration of Justice Act, Documentation.	ECHR art 6, (1) and (3) litra d.	
U 1989.775 Ø	Civil proceedings, Alien Act, Reunion of families.	ECHR Art. 8 and Rec. to the Conv. on Refugees, 1951, Final Act to UN Conf. 1951.	
U 1989.302 Ø	Criminal Code, The Administration of Justice Act, Asylum seeker in prison.	ECHR Art. 5,(1), litra f and UNHCR EX COM Concl. No. 44 XXXVII of 10 Oct. 1986 para. 2, litra f.	
U 1984.88 Ø	Civil proceedings, Dismissal.	ECHR Art. 11.	

EXAMPLES OF UNREPORTED JUDGMENTS AND RULINGS OF THE *HIGH COURTS* IN WHICH THE COURTS HAVE APPLIED THE EUROPEAN CONVENTION ON HUMAN RIGHTS OR REFERRED TO INTERNATIONAL LAW

No. of the case	Type of case	Invoked articles of the convention	Reference to ECHR judgments
VLK 1993. 404/93	Act of Tariffs (customs), Interrogation.	ECHR Art. 5, (2) and Art. 6, (1) and (3), litra a.	
ØLK 1993. S 2262/ 93	Criminal Code, The Administration of Justice Act, Capacity.	ECHR Art. 6, (1).	
VLK 1993. S 785/93	Extradition to criminal prosecution in Poland.	The extraterritorial effect of ECHR.	

No. of the case	Type of case	Invoked articles of the convention	Reference to ECHR judgments
VLK 1993. 2590/92	Act of Tariffs (customs), Interrogation.	ECHR Art. 5, (2) and Art. 6, (1) and (3), litra a.	
VLD 1992. 659/92	Criminal Code, Aliens Act, Expulsion.	ECHR Art. 6, (1) and (3), litra d.	
ØLD 1991. 387 & 388/90	Criminal Code, The Administration of Justice Act, Appointment of a counsel for the defence.	ECHR Art. 6, (3), litra c.	
ØLK 16 afd. 1989. 455/88	Civil proceedings, Reunion of families.	ECHR Art. 8.	
ØLK 16 afd. 1989. 423/88	Civil proceedings, Reunion of families.	ECHR Art. 8	
ØLK 17 afd. 1989. 406/89	Significance of conventions (International law) in national law. See also U 1990.13 (Jydebrødre-sagen).		
ØLK 3. afd. 1989. 211/89.	Criminal Code, The Administration of Justice Act, Capacity.	ECHR Art. 6, (1).	A 154
ØLK 3. afd. 1989. 188/1989.	Criminal Code, The Administration of Justice Act, Capacity.	ECHR Art. 6, (1).	A 154
ØLD 1989. 185/88	Civil proceedings, Taxation of income below EC poverty line.	CESCR Art. 11, (1) and CCPR Art. 2, (3).	
VLK 3 afd. 1989. 2581/88	Criminal Code, The Administration of Justice Act, Documentation of a policeman's report.	ECHR Art. 6, (1) and (3), litra d.	
VLK 8 afd. 1988 S 1249/88	Criminal Code, The Administration of Justice Act, Documentation.		Uses the grounds of A 110

ANNEX 2

EXAMPLES OF UNREPORTED JUDGMENTS AND RULINGS OF THE *CITY COURTS* IN WHICH THE COURTS HAVE APPLIED THE EUROPEAN CONVENTION ON HUMAN RIGHTS OR REFERRED TO INTERNATIONAL LAW

No. of the case	**Type of case**	**Invoked articles of the co nvention**	**Reference to ECHR judgments**
Cph City Court 398/1989 afd. K 151/90	Civil proceedings, Freedom of association.	ECHR Art. 11.	
Korsør City Court 1988. SS 113/88	Aliens Act, Reunion of family, Affirmed in U 1989. 775.	UN humanitarian considerations and ECHR Art. 8.	
Slagelse Criminal Court 1984. PS 575/84 & PS 590/84	Criminal Code, Limitations.	CCPR. Art. 14 litra c and ECHR Art. 6, (1).	
Slagelse Criminal Court 1985. SS 163/76 & SS 384/79	Criminal Code, Tax evasion Limitations.	CCPR. Art. 14 litra. c and ECHR Art. 6, (1).	
Cph City Court 1966. 21427/65	Criminal Code, Bearing the expenses of an interpreter.	ECHR Art. 6, (3), litra c.	

RULINGS OF THE OMBUDSMAN IN WHICH HE HAS APPLIED THE EUROPEAN CONVENTION ON HUMAN RIGHTS

No. in Ombuds-man's report	**Type of case**	**Invoked articles of the Convention**	**Reference to ECHR judgments**
Decision of 28.09.1993	Refusal of residence permit to two asylum seekers of different nationality who had married in DK.	ECHR Art. 8.	

Dcision of 15.07.1993	Allocation and categorization of inmates.	The European Standard Minimum Rules for the Treatment of Prisoners, 1987.	
FOB 1992. 363	*Ex officio* /The basis of valuation of the board receiving and treating complaints about administrative decisions.	The principles of ECHR.	
FOB 1992. 334	Social Legislation, Custody of Minors Act, Restriction of the father's right of contact without asking the child.	UN Convention on the Rights of the Child Art. 12.	
FOB 1988. 93	Refusal to grant a woman a temporary visa. Her husband was serving a longer sentence in Denmark.	ECHR. Art. 8.	
FOB 1983. 205	Parents' rights of contact when their children are placed in nursing homes.	ECHR Art. 8.	
FOB 1982. 156	Criminal Code, Aliens Act, Expulsion of a woman living in Denmark with her two children after the sentence had been served.	ECHR Art. 8.	

8. INCORPORATION AND IMPLEMENTATION OF HUMAN RIGHTS IN FINLAND

by Martin Scheinin,
University of Helsinki

1. STATUS OF HUMAN RIGHTS TREATIES - GENERAL CONSIDERATIONS

In Finland, the relationship between domestic and international law is generally understood as having been resolved according to the *dualistic* model. The relevant constitutional provisions (Section 33 of the Constitution Act of 1919 and Section 69 of the Parliament Act of 1928) are not very clear on this point as they can be understood to require parliamentary consent for the *adoption* of certain categories of treaties and thus to refer to the *monistic* method of automatic incorporation. The prevailing interpretation of these constitutional provisions is that Section 33 of the Constitution Act requires the consent of Parliament for concluding (through ratification or accession) certain categories of treaties. Section 69 of the Parliament Act is understood to make a distinction between the *approval* (participation in the ratification of or accession to a treaty) and the "bringing into force" of the treaty in Finland, that is, its domestic *implementation*.[1]

The most frequently used method of implementing international treaties in Finland is *incorporation* either through an act of parliament *in blanco* or through a similar government decree. In the first case, a government decree also accompanies the act of parliament. In some cases, only incorporation through a government decree is used even in relation to treaties which Parliament has given its consent to conclude.

---

[1] The classic study on the implementation of international treaties in Finnish constitutional law is Kaarlo Kaira's doctoral dissertation of 1932 (Kaira 1932). For short English language reports on the issue, see Saario 1979, Joutsamo 1983, Scheinin 1990 and the English summaries in Meres-Wuori 1990 and Scheinin 1991. For sources in Swedish, see Rosas 1973 and Sevón 1974.

M. Scheinin (ed.), International Human Rights Norms in the Nordic and Baltic Countries, 257–294.

The incorporating enactments usually simply state that the treaty provisions "are in force" domestically[2]. Because of the predominance of the incorporation method, Finland can be said to represent *de facto* monism[3], or *dualism in form but monism in practice*.

While based on the method of incorporation, the Finnish system contains features of transformation. Several human rights treaties have been implemented by enacting domestic legislation in order to achieve normative harmony with the treaty in question. This method has been used predominantly for two categories of human rights treaties namely treaties requiring the penalizing of certain acts (such as the Convention against All Forms of Racial Discrimination) and conventions of the International Labour Organisation. Even in these cases, the treaties themselves have been incorporated through government decrees.

A third method of implementing human rights treaties in Finland is *by reference*. This method is seen as special clauses in domestic pieces of legislation stipulating that international treaties are to be taken into account and, in some cases, given precedence in the application of the act in question. The method is used in other Nordic countries[4] as well and it is described as creating a "*monistic sector*" in an otherwise dualistic legal order.

According to the prevailing doctrinal understanding, approved by the leading authority on constitutional interpretation, the Constitutional Law Committee of Parliament[5], the hierarchical status of the incorporating act determines the formal domestic rank of the provisions in an international treaty (Opinion No. 2 of 1990, given in connection with the ratification and incorporation of the European Convention on Human Rights). This rule is, however, modified by the occasional use of the reference method which may result in the equal rank or even priority of a treaty incorporated by a lower norm, such as a government decree, in relation to a domestic act of parliament. As

---

[2] Examples of incorporating enactments of certain human rights treaties are presented in *Annex 1*. Of major human rights treaties, e.g., ECHR, CCPR, CEDAW, CRC and the European Social Charter have been incorporated through an act of Parliament, whereas CESCR and CERD through a government decree.

[3] This expression is used by Karapuu and Rosas, 1990, 201.

[4] See, Helgesen 1982, 53 and Aall 1989, 624.

[5] On some distinctive features of the Finnish Constitution, see, Scheinin 1993, 29-31. On the role of the Constitutional Law Committee of Parliament in particular, see, Länsineva 1991.

one and the same treaty may be the subject of both incorporation, amendments to existing acts of parliament (transformation) and of reference clauses in other acts of parliament, one could speak of double or even triple implementation.

The process of European integration causes further changes in the picture, since Finnish judges and authorities are obliged to examine the harmony between domestic acts of parliament and Community norms with direct effect and not to apply domestic provisions in cases of conflict. In connection with the European Economic Area, such an obligation was established through explicit priority clauses in the incorporating Act, approved by a qualified majority as an exception to the Constitution (Act of Parliament No. 1504/1993). No explicit priority clauses are needed in the incorporation Act of the Accession Treaty to the European Union, also approved as an exception to the Constitution (Act of Parliament No. 1540/1994), because the supremacy of community law is considered an essential part of the treaty obligations under the Accession Treaty.

2. DIRECT APPLICABILITY OF HUMAN RIGHTS TREATIES

2.1 Rules of Construction. In its opinion on the ECHR (No. 2 of 1990), the Constitutional Law Committee of Parliament emphasized that the method of incorporation warrants direct application of international treaties by domestic courts and authorities. The Committee also confirmed the following rules of construction:

- The hierarchical status of the domestic incorporating act of a treaty determines the formal rank of the treaty provisions in domestic law.
- The rules *lex posterior derogat legi priori* and *lex specialis derogat legi generali* are, in principle, applicable also in conflicts between incorporated treaty provisions and (other) domestic acts; this means that Parliament retains its *constitutional* authority in relation to the courts to enact new acts, even though they might conflict with Finland's international obligations and even though *international* obligations stipulate that such acts should not be enacted.
- Courts and authorities should resort to "human-rights-friendly" interpretations of domestic statutes, in order to avoid conflicts between domestic law and human rights treaties.

- Incorporated treaty provisions are in force in domestic law according to their contents in international law, e.g. in their authentic languages which are decisive in case of translation errors or ambiguities.
- International case law (by the European Court and Commission of Human Rights) is of importance to domestic courts and authorities.

The *rule of presumption*, i.e. the permission and duty of courts to assume that Parliament had no intention of derogating from treaty obligations unless such an intention is clearly expressed by Parliament, was not explicitly included in the Opinion. The specific wording of the *rule of interpretation* ("human-rights-friendly interpretation") may, however, also be understood to comprise this rule of construction.

In Finland, the doctrine of "self-executing" treaties is not used for the purpose of categorizing treaty provisions to "directly applicable" and "non-self-executing" provisions. The difference between direct applicability and interpretive effect (indirect application) is seen as a matter of degree, not as an all-or-nothing distinction. Previously, human rights treaties with a predominantly "programmatic" character (e.g. the UN Covenant on Economic, Social and Cultural Rights) were often incorporated through government decrees. This decision limited their direct application by the courts and authorities, as domestic acts of parliament would be norms of a higher hierarchical rank. In the mid-1980s, however, incorporation through act of parliament has become standard practice as far as human rights treaties are concerned.

A recent example is the European Social Charter that was incorporated in this manner and accompanied by a statement by the Social Affairs Committee of Parliament, calling for direct application of the treaty provisions (Opinion No. 14 of 1990). It is clear that the wording of the treaty affects the *concrete methods* of applying its provisions in Finland, but incorporation through act of parliament creates a *presumption* of "full" direct applicability.

2.2 The Constitutional Context. Finland has a written constitution with a brief catalogue of fundamental rights (Chapter II of the Constitution Act of 1919 and some scattered provisions elsewhere in the Constitution). Constitutional rights have been understood to be binding primarily on the *legislature*. Parliament has a special body, the Constitutional Law Committee, that hears legal experts and operates as a quasi-judicial body determining the relationship between proposed bills and the Constitution whenever doubts on the constitutionality of the bills occur.

Section 92 of the Constitution Act includes a provision stipulating that all judges and authorities have a duty not to apply *government decrees* that conflict with the Constitution or any acts of parliament. The Constitution is silent on the issue of the authority of the courts to examine the constitutionality of Acts of Parliament. The prevailing opinion is that Section 92 of the Constitution Act may be interpreted as a prohibition of such examinations. However, it has been stressed in the doctrine on constitutional law from the beginning of the 1970s and subsequently also by the Constitutional Law Committee of Parliament that all acts of parliament shall be interpreted in such a way that conformity with the Constitution is achieved. In everyday court practice, constitutional rights have never played a significant part and even today cases where constitutional provisions have been invoked by Finnish courts remain few in number.

The constitutional features described above contribute to the relatively limited role of constitutional rights in court practice, but these features do not legally or logically relate to international human rights treaties. As a considerable number of these treaties were incorporated through acts of parliament, Section 92 of the Constitution Act explicitly authorizes their direct application and precedence in cases where the domestic provision is of a hierarchically lower status than an act of parliament. Moreover, in relation to domestic acts of parliament, these human rights treaties are of the same status. Human rights treaties were, however, practically never cited in court decisions until the late 1980s, probably partly because of the tradition not to invoke constitutional rights in court.

Since 1988 or 1990, Finnish judges have become aware of the existence and applicability of human rights treaties. The number of relevant cases has grown, and human rights treaties are now being invoked by the courts more often than constitutional provisions. In the following, some examples of such court cases are presented.[6]

[6] For surveys of Finnish judicial decisions involving questions of international law, see Pellonpää 1990a and Scheinin 1993a. It is the intention of the editors of the Finnish Yearbook of International Law to publish similar surveys on a regular basis.

2.3 Human Rights Treaties in the Supreme Administrative Court. Already in 1979, the non-discrimination clause in Article 26 of the Covenant on Civil and Political Rights was mentioned in a *minority opinion* attached to a ruling by the Supreme Administrative Court (*KHO 1979 I 4*). The first cases in which the court itself referred to human rights treaties date back to 1988. The case *KHO 1988 A 48* was also related to the CCPR and the Supreme Administrative Court expressed, in general terms, its willingness to apply the provisions of the CCPR. The Court, however, came to the conclusion that the withdrawal of a passport was not in violation of Article 12 CCPR. In the case *KHO 1988 A 49,* the Court quashed an expulsion order on the basis that the person in question was a refugee according to the Convention on the Status of Refugees and could therefore not be expelled on the grounds resorted to by the Ministry of the Interior. The case illustrates that also treaties incorporated by government decree may be applied by courts.

The case *KHO 1993 A 25* related to the case *Torres v. Finland* (291/1988) in which the Human Rights Committee found that Article 9 (4) CCPR had been violated as Mr. Torres could not challenge the legality of certain deprivations of liberty under the Finnish Aliens Act in a court of law. In the domestic case for compensation that followed, the Supreme Administrative Court finally came to the conclusion that the Government of Finland was under an obligation to pay FIM 20,000 in compensation for the violation of the CCPR.[7]

Since the incorporation of the European Convention on Human Rights, Article 8 (the right to private life and family life) has become the human rights treaty provision cited most frequently in the Supreme Administrative Court. It is applied in the review of expulsion orders by the Ministry of the Interior, sometimes together with Article 3

[7] In a recent case by the Uusimaa Provincial Administrative Court (7 March 1995 No. 360/2) came to a similar conclusion in relation to the case *Vuolanne v. Finland* (265/1987), in which the Human Rights Committee also had found a violation of CCPR Article 9 (4). The Government was obliged to pay FIM 8,000 in compensation. A particular feature of this case is the fact that the Act on Military Discipline was *lex posterior* in relation to the incorporation Act of the CCPR. The Court resorted to the rule of presumption; "Even though the Act on Military Discipline was enacted after the incorporating Act of the Covenant entered into force, there was, taking into account the *travaux preparatoires* of the prohibition of appeal in Section 34 of the Act on Military Discipline, no intention to derogate from the right guaranteed by Article 9, paragraph 4, of the Covenant...".

(prohibition of torture and inhuman or degrading treatment). The Aliens Act (No. 378 of 1991) includes a reference to "international treaties binding on Finland" in Section 1, paragraph 1, and the case law of the Court gives the impression that the ECHR provisions are being applied as an integral part of the Aliens Act itself.

Just to mention some examples, the following cases were reported in the 1993 Yearbook of the Supreme Administrative Court:

- *KHO 1993 A 26*: The decision to expel a Russian homosexual person was quashed, because his permanent relationship with a Finn of the same sex was considered as part of his "private life" protected under ECHR Article 8 and because the possibility of inhuman or degrading treatment, contrary to Article 3 of the ECHR, could not be excluded if he was sent back to Russia.

- *KHO 1993 A 27*: The Court granted an extraordinary remedy by repealing its own previous decision upholding the expulsion order of a Romanian family, on the grounds that the birth of a new family member who was not mentioned by name in the expulsion order, was a new fact that could affect the outcome of the case, "taking into account the commitments by Finland to protect the unity of the family, family life and the best interest of the child, expressed in international treaties binding on Finland".

- *KHO 1993 A 28*: An almost identical case, except for the fact that the family was Russian.

- *KHO 1993 A 29*: The expulsion order relating to an Estonian family with several links to Finnish society and with a sick child was quashed, "taking into account" among other things Article 8 of the ECHR.

In addition to these published cases, the Supreme Administrative Court has in a number of cases quashed an expulsion order because of the risk of torture or other inhuman or degrading treatment. In these cases, the Court bases its rulings on Sections 1 and 41 of the Aliens Act, Article 7 of the CCPR and Article 3 of the ECHR. One recent case falling into this category was published by including it in the electronic data bank "Finlex".[8]

[8] KHO 20 April 1994 No. 1649. Some of the similar unpublished cases are KHO 7 April 1993 No. 1374, KHO 9 December 1993 No. 4953, KHO 17 June 1993 No. 2398, KHO 7 June 1993 No. 1756, KHO 7 September 1993 No. 3228, KHO 3 November 1993 No. 4351 and KHO 31 December 1993 No. 5602.

2.4 The Supreme Court. Before the Finnish ratification of the ECHR in May 1990, there were no references to international human rights treaties in the case law of the Finnish Supreme Court (KKO). In the case *KKO 1990:67* a reference to the CCPR was, for the first time, made in the descriptive part of the Supreme Court decision. The judgment itself, however, was based on other grounds.

The case *KKO 1990:93* and unpublished cases H90/220 of 9 August 1990, H90/350 of 21 November 1990, and H90/422 of 20 February 1991 all concerned the extradition of persons accused of hijacking an aeroplane in former Soviet Union. Through these cases, the Supreme Court established its willingness to apply international human rights norms where appropriate. In all of the four cases, the Court informed the Ministry of Justice in its opinions that there were no legal obstacles to extradition in the concrete cases, in the same connection stating that a rule of *non-refoulement,* directly binding on Finnish authorities, could be drawn from, *inter alia,* Article 3 of the ECHR and Article 7 of the CCPR.[9]

After these extradition cases the main emphasis in the application by the Supreme Court of human rights treaties has been on issues relating to criminal procedure, Article 14 of the CCPR and Article 6 of the ECHR. Without entering into discussions on the hierarchy of norms or on various presumptions, the Court has simply applied the abovementioned treaty provisions directly in order to fill certain gaps in the Finnish legislation on criminal procedure. Some examples of such cases are:

- In the case *KKO 1991:84* the Court stated that according to the principles laid down in Article 14 (3) (e) of the CCPR and in Article 6 (3) (d) of the ECHR, everyone charged with a criminal offence has the right to examine or to have examined witnesses used against him. As a person had been convicted on the basis of statements given in earlier trials, the Supreme Court remitted the case for retrial at the Municipal Court. An additional factor illustrating the importance of the case as the first Supreme Court judgment based on international human rights treaties, is the fact that the Court resorted to the treaties in question *ex officio*.

[9] The implications of these cases are analyzed in Hannikainen 1991.

- In the case *KKO 1992:73* the Court referred to Article 6 (1) of the ECHR and to Article 14 (1) of the CCPR guaranteeing the right to a fair trial, and to Article 6 (3) of the ECHR and Article 14 (3) of the CCPR, according to which everyone charged with a criminal offence has the right to be informed, in detail, of the nature and cause of the accusation or charge against him/her, and to have adequate time and facilities for the preparation of his/her defence. As the defendant had not been informed of the possibility that he could be found guilty of a more serious crime than the one mentioned in the charge, he had not been informed, in detail, of the charge against him and had not had adequate facilities for the preparation of his defence. Therefore, he could not be convicted of aggravated assault but only of assault. The Supreme Court shortened the sentence.

- In the case *KKO 1992:81* the Court resorted to Article 14 (3) (d) of the CCPR and Article 6 (3) (c) of the ECHR, concerning the right to free legal assistance when the interests of justice so require in its interpretation of Section 10, paragraph 2 of the Act on Free Legal Aid. As the injured party was assisted by a lawyer, there were specific reasons, as required by the domestic provision, to appoint a lawyer to assist the defendant even in a rather simple case.

- In the case *KKO 1993:19* the Supreme Court explicitly stated that the CCPR and the ECHR are "part of the law of the land". A summary procedure applied by the first instance court in a serious criminal case was in violation of CCPR Article 14 and ECHR Article 6. An English translation of the ruling is included below as *Annex 2*.

- Also the case *KKO 1994:26* is related to Article 6 of the ECHR but in this case with relation to civil rights and obligations in a law suit between private parties. The Court of Appeals had asked for an advisory opinion from the Labour Court and had thereafter decided the case without hearing the parties to the case again. The Supreme Court stated that this procedural conduct by the Court of Appeals had been erroneous and in its motivation for its conclusion it referred to case law under Article 6 of the ECHR and specifically mentioned the cases of *Feldbrugge* (Judgment of 29 May 1986, ECHR Series A 99) and *Kamasinski* (Judgment of 19 December 1989, ECHR Series A 168).

- The case *KKO 1995:7* can be seen as an indication of a trend towards a more frequent use of Strasbourg case law in the reasoning by the Finnish Supreme Court. Two defendants had been found guilty and convicted to short terms of imprisonment by the Court of First

Instance. Both appealed to the Court of Appeals, asking to have the sentences shortened and to receive free legal assistance. The Court of Appeals granted them free trial but denied them free legal assistance, because the Act on Free Legal Aid, as amended by Act No. 1668 of 1992, required specific reasons for appointing a government-paid lawyer in a simple criminal case. The Supreme Court granted leave of appeal but decided to uphold the ruling by the Court of Appeals. In support of this conclusion, the Supreme Court presented an analysis of case law by the European Court of Human Rights in relation to the right to free legal assistance under Article 6 of the ECHR.[10] The Supreme Court also referred to the rule of presumption by stating that the domestic provision in question had been enacted in 1992[11] and that the Law Affairs Committee of Parliament had approved the amendment in question after stating that everyone is entitled to legal assistance when the interests of justice so require.[12] According to the Supreme Court, this indicates that it has been ascertained that the Act is not in conflict with human rights treaties binding on Finland. Justices Mikko Tulokas and Gustaf Möller *dissented* and stated that the denial of free legal assistance in the Court of Appeals could in practice amount to a prohibition of appeal and was not acceptable when a defendant had been convicted to unconditional imprisonment.

- The Supreme Court Case *KKO 1993:58* relates to a different area, namely family law. It is so far the most evident example of a Supreme Court decision *not to apply* a domestic act of parliament because of reasons relating to human rights. Therefore, a somewhat closer analysis is presented below.

The case dealt with the establishment of paternity. As Mr A was married to Mrs B in 1975 when the child C was born, he was regarded as C's father based on legal presumption. Actually, Mrs B already lived together with Mr D in 1975, and the couple married in 1976, two months after A and B were divorced. In 1977, Mr D died.

Medical evidence strongly suggested that D was the father of the child. In 1990, A's paternity was nullified by a court. Because C was

---

[10] The cases *Pakelli* (Judgment of 25 April 1983, ECHR Series A 64), *Monnell and Morris* (Judgment of 2 March 1987, ECHR Series A 115), *Granger* (Judgment 28 March 1990, ECHR Series A 174) and *Quaranta* (Judgment of 24 May 1991, ECHR Series A 205).

[11] I.e., after the incorporation of the ECHR (1990) and the CCPR (1976).

[12] See, Report No. 12 of 1992 by the Law Affairs Committee of Parliament.

born before the 1975 Paternity Act entered into force, the death of D precluded, according to the wording of the Implementing Act of said Act, the possibility of instituting paternity proceedings. Such a conclusion would be problematic in the light of several human rights treaty provisions, including those of non-discrimination, the right to family life and a child's right to know his or her parents.

The majority, President Olavi Heinonen together with two other Justices in the five-member Chamber of the Supreme Court, classified the problem as one of *interpretation*. According to them, a literal interpretation of the Implementing Act would cause "unjustified inequality". The *ratio legis* of the Act could be realised only by deviating from its wording, that is, by allowing C to institute court proceedings to establish the question of paternity. According to the majority, such an interpretation was "in harmony with the principle illustrated by" Article 7 of the Convention of the Rights of the Child and with Articles 8 and 14 of the ECHR.

Supreme Court Justice Lauri Lehtimaja *concurred* and referred to the *ratio legis* as well as to the general equality clause in Section 5 of the Constitution Act. Then he referred to Articles 8, 6 and 14 of the ECHR and to Articles 7 and 8 of the Convention of the Rights of the Child, and continued:

> "On the basis of what has been said above and taking, in particular, into account the provisions of the above-mentioned conventions, falling within the legislative sphere and having been incorporated into domestic law through Acts of Parliament, Nos. 438 of 1990 and 1129 of 1991, which have been enacted at a later point than the Implementing Act of the Paternity Act, I am of the opinion that Section 7, paragraph 2, of the Implementing Act of the Paternity Act, restricting action in cases of death [of the potential father] is inapplicable in the case of C".

Supreme Court Justice Per Lindholm, also *concurring*, would have decided the case without any reference to human rights treaties or to the Constitution Act. According to him, the Implementing Act of the Paternity Act related to a certain transition period and Section 7, paragraph 2 of the Act, was therefore not applicable in a case in which the preconditions for instituting paternity proceedings had emerged only after the Paternity Act had entered into force.

These three opinions, all reaching the same conclusion, indicate that the Supreme Court may be unanimous when it concerns the need to comply with international human rights treaties, but the Justices have differing opinions concerning the appropriate juridical construction needed to reach this end. Justice Lehtimaja followed a "*direct application approach*" and put emphasis on the *lex posterior* rule. The majority, headed by President Heinonen, resorted to the "*interpretive effect approach*", emphasizing neither the formal domestic status of human rights treaties nor the formalistic *lex posterior* rule.

An additional feature of the majority opinion deserves attention, namely the absence of references to the domestic Constitution. Only Justice Lehtimaja made a reference to the equality clause in Section 5 of the Constitution Act. In the late 1980s and the early 1990s, international human rights treaties have gradually attracted the attention of Finnish courts, especially the highest ones. The number of references to the Constitution seems to *decline* together with this trend.

2.5 Other Courts and Authorities. In a historical perspective, the *Parliamentary Ombudsman* was clearly the first Finnish authority to systematically apply international human rights treaties in decision-making. This has been the case at least since 1987. The Finnish experience suggests that the institution of the Ombudsman might be particularly suitable for opening the eyes of courts of law and administrative authorities to "new" sources of law. The Ombudsman started to invoke the European Convention on Human Rights already prior to its ratification by Finland and later, the Ombudsman has also cited CSCE documents or other international human rights instruments other than treaties legally binding on Finland.

Today, *lower courts* and *administrative authorities* still apply human rights treaties somewhat sporadicly, in spite of the fact that they should do it *ex officio*. This emphasizes the responsibility of practising lawyers to invoke human rights treaties when appropriate.

As far as the highest courts are concerned, the above-mentioned Supreme Court case *KKO 1993:58* comes closest to finding a *conflict* between a human rights treaty and a Finnish act of parliament. As explained, even in that case the majority of the Court decided the case to be one of *interpretation*. Two recent cases by the Vaasa Court of Appeals deserve to be mentioned because they represent a different approach.

The cases *Vaasa Court of Appeals 29 August 1994 No. 1390 and 22 September 1994 No. 1643* both concerned the impartiality of a first instance court in a case where a Savings Bank acted as a party in the case and one or more of the lay members of the court of first instance were serving or had been serving on a board of trustees in the administration of the bank in question. In the first-mentioned case, the persons in question had resigned from their posts in the bank before the court case was initiated. The majority of the Court of Appeals therefore came to the conclusion that no breach of Article 6, paragraph 1 of the European Convention had occurred.[13] In an *obiter dicta* statement, the Court, however, stated:

> "The clause on the disqualification of judges in our national Code of Judicial Procedure and case law based on that provision conflict with Article 6 of the European Convention on Human Rights and case law based on that provision. The above-mentioned supranational norm together with the interpretation of the relevant case law supersede national legislation and national case law in this case."

In other words, the Court of Appeals stated that the ECHR has, at least in some cases, priority over Finnish acts of parliament. Another interesting feature of the ruling was that the Court in its reasoning explicitly referred to certain judgments of the European Court of Human Rights.[14]

Some four weeks later, the same Court of Appeals was faced with a similar case in which one of the lay members of the court of first instance had been nominated to a board of trustees in a bank while a case to which the bank in question was a party, was pending before the court. After his nomination to a position of confidence within the bank he participated in deciding the court case.

The Vaasa Court of Appeals quashed the judgment by the court of first instance and remitted the case for retrial. This conclusion was

---

[13] Two appeal court judges, including the President of the Vaasa Court of Appeals, were of the opinion that the composition of the first instance court had not met the requirements of Article 6 of the ECHR. They wanted to remit the case for retrial.

[14] The cases *Delcourt* (Judgment of 17 January 1970, ECHR Series A 11), *Piersack* (Judgment of 1 October 1982, ECHR Series A 53), *Sramek* (Judgment of 22 October 1984, ECHR Series A 84), *Langborger* (Judgment of 22 June 1989, ECHR Series A 155) and *Holm* (Judgment of 25 November 1993, ECHR Series A 279A). The same cases were also cited in judgment No. 1643 of 22 September 1994 by the same court.

motivated by the using of the same wording as in the *obiter* statement quoted above.[15] In addition, the Court reasoned:

> "The composition of the court of first instance did not meet the requirements for an independent and impartial tribunal according to Article 6 of the European Convention on Human Rights."

3. REFERENCES TO INTERNATIONAL SOURCES OTHER THAN TREATIES

The Finnish legal culture is usually described as positivist or legalistic[16]. One does not find instances of courts referring to "practical considerations" or extra-legal principles. Therefore, the use of the incorporation method may be understood as a precondition for the domestic applicability of international human rights instruments. This is a background explanation for the fact that Finnish courts in their rulings do not usually refer to judgments by the European Court of Human Rights, even in cases where the influence of existing international case law is clearly visible (see, e.g., the Supreme Court case KKO 1993:58).

This is not, however, the absolute truth. The following information relates to the relevance of sources other than treaties:

(a) International case law is used *within* the court in the preparation of rulings. To a great extent, this material remains inaccessible to the public and scholars, since it is considered part of the confidential negotiations held *in camera*.[17]

(b) There are occasional exceptions to the general rule, i.e. cases in which Finnish courts have actually cited non-treaty instruments in their rulings. In a ruling by the *Vaasa Court of Appeals* (26 May 1993 No. 1031) the principle of non-discrimination was established through a reference to, in equal terms, "the *Declaration* and Convention on Human Rights" (emphasis added), the latter term apparently relating to the ECHR. In the Supreme Court case KKO 1993:120, the court referred

[15] Because Finland is officially a bilingual country, court rulings are issued in the language (Finnish or Swedish) of the parties. Therefore, judgment No. 1643 of 22 September 1994 by the Vaasa Court of Appeals was issued in Swedish and thus easily accessible to Nordic readers.

[16] For a presentation of the prevailing doctrine on the sources of law, see Aarnio 1989, 222-247.

[17] This interpretation is based on Chapter 1, Section 7 of the Code of Judicial Procedure.

to an international treaty *not ratified* by Finland, and to (unspecified) *foreign case law*, as sources "for the determination of valid customary international law". A third example comes from the Supreme Administrative Court which, in a series of expulsion cases (8 November 1994, Nos. 5496-5502), quashed the expulsion orders of seven Zairians after referring to a memorandum prepared by the UNHCR and to a specific case decided by the UN Committee Against Torture. This material was used as additional *information* affecting the over all consideration required in expulsion cases by Section 41, paragraph 1, of the Aliens Act.

(c) The Parliamentary Ombudsman has also shown much willingness to apply other sources of international human rights law than treaties binding on Finland. The Ombudsman referred to the ECHR already prior to its ratification by Finland (14 April and 8 May 1989). In some instances he/she has also invoked some of the human rights commitments included in CSCE Documents (18 August 1988, 9 January 1990 and 23 February 1993) and the UN Standard Minimum Rules for the Treatment of Prisoners (15 June 1988).

(d) Legislators are, of course, also free to use other international instruments than binding treaties as "standards" for domestic legislation. Occasionally, such an effect may be far-reaching in the sense that an international treaty not (yet) ratified by Finland is presented as an obstacle for enacting a specific piece of legislation. Such a position was indeed taken in relation to ILO Convention No. 169 on Indigenous Peoples in Opinion No. 30 of 1993 by the Constitutional Law Committee of Parliament, where the Government bill would have had negative consequences for the fishing rights of the Sami People.

These examples illustrate that the "legalistic" legal culture does not exclude the operation of non-treaties or treaties not ratified or incorporated by Finland as so-called standards[18], i.e. factors formally outside the domestic legal order but having, at least, *interpretive effect* on the application of law.

---

[18] On the use of this concept, see Scheinin 1991, 354 and Pentikäinen 1994, 71.

4. ASSESSMENT OF LAW AND PRACTICE

Until the ratification of the European Convention on Human Rights, the general application of the incorporation method was a "Sleeping Beauty" in the Finnish legal system. Since 1990, a rapid growth in the number of court references to international human rights instruments has been visible, and the references are not limited to the ECHR. In many court cases, the invoked human rights provisions have had an effect on the outcome of the case.

4.1 Human Rights Treaties and Legislators. It has already been mentioned that one may find references to non-ratified human rights treaties in parliamentary proceedings, exemplifying their operation as standards for national law-making. Quite naturally, the main emphasis has, also in the field of legislation, been on binding treaties, the European Convention on Human Rights and the Covenant on Civil and Political Rights in particular.

Before Finland ratified the ECHR in 1990, an in-depth study on the compliance of Finnish legislation with the ECHR and Strasbourg case law was conducted. Several acts of parliament were amended, for instance with respect to pre-trial investigation and aliens' rights.[19]

Another category of legislative amendments influenced by Finland's international human rights commitments relates to the domestic responses to findings by international treaty bodies, notably the Human Rights Committee established under the CCPR. The cases *Vuolanne v. Finland* (265/1987)[20] and *Torres v. Finland* (291/1988)[21] where the Human Rights Committee found violations of Article 9 (4) of the CCPR, both contributed to the rapid amendment of the acts in question, in the latter case even prior to the final views were given by the Committee. In the Government bill on the amendment of the Act

---

[19] A detailed account on the legislative amendments is presented in Pellonpää 1990. The amendments were largely initiated by a special study prepared for the Ministry of Justice by Prof. Matti Pellonpää, the current member of the European Commission of Human Rights with Finnish nationality (see, Pellonpää 1988).

[20] Report of the Human Rights Committee 1989, 249-258.

[21] Report of the Human Rights Committee 1990 vol. II, 96-100.

on Military Discipline, direct reference is made to the Committee's views in the *Vuolanne* case.[22]

But not only findings of violations have influenced the amendments of legislation. The introduction of a new subject, "ethics", a clearly nondenominational alternative to the instruction in the Lutheran religion in Finnish public schools, was partly influenced by the criticism expressed by the Human Rights Committee in the case *Hartikainen et al. v. Finland* (40/1978), even though the Committee came to the conclusion that no actual violation of Article 18 (4), CCPR had taken place.[23]

The case *Järvinen v. Finland* (295/1988) had similar consequences. According to the applicant, the 16-month term of alternative service required of conscientious objectors was discriminatory compared to the 8- to 11-month duration of military service. The Human Rights Committee took the view that the distinction had objective and reasonable justification, as the prolongation of the term of civilian service was introduced in connection with the discontinuation of a system aimed at examining the genuineness of an objector's convictions. In the same connection, the Committee expressed concern about the arrangement that "works to the detriment of genuine conscientious objectors"[24]. When the Finnish legislation on conscientious objection was revised the following year, the term of alternative service was shortened to 13 months. In the Government bill, the critical remarks of the Human Rights Committee are included as one reason for this amendment.[25]

The above-mentioned examples show the impact of individual complaints to international treaty bodies on legislation. In recent years, there have been several other examples of human rights treaties influencing the legislative process. Opinion No. 30 of 1993 by the Constitutional Law Committee of Parliament has already been

---

[22] Government Bill No. 100 of 1989, 1-2. In Government Bill No. 29 of 1990 on amendments to the Aliens Act, relating to the *Torres* case, there is a statement that "it has become evident" that Article 9 (4), CCPR is applicable in relation to all deprivations of liberty (p. 2).

[23] Human Rights Committee, Selected Decisions 1985, 74-76. See, also, Report of the Human Rights Committee 1983, 255-256 (a letter from the Finnish Government on follow-up action), de Zayas & Möller 1986, 388-389, McGoldrick 1991, 203-204.

[24] Report of the Human Rights Committee 1990 vol. II, 101-105 (paragraph 6.5).

[25] Government Bill No. 149 of 1991, 8.

mentioned as a case in which a non-ratified treaty (ILO Convention No. 169) was seen as an obstacle to the enactment of new legislation. In two recent cases, two Parliamentary Committees have resorted to human rights treaties binding on Finland as affecting the scope of discretion by Parliament in enacting domestic legislation.

In Government Bill No. 209 of 1994 certain amendments were proposed to the Sickness Insurance Act. A consequence of the amendments would have been that income-based maternity benefits and the parents' benefits of the mother would have been calculated according to different rules than the parents' benefits enjoyed by the father.[26] At least in some cases, women would have received lower benefits than men in the same situation. The Constitutional Law Committee of Parliament stated in its Opinion No. 21 of 1994 that such legislation would be in conflict with Article 26 of the Covenant on Civil and Political Rights and also with the equality clause in Section 5 of the Finnish Constitution Act.

Government Bill No. 341 of 1994 included a proposal for an Aliens Affairs Data Systems Act. During the Parliamentary proceedings both the Ombudsman for Data Protection and certain human rights specialists expressed criticism of the proposal. Referring, *inter alia*, to the European Convention on Human Rights, the Administrative Affairs Committee of Parliament proposed in its Report No. 22 of 1994 that the Bill be rejected.

In both cases, Parliament decided to reject the Government Bill.

4.2 Weaknesses in the Finnish System of Treaty Implementation. Three weaknesses in the Finnish system of treaty implementation can be identified:

(a) Human rights treaties are, in general, incorporated by an act of parliament and within domestic law they have the formal status of ordinary acts of parliament. The positive aspect of this feature is that it gives international human rights treaties a firm position as a part of the system of domestic law. A negative aspect is that judges might, in certain cases, be tempted to overlook human rights treaty provisions because of the *lex posterior* rule. The Agreement on the European

[26] According to Finnish law, only the mother may enjoy the benefits during a certain period of time before and after the birth of the child (maternity benefit), after which period either the mother or the father may receive the benefits (parents' benefit).

Economic Area and the membership of the European Union both including the possibility for a Finnish judge not to apply an act of parliament due to inconsistency with certain international norms, may probably create discussions of the need to elevate the hierarchical status of human rights treaties within the system of domestic law.

(b) Some of the human rights treaties were originally incorporated through government decrees, only. This is the case for, e.g. the Covenant on Economic, Social and Cultural Rights, the Convention and Protocol on the Status of Refugees and the Convention for the Elimination of Racial Discrimination. As a consequence, judges and administrative authorities are, *prima facie*, under an obligation to give priority to domestic acts of parliament in cases of conflict. This problem is mitigated by the occasional use of statutory provisions representing the *reference* method and by the doctrine of *human rights friendly interpretation.*

(c) Even today, only a minority of the legal profession is aware of the contents and relevance of international human rights norms. This is, at least in part, due to the old-fashioned and partly ambiguous standard formulation used in the incorporation enactments and to practical limitations in the accessibility of international instruments and case law.

5. THE CONSTITUTIONAL RIGHTS REFORM

Since the mid-1980s, the Finnish Constitution has been the subject of a rather rapid process of reform and amendment. The next step in this process will be a complete and extensive amendment of Chapter II of the Constitution Act, which relates to fundamental rights. This reform will enter into force in 1995.

In 1989, a Governmental Commission was established to revise Chapter II of the Constitution Act relating to fundamental rights. In early 1992, the Commission presented its report which, after some re-drafting, was presented to Parliament (Government Bill No. 309 of 1993).

International human rights treaties have served as a source of inspiration for the reform[27]. The inspiration does not relate only to the concrete wording of the various material provisions on fundamental rights but also to the methods of giving legal protection to constitutional rights. Several of the proposed constitutional provisions make reference *both* to constitutional *and* to (international) human rights, thus giving *semi-constitutional status* to human rights treaties. The clauses in question relate to the duty of public authorities to ensure the realization of constitutional and human rights (proposed Section 16 a of the Constitution Act), to the limitations on derogations in times of public emergencies (also Section 16 a), and to the duties of the Parliamentary Ombudsman (Section 49), the Chancellor of Justice (Section 46) and the Constitutional Law Committee of Parliament (Section 46 of the Parliament Act).

The new provisions on constitutional rights will be more detailed than the 1919 provisions. It is expected that the reform will strengthen the possibility of courts and authorities to apply constitutional provisions directly, even though the prohibition of courts to examine the constitutionality of acts of parliament will be maintained as an institution. The text of the proposed new Chapter II of the Constitution Act is reproduced below as Annex 3, in the form in which it was approved by Parliament on 17 February 1995 and was unanimously confirmed by the new Parliament on 13 June 1995.

6. PRACTICAL ASPECTS OF IMPLEMENTATION

International treaties ratified by Finland are published in the Treaty Series of the official Collection of Statutes, usually in four languages (Finnish, Swedish and two authentic languages, often English and French). In addition, the privately published Lawbook (*Suomen Laki - Finlands Lag*) includes the following human rights instruments (in the 1994 edition of the Finnish language volume II): the European Convention on Human Rights and its Protocols, the two 1966 UN Covenants and the Universal Declaration of Human Rights. The availability of the official Treaty Series is limited, and most lawyers

[27] On the role of international human rights treaties as a background factor for the constitutional reform project, see Viljanen 1991.

and judges usually rely on the Lawbook (and, unfortunately, just on its volume I).

In June 1994, a 800-page compilation, prepared by the Finnish League for Human Rights and composed of 100 international human rights instruments was published (*Ihmisoikeudet - sata kansainvälistä asiakirjaa*). The majority of the texts are in Finnish and the rest in English. Already in March 1995, a somewhat revised second edition was published.

The Ministry of Justice and the Finnish Lawyers' Association cooperate in the production of a database (FEIT) of Finnish language summaries of all judgments by the European Court of Human Rights. At the moment, approximately two thirds of all the judgments have been included. In the future, also summaries of the final opinions of the UN Human Rights Committee will be accessible (in English) in the database FEIT which is part of the data bank Finlex. Finlex is run by the Government Computer Centre and it is accessible by courts, administrative authorities, law firms, universities etc. Unfortunately, it is too expensive for many potential users.

The judgments of the European Court of Human Rights are available in many libraries or institutions. The documentation produced by other human rights treaty bodies is, in practice, accessible only to specialists who know what they need.

Various governmental and non-governmental bodies organise training courses in human rights law for, for instance, judges, administrative authorities, social workers and teachers. In recent years, however, the emphasis has shifted to training courses in European Community Law.

REFERENCES

Aall, Jørgen, "Menneskerettighetskonvensjonene som rettskildefaktor i intern norsk rett." *Tidsskrift for Rettsvitenskap*, vol. 102 (1989): 613-639.

Aarnio, Aulis: *Laintulkinnan teoria. Yleisen oikeustieteen oppikirja.* [The Theory of Statutory Interpretation. A Textbook in Legal Theory] WSOY, Juva 1989.

Hannikainen, Lauri, "How to Interpret, and What to Do to, the Treaty on Aircraft Seizures with the Soviet Union", in *Finnish Yearbook of International Law*, vol. II (1991): 538-558.

Helgesen, Jan, *Teorier om "folkerettens stilling i norsk rett".* Aschehoug & Co., Oslo 1982.

Human Rights Committee, Selected Decisions under the Optional Protocol. Second to sixteenth sessions. United Nations, New York 1985.

Ihmisoikeudet - sata kansainvälistä asiakirjaa [Human Rights - 100 International Instruments]. Edited by Lauri Hannikainen *et al.* Painatuskeskus, Helsinki 1994 (Second edition, 1995).

Joutsamo, Kari, "The Direct Effect of Treaty Provisions in Finnish Law", in *Nordic Journal of International Law*, vol. 52 (1983): 34-44.

Kaira, Kaarlo: *Valtiosopimusten tekemisestä ja voimaansaattamisesta Suomen oikeuden mukaan.* [On Concluding and Implementing International Treaties According to Finnish Law] Otava, Helsinki 1932.

Karapuu, Heikki -- Rosas, Allan: "Economic, Social and Cultural Rights in Finland". In Rosas (ed.) 1990.

Lehtimaja, Lauri: "International Human Rights and Domestic Legality: Experiences of the Finnish Parliamentary Ombudsman". In Rosas (ed.) 1990.

Länsineva, Pekka, "The Constitutional Committee of Parliament: The Finnish Model of Norm Control", in Sakslin (ed.) 1991.

McGoldrick, Dominic: *The Human Rights Committee. Its Role in the Development of the International Covenant on Civil and Political Rights.* Clarendon Press, Oxford 1991.

Meres-Wuori, Ora: *Toimivaltasuhteet kansainvälisiä sopimuksia tehtäessä.* [Distribution of Powers in the Conclusion of International Treaties] Finnish Lawyers' Publishing Company, Helsinki 1990.

Pellonpää, Matti, *Euroopan neuvoston ihmisoikeussopimus Suomen näkökulmasta.* [The European Convention on Human Rights from a Finnish Point of View] Oikeusministeriön lainvalmisteluosaston julkaisu, No. 21 of 1988.

Pellonpää, Matti, "The Implementation of the European Convention on Human Rights in Finland", in Rosas (ed.) 1990.

Pellonpää, Matti, "Finnish Judicial Decisions Involving Questions of International Law, 1988-1989", in *Finnish Yearbook of International Law*, vol. I (1990): 555-564 (Pellonpää 1990a)

Pentikäinen, Merja, *Human Rights Commitments within the CSCE Process: Nature, Contents and Application in Finland*. Publications of the Advisory Board for International Human Rights Affairs, No. 3, Helsinki 1994 (2nd edition).

Perusoikeuskomitean mietintö [Report by the Government Commission on Constitutional Rights]. Komiteanmietintö 1992:3.

Report of the Human Rights Committee. United Nations General Assembly Official Records, Supplement A/38/40. New York 1983.

Report of the Human Rights Committee. United Nations General Assembly Official Records, Supplement A/44/40. New York 1989.

Report of the Human Rights Committee, volume II. United Nations General Assembly Official Records, Supplement A/45/40. New York 1990.

Rosas, Allan: "Några synpunkter på införlivandet av internationella fördrag med finländsk rätt." *Tidskrift utgiven av Juridiska Föreningen i Finland,* vol. 109 (1973): 506-514.

Rosas, Allan (ed.), *International Human Rights Norms in Domestic Law; Finnish and Polish Perspectives.* Finnish Lawyers' Publishing Company, Helsinki 1990.

Saario, Voitto: "Kansainväliset sopimukset ja valtionsisäinen oikeusjärjestys", in *Festschrift Aarne Nuorvala.* Suomalainen Lakimiesyhdistys, Vammala 1982.

Sakslin, Maija (ed.), *The Finnish Constitution in Transition.* The Finnish Society of Constitutional Law, Tampere 1991.

Scheinin, Martin: "The Status of Human Rights Conventions in Finnish Domestic Law". In Rosas (ed.) 1990.

Scheinin, Martin, *Ihmisoikeudet Suomen oikeudessa* [Human Rights in Finnish Law]. Suomalainen Lakimiesyhdistys, Jyväskylä 1991.

Scheinin, Martin, "Constitutional Law and Human Rights", in Juha Pöyhönen (ed.), *An Introduction to Finnish Law.* Finnish Lawyers' Publishing Company, Helsinki 1993.

Scheinin, Martin, "Finnish Judicial Decisions Involving Questions of International Law, January 1990 - June 1992", in *Finnish Yearbook of International Law,* vol. IV (1993): 501-507. (Scheinin 1993a).

Sevón, Leif, "Om konventionsstyrd lagstiftning". *Tidskrift utgiven av Juridiska Föreningen i Finland,* vol. 110 (1974): 194-206.

Viljanen, Veli-Pekka, "The International Challenge to the Finnish System of Fundamental Rights", in Sakslin (ed.) 1991.

de Zayas, Alfred & Möller, Jakob Th., "Optional Protocol Cases Concerning the Nordic States before the United Nations Human Rights Committee. *Nordic Journal of International Law,* vol. 55 (1986): 384-400.

ANNEXES

1. Examples of Finnish Incorporation Acts.
2. Supreme Court Ruling 1993:19.
3. New Chapter II of the Constitution Act and amendments to the Parliament Act.

ANNEX 1

EXAMPLES OF FINNISH INCORPORATION ACTS

1. ACT NO. 438 OF 4 MAY 1990 (FINNISH TREATY SERIES 18/ 1990)

ACT
ON THE APPROVAL[1] OF CERTAIN PROVISIONS IN THE CONVENTION FOR THE PROTECTION OF HUMAN RIGHTS AND FUNDAMENTAL FREEDOMS AND IN ITS PROTOCOLS

In accordance with decision of Parliament made in the manner stipulated in Sections 67 and 69 (1) of the Parliament Act[2], the following is enacted:

1 §

The provisions of the Convention for the Protection of Human Rights and Fundamental Freedoms, concluded in Rome on 4 November 1950, as amended by its Protocols 3, 5 and 8, and of its Protocols 1, 2, 4, 6 and 7 are, as far as they fall within the domain of legislation, in force as they have been agreed upon.

2 §

This Act enters into force at a point of time prescribed by a Government Decree.

---

[1] It is a standard practice to use the inappropriate word "approval" in the title of incorporation acts. It is to be noted that Parliament makes a *separate* decision through which it gives it consent to ratification, and the Act really relates to domestic implementation.

[2] This phrase indicates that a qualified majority was required as the competencies of the European Court of Human Rights and the Committee of Ministers under the Convention were considered to alter the constitutional rules of sovereignty and distribution of powers, see Opinion No. 2 of 1990 by the Constitutional Law Committee.

2. *ACT NO. 843 OF 5 APRIL 1991 (FINNISH TREATY SERIES 43/ 1991)*

ACT
ON THE APPROVAL OF CERTAIN PROVISIONS IN THE EUROPEAN SOCIAL CHARTER AND IN ITS ADDITIONAL PROTOCOL

In accordance with decision of Parliament the following is enacted:

1 §

The provisions of the European Social Charter, concluded in Turin on 18 October 1961, and of its Additional Protocol are, as far as they fall within the domain of legislation, in force as they have been agreed upon.

2 §

This Act enters into force at a point of time prescribed by a Government Decree.

ANNEX 2

SUPREME COURT RULING 1993:19[3]

RULING BY THE SUPREME COURT OF FINLAND, 12 FEBRUARY 1993
RULING NO. 446, FILE NO. R 92/54

COURT PROCEDURE - CRIMINAL CASE
Under the circumstances described in the statement of reasons by the Supreme Court, a court had the duty to investigate *ex officio* whether a defendant in a criminal case had adequate time for the preparation of his defence. (Dissent)

PROCEEDINGS BEFORE LOWER COURTS
Decision of the Parikkala Court of First Instance, 20 February 1991
On the basis of the charges raised by the Public Prosecutor and with the concurrence of the Post Office Bank as the complainant, the Court of First Instance has declared that it has been established that A. had

1) in Parikkala, Rautjärvi, Punkaharju and Joensuu between 8 August and 29 October 1990, in order to obtain illegal material benefit, deliberately deceived the personnel of several shops into selling him products or offering him services against payment by bankcard while hiding the fact that he had no money on his account with the Post Office Bank in order to make a final payment and thus causing the Bank a financial loss of FIM 20,317.39,

2) in Parikkala on 13 October 1990, together with other persons stolen two car stereos, a walkie-talkie and a fire extinguisher, worth FIM 4,400, detaching them from trucks owned by Parikkalan Kuljetus ky, a transport company,

3) in Parikkala on 28 November 1990, after penetrating into a factory hall owned by Kalustepalvelu R. Lötjönen by using a key he had found, together with other persons stolen from the premises foodstuffs, a breathalyser, forms for registering change of ownership of vehicles anda safe, which was worth FIM 3,000 and contained a deposit receipt from a bank and loan documents, and had tried to force the safe open with an axe, two hammers and two screwdrivers, of which one hammer and one screwdriver were owned by one of the persons present, and having failed in his efforts had dropped the safe into a lake, and

4) in Rautjärvi on 9 December 1990, after first forcing a door with a crowbar and failing to open it, then dislodging a window and its frame and penetrating into the church of the Parish of Simpele, stolen a money box for missionary work and the FIM 300 therein, in other words, had stolen property worth FIM 460.

The offences of which A. was found guilty under item 1 amounted to the continuation of one offence.

---

[3] Translation by translator Heljä Tilli of the ruling as published in the Yearbook of the Supreme Court (Korkeimman oikeuden ratkaisuja 1993 I, Helsinki 1993, pp. 74-82).

Therefore the Court of First Instance sentenced A. under Chapter 28 Section 1 (1) (498/72), Chapter 36 Section 1 (1) (498/72) and Chapter 7 Section 2 of the Penal Code to 80 days' imprisonment for the continued fraud referred to in item 1; to 60 days' imprisonment for the theft referred to in item 2 ; to 3 months' imprisonment for the theft referred to in item 3; and to 60 days' imprisonment for the theft referred to in item 4.

The Court of First Instance combined the sentences under items 3 and 4 to a term of 3 months' and 20 days' (unconditional) imprisonment and the sentences under items 1 and 2 together with the 3 months' conditional sentence passed for theft by the Court of First Instance on 28 November 1990 the probation period of which ended on 30 June 1992 to a term of 4 months and 15 days' imprisonment; under Chapter 3 Section 11 of the Penal Code one day having been deducted from the latter sentence. The latter sentence of imprisonment is conditional, with the probation period ending on 31 December 1992.

The Court of First Instance also ordered A. to pay the Post Office Bank FIM 20,513.11, with a 16 per cent interest starting from 3 December 1991, in compensation for the damage he caused, and FIM 250, with a 16 per cent interest starting from 20 February 1991, in compensation for legal expenses.

Extraordinary Appeal to the Court of Appeal of Kouvola

In his petition of 7 March 1991 to the Court of Appeal, A. stated the following:

1) He was summoned to appear before the 20 February 1991 session of the Court of First Instance with respect to the acts referred to in items 2 and 4. In his presence during the hearing the prosecutor demanded that he be punished and ordered to pay compensation for the acts cited in items 1 and 3. Decision was given in the first hearing of the case. A. held that he did not have the adequate time and facilities to prepare his defence provided for in the Convention for the Protection of Human Rights and Fundamental Freedoms.

2) As regards item 1 in the decision of the Court of First Instance, the charge did not specify that A. had deceived a person. However, according to the statement of reasons by the Court, A. had deceived the personnel of a number of shops. Consequently, the act of which the Court of First Instance found A. guilty went beyond the charge, and A. was not able to respond to this extension during the hearing.

3) After the charges were read out the procedure was continued by the judge who requested those defendants to raise their hands who did not wish to renew the statements that they had made in the pre-trial investigation. This was followed by the judge's request for those defendants to raise their hands who contested the charge in part. The events referred to in the charge and the statements made in the pre-trial investigation were not pursued in more detail. After the charges were read out A. did not fully comprehend to which events the court was referring. As to item 3, he would have wanted to say that he had not participated in attempts to open and destroy the safe. As regards item 4, A. would have wanted to say that the act was not planned, but the person who was with him had stolen the chandelier on his own initiative and that they later divided the money between them. A. would also have wanted to explain the reasons leading to the offences and state the fact that he had withdrawn from committing them. A. held that his views of the charges were not sought as required under Chapter 14 Sections 3 and 4 of the Code of Procedure and the Court had not ensured a full hearing.

4) A. was not able to understand the instructions for appeal, which were given orally by the judge, and he did not receive written instructions prescribed in Chapter 25 Section 3 (2) of the Code of Procedure. He contacted the public defender on 1 March 1991 in order to appeal the decision, which had already become final.

A. held that the procedural errors mentioned in points 1 to 4 affected the outcome of the case. A. has therefore demanded that the decision by the Court of First Instance, which is legally valid, be annulled because of a procedural error and, as far as the case concerns him, the case be remitted to the Court of First Instance.

Decision of the Court of Appeal

The Court of Appeal stated on point 1 that A. appeared in person before the Court of First Instance. Under Chapter 11 Section 22 (1) of the Code of Procedure, summoning is not necessary in such criminal proceedings because the claim based on a criminal offence was made against a person who appeared in court in person. This means that the charges against A. referred to in items 1 and 3 were raised legally.

The European Convention for Human Rights and Fundamental Freedoms states in Article 6 (3)(b) that a person charged with a criminal offence has the right to have adequate time and facilities for the preparation of his defence. A. did not raise the question before the Court of First Instance that he was unable to respond to the charges concerned. There was no essential difference between either count and the statements made by A. in pre-trial investigation. On the basis of the pre-trial investigation it was deemed that A. had confessed to the charges on both counts. Consequently there were no reasons under the European Convention on Human Rights that the Court should have taken into account *ex officio*.

Concerning point 2 the Court of Appeal observed that the charges corresponding to item 1 in the decision by the Court of First Instance claimed that A. was guilty of buying products and services in a number of shops, in order to obtain unlawful material benefit, and had overdrawn his account by IM 20,459.92. In finding A. guilty of fraud the Court of First Instance used the expression "deceived the personnel of a number of shops into selling him products and offering him services against payment by bank card while hiding the fact that he had no money on his account with the Post Office Bank". The Court of First Instance also held that by hiding his lack of means A. had deceived the personnel of the shops referred to in the charge. Therefore, the Court of First Instance had not convicted A. of an act to which A. did not have opportunity to respond on account of the charge made against him during the hearing of the case.

As regards point 3, the Court of Appeal observed that the examination of the charges and of the pre-trial investigation report in the court through the defendants raising their hands as described by A. was not satisfactory, and in most cases such an investigation cannot be deemed to correspond to the full investigation required by Section 4 of the Code of Procedure. However, the court record shows that, when specifically asked, A. did not wish to comment on the matter. There was no significant inconsistency between the charges and the pre-trial investigation report; A. essentially confessed to the acts referred to in the charges in the pre-trial investigation. Even though the court hearing had taken place as described by A, it could not be presumed that, with due regard to the extent to which the case has been proven, the error had essentially affected the outcome of the case.

As regards point 4, the Court of Appeal observed that the Court of First Instance had, according to A, given him oral instructions for appeal which he however could not comprehend. A. had stated that he had not received any instructions for appeal in writing. If this was the case, the procedure was incorrect. However, A. could merely on the basis of the oral instructions have registered his intent to appeal.

The Court of Appeal has sent the documents of the case to the public prosecutor for information and for investigation in order to establish whether points 3 and 4 indicate such incorrect procedure which does not lead to the annulment of the judgment on the basis of a grave procedural error.

On these grounds the Court of Appeal has dismissed the extraordinary appeal.

APPEAL TO THE SUPREME COURT

Leave of appeal was granted on 18 February 1992. The Supreme Court ordered in its interim decision on 27 February 1992 that, as regards the sentence of imprisonment, the ruling of the Court of First Instance not be enforced or the enforcement measures not be continued.

In his petition A. has reiterated the claims presented to the Court of Appeal. The public prosecutor has provided a reply. The Post Office Bank has not responded to the request for reply. The judge of the Court of First Instance has given an explanation. A. has made a rejoinder.

RULING BY THE SUPREME COURT, 12 FEBRUARY 1993

Statement of reasons

Points 1, 3 and 4 of the decision made by the Court of Appeal.

At the time of the hearing by the Court of First Instance A. was no older than 19. He did not have legal assistance. The charges made against him were serious and carried the possibility of a sentence of imprisonment, which could also be unconditional.

Under Article 14 (3)(b) of the Covenant on Civil and Political Rights, and Article 6 (3)(b) of the Convention for the Protection of Human Rights and Fundamental Freedoms a defendant in a criminal case has the right to have adequate time and facilities for the preparation of his defence. It has not been established in the case that A. was summoned for the offences cited in items 1 and 3. Consequently A. was not able to prepare his defence concerning those items, because the charges were, in accordance with Chapter 11 Section 22 of the Code of Procedure, submitted only in court. Before the Court of First Instance A. did not remark that he had not been summoned for all items and that he had not been able to prepare his defence. But neither did the court, *ex officio*, investigate whether A. had been summoned for each offence cited in the charges and, if so, at what time this had taken place.

A court has the duty to ensure that a defendant in a criminal case benefits from the minimum rights provided for in international treaties which are part of the law in force, including the right to have adequate time and facilities for the preparation of his defence. If it transpires that the defendant has not had enough time to prepare his defence, the court must draw his attention to the possibility that the case can be postponed, and postpone it if so requested by the defendant.

The Court of First Instance decided the case as regards items 1 and 3 without examining whether A. had had adequate time to prepare his defence. As a result of this omission by the Court of First Instance, A. did not benefit from his minimum right as a defendant in a criminal case. A procedural error has therefore been made in the case.

For the consideration of the charges and the hearing of A. regarding them the judge of the Court of First Instance requested those present wishing to add or change their statements in the pre-trial investigation reports to raise their hands. As A. did not raise his hand, the judge asked it to be recorded that A, among other persons, renewed the statement he had made in the pre-trial investigation. Then the judge asked those defendants who denied the charges to raise their hands. As A. did not raise his hand, the judge asked it to be recorded that A, among other persons, admitted to the charges. In case he had misunderstood the intentions of the parties, the judge requested that the parties speak up no later than the decision-making began in order to have their recorded statements corrected. The court record also shows that, when asked individually, A, for one, did not have any comment to make. Finally, the judge asked whether anyone wished to speak. None of the parties spoke in this instance. There is a record of A. having spoken separately only of some details of the act referred to in item 3.

The purpose of hearing a defendant in a criminal case, as stipulated in Chapter 14 Section 3 of the Code of Procedure, is to have his account of the events described in the charges and of the judicial assessment of the events as well as to afford him an opportunity to present his views on the possible sanctions. The hearing of the defendant and the obligation imposed by Chapter 14

Section 4 of the Code of Procedure on the court to ensure a full enquiry require that the questions asked for the purpose of enquiry are posed individually to each defendant in such a manner that the defendant even without legal assistance is able to understand the question and to give his account and views.

The enquiry by the Court of First Instance did not ensure that each defendant was aware of the various stages of the proceedings and of the issues under consideration at a particular moment. A. says that he was not aware of these matters. It is likely that the other members of the court, excluding the presiding judge, had to rely for their decision mainly on the judge's account of the content of the pre-investigation material. Consequently, the procedure neither complied with the provisions of Chapter 14 Sections 3 and 4 of the Code of Procedure on the hearing of the defendant and on the full and comprehensible examination of the case nor with the provisions on fair and public trial of Article 6(1) of the Convention for the Protection of Human Rights and Fundamental Freedoms and of Article 14 (1) of the International Covenant on Civil and Political Rights. Therefore, this is another procedural error in the case.

According to the information received on the case, the Court of First Instance issued instructions for appeal orally when pronouncing the judgment. Chapter 25 Section 3 (2) of the Code of Procedure requires that a party present be given instructions for appeal also in writing, unless this is considered manifestly unnecessary. A. says that he did not receive those instructions in writing. As A. appeared in court without legal assistance, the issuing of written instructions was not manifestly unnecessary. The omission of the Court of First Instance to provide A. with instructions for appeal in writing was a procedural error.

As a result of the procedural errors in the case, A. did not have adequate possibilities to defend himself and to submit to the court his views which might have had a bearing on the determination and conditionality of the punishment. The errors in the procedure have prevented or in the minimum contributed to the difficulty for A. to appeal against the unconditional sentence he received. It may therefore be presumed that the procedural errors had an essential effect on the outcome of the proceedings.

Point 2 in the decision of the Court of Appeal.

The Supreme Court upholds the decision of the Court of Appeal together with the grounds given.

Applicable legislation

Chapter 31 Section 1 (4) of the Code of Procedure.

Resolution

The decision of the Court of Appeal is quashed.

The decision of the Court of First Instance is annulled as regards A. The case is remitted to the Court of First Instance of Parikkala, where A. must have it re-examined by notifying the Court to that effect no later than 15 March 1993. If this is not done, the decision to nullify becomes void and the judgment pronounced by the Court of First Instance becomes final also for A.

The prohibition against enforcement becomes void.

Members of the Supreme Court taking the decision: President Heinonen, Justices Roos, Taipale, Suhonen and Tulokas (dissenting)

Report by the presenting official and statement by the dissenting member of the Court

Acting Judicial Secretary Haapaniemi: It is proposed that the Supreme Court give the following decision:

ANNEX 2

Grounds

Point 1 of the decision of the Court of Appeal

According to Chapter 11 Section 22 (1) of the Code of Procedure summoning is not necessary in criminal proceedings in cases where a claim based on a criminal offence is made against a person who is present in court. It has not been established in the case that A. was summoned for the offences referred to in items 1 and 3 of the decision of the Court of First Instance; a charge of those offences was brought against A. who was present in the proceedings before the Court of First Instance. Under Article 14 (3)(b) of the International Covenant on Civil and Political Rights and Article 6 (3)(b) of the Convention for the Protection of Human Rights and Fundamental Freedoms, a defendant in a criminal case has the right to have adequate time and facilities for the preparation of his defence. Consequently, a defendant in a criminal case has, notwithstanding the provision of Chapter 11 Section 22 (1) of the Code of Procedure, the right to have adequate time to prepare his defence. If necessary, the court must, under Chapter 16 Section 4 (1) of the Code of Procedure, postpone the hearing, in order to allow the defendant a possibility to prepare his defence.

A, who appeared before the Court of First Instance without legal assistance, did not comment on inadequacy of time for preparation and the Court did not examine *ex officio* whether A. had had enough time to prepare his defence. The Court of First Instance was therefore unable to consider whether to postpone the case as a result. In its assessment whether to conduct the proceedings in such a manner as to examine *ex officio* whether the defendant has had adequate time for the preparation of his defence, the court must consider whether reasons exist for doing so in order to ensure the defendant the minimum rights afforded to him in international human rights treaties which are part of the law in force. Reasons for doing so may be that the defendant contests the charges, that the evidence is insufficient or conflicting, that the offence carries serious consequences, that the case gives rise to difficult legal problems and that a defendant who is present without legal assistance is in need of such assistance for personal reasons. In considering whether the Court of First Instance should in this case have examined *ex officio* whether A. had had adequate time to prepare his defence, the Supreme Court takes account of the fact that A. did not have legal assistance and that the foreseeable punishment for him was an unconditional sentence of imprisonment. Under these circumstances, the fact that there where no essential inconsistencies between the charges and the accounts given by A. in the pre-trial investigation was not of crucial significance. Consequently, the Court of First Instance should have examined *ex officio* whether A. had had enough time to prepare his defence and whether he had wanted to have the case postponed for that purpose. Because the Court of First Instance omitted to do so, a procedural error has been made in the case.

A judgment may be quashed on the basis of a procedural error referred to in Chapter 31 Section 1 (4) of the Code of Procedure only in cases where it is found or it may be presumed that the error has essentially affected the outcome of the case. In his petition, A. stated that, as regards the offence referred to in item 3 in the decision of the Court of First Instance, he did not participate in efforts to open and hide the safe, as regards the offence in item 4, that the theft was not planned and a person under fifteen had on his own initiative stolen the chandelier and the money, the money being divided between them later. A. had wanted to explain the reasons leading to the offences and that he had refrained from committing them. The matters raised by A. are such that they should have been taken into account by the court in considering the sentence under Chapter 6 Section 1 of the Penal Code. This Section states that when determining the sentence account must be taken of all aggravating and extenuating circumstances.

The Supreme Court holds that the reasons described by A. in his petition would not have affected the legal material available to the Court of First Instance to such an extent as to have the Court of First Instance to rely on essentially different grounds for its decision on the sanction. Consequently it cannot not be presumed that the procedural error has had an essential effect on the outcome of the case.

Point 2 of the decision of the Court of Appeal

The Supreme Court upholds the decision of the Court of Appeal together with the grounds given.

Point 3 of the decision of the Court of Appeal

According to the information received in the case the consideration of the charges and the hearing of A. took place in the manner that the judge of the Court of First Instance requested those defendants present wished to add to or to alter the statements which they had made in the pre-trial investigation to raise their hands. As no one raised his hand, the judge asked it to be recorded that in his interpretation the defendants had renewed the statements unaltered which they had made in the pre-trial investigation. The judge then requested those defendants to raise their hands who contested the charges. As no one raised his hand the judge asked it to be recorded that the defendants had admitted to the charges. Then the judge requested that, if he had misunderstood the intentions of the parties, they speak up no later than the proceedings reach the decision-making stage in order to correct their written statements. The judge also enquired whether A, among other defendants, had anything to say. As none of the defendants wished to speak, the judge asked it to be recorded that, when specifically enquired, A. among other persons did not have anything to say. Before leaving the case for decision by the court the judge still asked whether anyone wished to speak. None of the parties spoke.

The purpose of hearing a defendant in a criminal case, as stipulated in Chapter 14 Section 3 of the Code of Procedure, is to have the defendant's account of the events described in the charges and of the judicial assessment of those events as well as to afford him an opportunity to present his views on the possible sanctions. To hear the defendant and to fulfil the obligation imposed on the court by Chapter 14 Section 4 of the Code of Procedure to ensure a full enquiry it is usually necessary that the defendant replies in words. Therefore the procedure used by the Court of First Instance cannot be considered appropriate. However, A. did not use the opportunity offered to him to speak. Also, A's views on the charges made against him did not remain unknown. Consequently the Supreme Court holds that the procedure by the Court of First Instance did not amount to a procedural error.

Point 4 of the decision of the Court of Appeal

According to the information available in the case, the Court of First Instance gave oral instructions for appeal when pronouncing the judgment. Chapter 25 Section 3(2) requires that, in addition, the parties present be given instructions for appeal in writing unless this is manifestly unfounded. A. has alleged that he did not understand the oral instructions and received no instructions in writing. As the alleged error did not have an effect on the outcome of the decision of the Court of First Instance, the complaint on the basis of a grave procedural error is dismissed.

Resolution

The outcome of the decision of the Court of Appeal is upheld.

The prohibition against enforcement becomes void.

Justice Tulokas: I approve the report.

ANNEX 3

THE CONSTITUTIONAL RIGHTS REFORM[4]

ACT
AMENDING THE CONSTITUTION ACT OF FINLAND
NO. 969 OF 17 JULY 1995

In accordance with decision of Parliament made in the manner stipulated in Section 67 of the Parliament Act,

Sections 22 a (2), 23 d (1) and 78 to 81 of the Form of Government Act shall be *repealed,*

Section 22 a (2) as amended by the Act (570/87) of 26 June 1987 and Section 23 d (1) as amended by the Act (1074/91) of 22 July 1991,

Section 1, Chapter II, Section 46 (1) and Section 49 (1) shall be *amended,*

Chapter II as partly amended by the Act (592/72) of 28 July 1972 and Sections 46 (1) and 49 (1) by the Act (1221/90) of 21 December 1990,

a new second paragraph shall be *added* to Section 49, as amended by the Act (176/57) of 26 July 1957 and by the said Act of 21 December 1990, the present paragraphs 2 to 4 thus becoming paragraphs 3 to 5, and a new third paragraph shall be added to Section 75, as follows:

SECTION 1

Finland is a sovereign republic the constitution of which shall guarantee the inviolability of human dignity and the freedom and the rights of the individual as well as promote justice in society.

The democratic constitution of Finland is confirmed in this Constitution Act and in other Constitutional Acts.

II. FUNDAMENTAL RIGHTS

SECTION 5

All persons shall be equal before the law.

No distinction shall be made without acceptable reason on the basis of sex, age, origin, language, religion, conviction, opinion, health, disability or for other reason related to person.

Children shall be treated equally as individuals, and they shall be allowed to influence matters affecting them according to their level of maturity.

---

[4] Unofficial translation by translator Heljä Tilli.

Equality between the sexes shall be promoted in activities in society and in working life, especially as regards the determination of remuneration and other conditions of employment, as prescribed and specified by an Act of Parliament.

SECTION 6

Everyone shall have the right to life and personal liberty, physical integrity and security of person.

No one shall be sentenced to death, tortured, or treated in any other manner which violates human dignity.

No one shall be subjected to interference with his or her personal integrity or to deprivation of liberty arbitrarily or without grounds prescribed by an Act of Parliament. A punishment entailing deprivation of liberty shall be imposed by a court of law. The lawfulness of any other form of deprivation of liberty may be submitted to judicial review. The rights of persons deprived of their liberty shall be secured by an Act of Parliament.

SECTION 6 A

No one shall be held guilty of a criminal offence or sentenced to a punishment for an act which was not punishable under an Act of Parliament at the time when it was committed. No greater punishment shall be imposed for an offence than was prescribed by an Act of Parliament at the time when it was committed.

SECTION 7

Finnish citizens and foreigners lawfully residing in Finland shall have the right to freedom of movement and to choose their place of residence.

Everyone shall have the right to leave the country. This right may be restricted by an Act of Parliament in order to ensure legal proceedings or the enforcement of a sentence or to secure the fulfilment of the obligation to carry out national defence.

Finnish citizens shall not be prevented from entering the country, not be expelled from the country, or extradited or transferred to another country against their will.

Provisions on the right of foreigners to enter Finland and to reside in the country shall be given by an Act of Parliament. A foreigner shall not be expelled, extradited or returned if, as a result, he or she faces a risk of a death sentence, torture or other form of treatment in violation of human dignity.

SECTION 8

Everyone's private life, honour and home shall be secured. More specific provisions on the protection of personal data shall be prescribed and specified by an Act of Parliament.

The secrecy of letters, telephone conversations and other confidential communications shall be inviolable.

Measures which are necessary to secure fundamental rights or to investigate crime and which extend to the sphere of home may be prescribed by an Act of Parliament. Necessary restrictions may, in addition, be provided by an Act of Parliament on the secrecy of communications in the investigation of offences which endanger the security of society or home, in legal proceedings and in security checks as well as during deprivation of liberty.

SECTION 9

Everyone shall have the right to freedom of religion and conscience.

The right to freedom of religion and conscience shall include the right to profess and to practise a religion, the right to express a conviction, and the right to belong or not to belong to a religious community. No one shall be obliged to participate in religious practice against his or her conscience.

SECTION 10

Everyone shall have the right to freedom of expression. The right to freedom of expression shall include the right to impart, publish and receive information, opinions and other communications without prior interference by anyone. More specific provisions on the exercise of the right to freedom of expression shall be given by an Act of Parliament. Restrictions concerning pictorial programmes necessary to protect children may by prescribed by an Act of Parliament.

Documents and other records in the possession of authorities shall be public, unless public access to them has been restricted separately by an Act of Parliament for compelling reasons. Everyone shall have the right to information in public documents and records.

SECTION 10 A

Everyone shall have the right to hold meetings and demonstrations without obtaining permission and to attend them.

Everyone shall have the right to freedom of association. The right to freedom of association shall include the right to found an association without permission, belong or not to belong to an association and to participate in the activities of an association. Similarly, the right to form and to join trade unions and the right to organise in order to protect other interests shall be secured.

More specific provisions on the exercise of the rights to freedom of association and assembly shall be given by an Act of Parliament.

SECTION 11

Every Finnish citizen who before the voting year has attained the age of eighteen shall have the right to vote in national elections and referendums. Separate constitutional provisions shall govern eligibility in national elections.

Every Finnish citizen and every foreigner with permanent residence in Finland who before the voting year has attained the age of eighteen shall have the right to vote in local elections and local referendums, as prescribed by an Act of Parliament. Provisions on the right to participate in local government in other ways shall be given by an Act of Parliament.

It shall be the duty of all branches of government to advance the opportunities of individuals to participate in activities in society and in decision-making affecting them.

SECTION 12

Everyone's property shall be protected.

Provisions on the appropriation of property for public purposes and against full compensation shall be given by an Act of Parliament.

SECTION 13

Everyone shall have the right to primary education free of charge. Provisions on compulsory education shall be given by an Act of Parliament.

In accordance with more specific provisions in an Act of Parliament, the various branches of government shall ensure all persons an equal opportunity, corresponding to their abilities and particular needs, to receive education other than primary education as well as to improve themselves without being prevented by the lack of means.

The freedom of sciences, arts and superior education shall be protected.

SECTION 14

The national languages of Finland are Finnish and Swedish.

Everyone's right to use his or her own language, whether Finnish or Swedish, before a court and other authorities, and to have the documents in that language shall be guaranteed by an Act of Parliament. All branches of government shall look after the cultural and societal needs of the Finnish and Swedish speaking populations in Finland according to the same criteria.

The Sami as an indigenous people and Romanies and other groups shall have the right to maintain and develop their own languages and cultures. The right of the Sami to use the Sami language before authorities shall be prescribed by an Act of Parliament. The rights of those using sign language and of those who are in need of interpretation or translation because of a disability shall be secured by an Act of Parliament.

SECTION 14 A

All shall be responsible for nature and its diversity, for the environment and for the cultural heritage.

The branches of government shall strive at securing everyone the right to a healthy environment as well as an opportunity to influence decision-making affecting his or her living environment.

SECTION 15

Everyone shall have the right under law to acquire a living through work, occupation or trade of his or her choice. The branches of government shall ensure the protection of labour.

All branches of government shall promote employment and strive to guarantee everyone the right to work. The right to vocational education and retraining for employment shall be provided by an Act of Parliament.

No one shall be dismissed from work without reasons stipulated in an Act of Parliament.

SECTION 15 A

Everyone who cannot acquire the security required by a life in dignity shall have the right to necessary means of subsistence and care.

Everyone shall be guaranteed by an Act of Parliament the right to the security of basic livelihood in time of unemployment, illness, inability to work and old age as well as on the grounds of child birth and loss of provider.

All branches of government shall, in accordance with more specific provisions provided by an Act of Parliament, secure everyone adequate social welfare and health services. Government shall also support the opportunities of families and others responsible for the care of children to secure the child's welfare and individual growth.

It shall be the duty of all branches of government to promote everyone's right to housing and to support attempts by persons to find housing on their own initiative.

SECTION 16

Everyone shall have the right to have his or her case heard appropriately and without undue delay by a court of justice or other authority competent under an Act of Parliament as well as the right to have a decision relating to his or her rights and duties reviewed by a court or other independent tribunal.

Publicity of the proceedings as well as the right to be heard, to receive a decision with stated reasons and to appeal the decision as well as any other safeguards of fair trial and good government shall be secured by an Act of Parliament.

ANNEX 3

SECTION 16 A

All branches of government shall secure the implementation of fundamental rights and human rights.

Such temporary exceptions to fundamental rights may be prescribed by an Act of Parliament as are necessary during an armed attack to Finland as well as under exceptional circumstances that threaten the life of the nation and are comparable under an Act of Parliament in gravity to an armed attack, and as are in compliance with Finland's international human rights obligations.

SECTION 46

The Chancellor of Justice shall oversee that authorities and public officials in the performance of their duties as well as employees of public corporations and other persons in the discharge of public functions observe the law and fulfil their obligations in such a manner as not to violate anyone's lawful rights. In discharging his or her functions the Chancellor of Justice shall also oversee the implementation of fundamental rights and human rights.

- -

SECTION 49

A Parliamentary Ombudsman shall be elected for a term of four years at a time in a regular session of Parliament. A person shall be elected who is known to be well versed in law. The election shall be carried out following the same procedure as is used for the election of the Chairman of Parliament. A Deputy Parliamentary Ombudsman, who assists the Parliamentary Ombudsman and discharges his or her duties as necessary, and an Assistant Parliamentary Ombudsman, who discharges the duties of the Deputy Parliamentary Ombudsman when the latter is disqualified, shall be elected for an equal term of office using the same procedure. In case the Parliamentary Ombudsman dies or resigns before the expiration of the term of office, Parliament may elect a new Parliamentary Ombudsman for the remaining term of office.

The duty of the Parliamentary Ombudsman is, in accordance with the regulations approved by Parliament for the Parliamentary Ombudsman, to oversee that the courts of law, other authorities and public officials in the performance of their duties as well as employees of public corporations and other persons in the discharge of public functions observe the law and fulfil their obligations. In discharging his or her functions the Parliamentary Ombudsman shall also oversee the implementation of fundamental rights and human rights.

- -

SECTION 75

- -

The right to be exempted on the grounds of conviction from military defence shall be provided by an Act of Parliament.

This Act shall enter into force on 1 August 1995

ACT
AMENDING THE PARLIAMENT ACT
NO. 970 OF 17 JULY 1995

In accordance with decision of Parliament made in the manner stipulated in Section 67 of the Parliament Act,

Sections 66 (7), 67 (3) and 73 (3) of the Parliament Act shall be *repealed,*

Section 66 (7) as amended by the Act (818/92) of 28 August 1992 and Section 73 (3) as amended by the Act (577/87) of 26 June 1987, and

Sections 46 (1), 73 (1) and 74 shall be *amended,*

Section 73 (1) as amended by the above Act (577/87) of 26 July 1987 and Section 74 as amended by the Act (576/87) of 26 June 1987, as follows:

SECTION 46

The Constitutional Law Committee shall prepare those matters referred to it which relate to the enactment, amendment, interpretation or repeal of the Constitution or to any legislation which is closely associated with the Constitution. It shall be the duty of the Committee to provide opinions on the Bills and other matters submitted to it for scrutiny as to their compliance with the Constitution and their relationship with international human rights treaties.

- -

SECTION 73

Parliamentary proceedings regarding a Bill which is left in abeyance shall be initiated by the session to which it was left in abeyance.

- -

SECTION 74

The fact that a Bill was left in abeyance or was not ratified shall not preclude a Government proposal or a private member's bill in the matter which was the subject of the Bill or the Act. If as a result of such a proposal or private member's bill a new Act of Parliament has been passed, the Bill which was left in abeyance or the unratified Act which was submitted to Parliament shall be void.

This Act shall enter into force on 1 August 1995

9. Incorporation and Implementation of Human Rights in Sweden

by Göran Melander,
University of Lund

1. STATUS OF HUMAN RIGHTS TREATIES - GENEREL CONSIDERATIONS

International considerations are important parts of the Swedish image. In spite hereof Sweden is a so-called dualistic country concerning the relation between international law and municipal law. Treaties ratified by Sweden will be of relevance on the domestic scene, only if the treaty has been incorporated or transformed into Swedish legislation. In cases of discrepancies between Swedish legislation and international obligations the former will prevail.

Unlike the situation in many other democracies there is no provision in the Swedish Constitution with respect to the question of the relationship between international law and municipal law. In the Constitution of 1809 there was only an article on treaty making power: It lay within the power of the Government to conclude a treaty with another state. In certain cases the Government was in need of an approval by Parliament (Art. 12). The same principle applies according to the new Constitution of 1974. It is prescribed that the Government is entitled to enter into an agreement with another state and with an inter-governmental organization (Chapter 10, Section 1) and that the Government sometimes must get the approval of Parliament before the conclusion of the treaty (Chapter 10, Section 2). The latter provision can be said to reflect Article 46 of the 1969 Vienna Convention on the Law of Treaties.

The way in which it has been established that Sweden is a dualistic country is somewhat remarkable, *viz.* by a number of consequent judgments by the Supreme Court. The first judgment was delivered in

M. Scheinin (ed.), International Human Rights Norms in the Nordic and Baltic Countries, 295–305.

1942.[1] In that case the question of state immunity from jurisdiction was at stake. The Supreme Court stated that in international customary law an indisputable rule of state immunity existed, but that there did not exist any Swedish legislation on the subject. The Court argued that there were no reasons to conclude that Swedish law should have an opposite standpoint ("*att svensk rätt i själva denna principfråga intoge en motsatt ståndpunkt*"), from which followed that immunity from jurisdiction was granted.

The clear establishment of Sweden as a dualistic state came in three judgments by the Labour Court (1972), the Supreme Court (1973) and the Supreme Administrative Court (1974) respectively.[2] The common element of the three cases is that the plaintiff invoked provisions in an international treaty, the European Convention on Human Rights, and that the three courts refused to apply the Convention, in more or less the same language. It was stated that a treaty which has been ratified by Sweden is of no relevance for the application of law in Sweden, if it has not been incorporated or transformed to municipal law. Such an incorporation or transformation had not been undertaken with respect to the European Convention![3]

It is true that the Swedish Parliament had approved that the Swedish Government ratified the European Convention on Human Rights. It is also true that when getting such approval it had been stated in the Bill to Parliament that there was no discrepancy between the then existing Swedish law and the Convention (a statement of harmony of standards) and that no further action was needed for the ratification of the Swedish Government.

In Sweden there are two (or perhaps three) methods for the incorporation or implementation of a treaty into Swedish law. A first

---

[1] NJA 1942 p. 65.

[2] AD 1972 p. 75; NJA 1973 p. 423; RÅ 1974 p. 121.

[3] "En av Sverige biträdd internationell överenskommelse gäller ej direkt för den inomstatliga rättstillämpningen i vårt land, utan de rättsliga principer, som kommit till uttryck i överenskommelsen, måste för att bli gällande rätt i vårt land, i den mån så erfordras, upptagas i en motsvarande svensk lagstiftning (transformering). Någon mot art 2 i tilläggsprotokollet 20.3.52 till Europarådets konvention angående skydd för de mänskliga rättigheterna och grundläggande friheterna svarande svensk transformeringslag har icke kommit till stånd. Förpliktelse har således icke uppkommit för skolstyrelsen att i sin verksamhet iakttaga reglerna i tilläggsprotokollet". RÅ 1974 p. 121.

method is referred to as "incorporation" (*inkorporation*).[4] The method means that a Swedish law is promulgated by which it is declared that a treaty should have force as municipal law. The method has been used, for instance an Act of 1976 on Immunities and Privileges in Certain Cases (*Lag om immunitet och privilegier i vissa fall*),[5] and it is, of course, most satisfactory in order to avoid any discrepancies between international obligations and municipal law, as the authorities which have to apply the law will have to make use of the treaty in its authentic versions. [6]

A second method of incorporation is referred to as "transformation" and appears in two different shapes. "Transformation through translation" means that the treaty is being translated into Swedish and that the Swedish version is promulgated as Swedish law. The only risk for a discrepancy lies in the fact that the treaty may be translated erroneously. If so, the Swedish (wrongly translated) version will prevail, because this is the version which has been adopted by Parliament. [7]

In its second shape transformation means the following. It may be realized that no corresponding Swedish law exists or that municipal law is not exactly in conformity with the treaty in question. In the first case it is considered necessary to promulgate a law which is drafted against the background of the treaty. When, for instance, Sweden ratified the UN Convention on the Continental Shelf a Swedish Act on the Continental Shelf was promulgated, which gave provisions on the Swedish continental shelf. On other occasions, it may be realized that

---

[4] The terminology used is confusing. It is, however, established language that a treaty must be incorporated (*införlivad*) in order to be of relevance in Swedish law. One method by which a treaty can be incorporated (*införlivad*) is by incorporation, i.e. the English word for *införlivade*!

[5] SFS 1976 : 661.

[6] The same method has been used in Law on International Railway Traffic. It is prescribed that the treaty, attached to the law, should be applied in its French version (*Convention relative aux transports internationaux ferrovaires (COTIF)*). It should be noted that according to the Swedish Constitution and other Swedish laws there is no obstacle for making use of texts in other languages.

[7] Admittedly, it is a most difficult task to translate a legal text. Besides, it is not possible to avoid pure mistakes. For instance, there is an amazing mistake in the original translation of the title of the European Convention on Human Rights and Fundamental Freedoms. The word "freedoms" (*friheter*) has been translated with *skyldigheter* (obligations) which after all is not the same thing. See. Prop. 1952:65; SÖ 1952:35.

domestic law partly will have to be amended in order to be in conformity with the treaty. When Sweden was about to ratify the 1967 European Convention on the Adoption of Children it was realized that the then existing provision in the Code of Parents (*föräldrabalken*) with respect to the obligation to get the permission of the biological parents did not correspond with the European Convention. Accordingly, that Section of the Code of Parents was amended, whereupon the Government could ratify the Convention.[8] When this method is being used, there are obvious risks for discrepancies between international obligations and municipal law. For instance, Article 33 para. 2 of the 1951 Convention relating to the Status of Refugees prescribes exceptions to the principle of non-refoulement. A refugee may be returned to his country of origin, *inter alia* if he has been convicted of "a particularly serious crime" (*ett synnerligen allvarligt brott*). In the Aliens Act of 1954 which took the 1951 Refugee Convention into consideration, the corresponding phrase used was "particular serious criminality" (*synnerligen grov brottslighet*). The different phrasing led to cases of refoulement of refugees, who were guilty of a number of petty crimes but not of a particularly serious crime.

The third method - if that can be seen as a method - is a statement of "harmony of standards". In the Bill to Parliament, when the Government is asking for the approval to ratify a treaty, it may be stated that all Articles of the treaty already form part of Swedish law. Accordingly, it is said that no further action is needed and there are no obstacles for a Swedish ratification.

The last mentioned method has been used when Sweden has ratified human rights treaties. It has been argued that the rules of the treaties already formed part of Swedish law - and it came as a great surprise when the Labour Court, the Supreme Court and the Supreme Administrative Court all of a sudden declared that the human rights treaties did not form part of municipal law. The question could rightly be asked, what Parliament is doing when it approves the ratification of a treaty.

The peculiar view-point that a ratified treaty is of no significance unless it has been "incorporated" or "transformed" into Swedish law is

---

[8] It may, of course, be argued that only the Article of the Convention which has given rise to an amendment of the Swedish law has been "transformed". With respect to all other Articles in the treaty "harmony of standards" has been found.

still upheld by some authorities. In an actual case on asylum concerning a family from former Yugoslavia, an important question is the relevance of the UN Convention of the Rights of the Child. The agent of the family, the Office of the UNHCR and others have advocated that an execution of the deportation order would lead to the separation of the family and that such consequences would go contrary to the Convention of the Rights of the Child. The argument has been neglected by the Aliens Board (the last instance in such cases) with the motive that courts and administrative authorities are not bound to apply the Convention because it is not part of Swedish law. The Aliens Board makes references to the relevant Bill to Parliament in which it is stated that Swedish law is in conformity with the Convention. The Aliens Board concludes that the Convention does not create any obstacles against the application of the Aliens Act in accordance with the *existing practice*.

However, the rules which can be said to have been established in the beginning of the 1970s has since long been abandoned. The turning-point came in a decision by the Supreme Court in 1983 (the *Tsesis Case*). The Supreme Court clearly stated - with reference to the *travaux préparatoires* in the relevant law - that significance must be attached to the text of the convention which lies behind the Swedish law, as well as municipal and international legal practice must be used when interpreting the Swedish Act. Swedish municipal law must be interpreted in light of the treaty behind it.

The new principle has later been confirmed by the Supreme Court in a number of judgments. In various Bills to Parliament it has been stressed that the ratification of a treaty (and the method "harmony of standards") means that Sweden is under an international obligation to respect the treaty loyally, also if the treaty will not be expressed in a Swedish law. It has also been repeatedly stated, that courts and administrative authorities are under an obligation to follow and respect the practice which is being developed by various treaty bodies (like the European Court of Human Rights with respect to the European Convention on Human Rights, the UN Human Rights Committee with respect to the UN Covenant on Civil and Political Rights, etc.).

Accordingly, the principle to interpret Swedish law against the background of a ratified treaty has slowly been accepted by courts and authorities. It is reasonable to conclude, that one reason is the surprisingly great number of cases against Sweden, brought before the

European Commission of Human Rights and the European Court of Human Rights.

2. CASES DECIDED BY THE EUROPEAN COURT OF HUMAN RIGHTS AND THEIR CONSEQUENCES

All started with the *Sporrong-Lönnroth case*.[9] The European Court found that Sweden had acted in violation of Article 1 of Additional Protocol 1 (11 votes to 10), which was remarkable enough. More serious was, however, that the Court unanimously stated, that Sweden had violated Article 6 of the Convention by not granting the applicants access to court. In a number of subsequent cases the Court has likewise stated that Sweden had acted in violation of Article 6, when the applicants had been refused access to a court.[10] The underlying problem was that the Swedish administrative system did not fit in with certain provisions of the European Convention. There were a number of situations when the decision in the first instance could be taken by a county administration (*länsstyrelse*) with a right to appeal to the Government.

It was finally accepted that Sweden had to amend its legislation. A particular law was promulgated, the Act of 1988 regarding Judicial Review of Certain Administrative Decisions (*Lag om rättsprövning av vissa förvaltningsbeslut*). The law was a direct consequence of the cases lost by the Government before the Strasbourg organs. The Act means that a request for judicial review shall be handed in to the Supreme Administrative Court (*Regeringsrätten*). If the Court were to find that the administrative decision is contrary to a rule of law, the Court shall quash the decision and, if necessary, refer the matter back to the authority which took the decision.

Another problem for Sweden concerned the provisions on remand in custody in the Swedish Code of Procedure. In the *Skoogström Case*[11] it was argued that the applicant had not been brought promptly before

---

[9] Judgment of 23 September 1982, ECHR, Series A, No. 52.

[10] E.g., the cases *Bodén and Pudas*, Judgments of 27 October 1987, ECHR, Series A, No. 125 (A and B), and *Tre Traktörer AB*, Judgment of 7 July 1989, ECHR, Series A, No. 159.

[11] Jugdment of 2 October 1984, ECHR, Series A, No. 83.

a judge or other officer authorized by law to exercise judicial power in contradiction with Article 5, para. 3 of the European Convention. In its report the Commission of Human Rights unanimously expressed the opinion that there had been a breach of Article 5, para. 3. The case was referred to the Court, whereupon a friendly settlement was reached. The Swedish Government undertook to amend the Code of Procedure, and the case was struck of the list of the Court.

The Swedish Code of Procedure became amended in April 1988. The new legislation means that any person deprived of his or her liberty on reasonable suspicion of having committed an offense, must be brought before a judge within four days. In order to make the reform possible, it has been necessary to have prosecutors and judges on duty during weekends and holidays. The reform is costly, but motivated by Sweden's interest to live up to the provisions of the European Convention.

Sweden has also had problems with the right of a fair trial according to Article 6, para. 1, of the European Convention. In the *Ekbatani Case*[12] a District Court had found the applicant guilty of a minor offense and sentenced him to a fine. The applicant appealed to a Court of Appeal, claiming that he had not committed the act alleged to constitute the criminal offense. The applicant formally requested the hearing of new witnesses on the ground that his credibility needed thorough examination. The request was rejected and in accordance with the Swedish Code of Procedure the Court of Appeal held no hearing. It confirmed the District Court's judgment.

The applicant submitted a petition to the European Commission of Human Rights. In its judgment the European Court of Human Rights found that the refusal by the Court of Appeal to hold a hearing constituted a breach of Article 6, para. 1 of the European Convention and the right to a fair trial. The judgment necessited another amendment of the Swedish Code of Procedure.

As from 1 January 1995 a change has taken place. The European Convention on Human Rights has been "incorporated" into Swedish law, according to which the Convention is valid as Swedish law. It is a positive reform and discrepancies between that Convention and municipal law may be impossible.

---

[12] Judgment of 26 May 1988, ECHR, Series A, No. 134.

In the Bill to Parliament some motives were given why only the European Convention on Human Rights would be incorporated and not other human rights treaties. One reason was that the existing method, i.e. "harmony of standards" is uncommon in Europe. Accordingly, it is logical that Sweden incorporates the Convention by which the significance of the Convention is stressed and by which it will be possible for courts and administrative authorities to directly apply the Convention.

A second argument was that the European Convention forms part of the common principles of law which are included in the European Union. By accepting the EEA Agreement, Sweden was under an obligation to interpret provisions in the agreement in the same way as the European Court of Justice, i.e. in light of the European Convention on Human Rights.

In the Bill it was also explained why only the European Convention on Human Rights would be incorporated. It was stated that the European Convention is unique in so far as its application is built upon a pronounced legal basis which includes a submission by individuals before a court. The continuous practice established by the Court in Strasbourg also means that the various Articles in the Convention will be more and more specified. In this respect there was a difference with respect to other human rights treaties.[13]

The given motives to differentiate between the European Convention on Human Rights and other human rights treaties are not convincing. There are good reasons to "incorporate" all other human rights treaties into municipal law as well. By making use of the same method further painful decisions, like the one taken by the Aliens Board and referred to above, could be avoided - as long as the individual members of the Board are unwilling to adapt to existing practice, and make use of treaties when interpreting Swedish laws.

ANNEXES

1. Act Regarding Judicial Review of Certain Administrative Decisions.
2. Chapter 2, Section 23 of the Constitution Act
3. Act on the Incorporation of the European Convention on Human Rights

---

13 Prop. 1993/94:11, p. 34 f.

Annex 1

ACT
REGARDING JUDICIAL REVIEW OF CERTAIN ADMINISTRATIVE DECISIONS

issued on 21 april 1988

According to decision by Parliament the following provisions are laid down.

JUDICIAL REVIEW
Section 1

At the request of a private party in such administrative proceedings before the Government or an administrative authority as pertain to any situation envisaged by Chapter 8, Articles 2 and 3 of the Instrument of Government, the Supreme Administrative Court is to review the issue whether the decision in the case is contrary to any legal provision.

Judicial review may pertain only to such decisions as

imply exercise of public authority regarding a private subject,

may otherwise be reviewed by court only following a request for relief for substantive defects and which could not otherwise have become subject to review.

EXCEPTIONS
Section 2

This Act does not apply to decisions by boards, the composition of which is determined by law and which are presided over by a permanent judge or a former permanent judge.

Neither does this Act apply to

1. decisions by a regional tenancies tribunal, a regional rent tribunal or a supervisory board,
2. decisions pertaining to Swedish citizenship,
3. decision pertaining to entry and sojourn of aliens in the realm,
4. decisions pertaining to calling up or service or conscripts or reserve personnel in the armed forces,
5. decisions under the Act (1966:413) on unarmed national service,
6. decisions regarding taxes and duties,
7. decisions under the Act (1974:922) on measures pertaining to the credit market or decisions pertaining to questions of general reduction of liquidity or general price control,
8. decisions under the Act (1982:513) on restrictions on the exportation of military equipment, etc.,
9. decisions under the Act (1983:1034) regarding control of the manufacturing of military equipment etc. other than decisions that concern revocation of permits

10. decisions regarding authorization to exercise such activities as are envisaged by section 1, 3-5, of the Act (1984:3) on nuclear activities.

REQUEST

Section 3

A request for judicial review shall be handed in to the Supreme Administrative Court. The request must have reached the Court not later than three months after the day on which the decision was handed down.

EXECUTION OF ADMINISTRATIVE DECISIONS

Section 4

An administrative decision shall apply although a judicial review may take place. The Supreme Administrative Court may decide, however, that the decision shall not apply.

THE DECISIONS OF THE SUPREME ADMINISTRATIVE COURT

Section 5

If the Supreme Administrative Court were to find that the administrative decision is contrary to a rule of law, the Supreme Administrative Court shall quash the decision and, if necessary, refer the matter back to the authority which took the decision. Otherwise the decision will remain in force.

THE COMPOSITION OF THE SUPREME ADMINISTRATIVE COURT

Section 6

In cases concerning judicial review, the quorum of a division of the Supreme Administrative Court shall be three councellors, if the matter is simple. The quorum required for a division to decide to reject a request for judicial review, which has reached the court too late, is three councellors. In other instances the Act (1971:289) on Administrative Court will apply.

This Act comes into force on 1 June 1988. It shall apply to decisions taken as of its entry into force until the end of 1991.

On behalf of the Government

Kjell Olof Feldt

Anna-Greta Leijon
(Ministry of Justice)

ANNEX 2

(Unofficial translation)

CONSTITUTION ACT

(Excerpt)

Chapter 2, Section 23:

No law or other regulation may be enacted contrary to Sweden's obligations as follow from the European Convention on Human Rights and Fundamental Freedoms.

LAW

ON THE EUROPEAN CONVENTION FOR THE PROTECTION OF HUMAN RIGHTS AND FUNDAMENTAL FREEDOMS

(1994:1219)

The European Convention of the 4th of November of 1950 on Human Rights and Fundamental Freedoms, with the changes therein brought about by the additional Protocols no. 3, 5 and 8, as well as the additions made by the additional Protocols no. 1, 2, 4, 6 and 7 to the convention shall be valid law in this country.

The original versions of the Convention, in English and French, are together with a Swedish translation included in this law as an enclosure.

This law enters into force on January 1st, 1995

CHART OF RATIFICATIONS

The following chart gives information on the ratifications and signatures by Nordic and Baltic countries of major human rights treaties originating from either the United Nations or the Council of Europe. The information given represents the situation on 1 August 1995. The years given in the chart indicate either the year when the treaty entered into force in relation to the State in question or, in case the treaty has not entered internationally into force, the year of ratification by the State in question.

A. UNITED NATIONS	*Den*	*Est*	*Fin*	*Ice*	*Lat*	*Lit*	*Nor*	*Swe*
Covenant on Economic, Social and Cultural Rights	1976	1992	1976	1979	1992	1992	1976	1976
Covenant on Civil and Political Rights	1976	1992	1976	1979	1992	1992	1976	1976
First Optional Protocol (Individual Complaints)	1976	1992	1976	1979	1994	1992	1976	1976
Second Optional Protocol (Death Penalty)	1994		1991	1991			1991	1990
Convention on the Elimination of All Forms of Racial Discrimination	1972	1991	1970	1969	1992		1970	1972
Article 14 (Individual Complaints)	+		+	+			+	+
Convention on the Suppression and Punishment of the Crime of *Apartheid*		1991			1992			
Convention on the Elimination of All Forms of Discrimination against Women	1983	1991	1986	1985	1992	1994	1981	1981
Convention against Torture and other Cruel, Inhuman or Degrading Treatment or Punishment	1987	1991	1989	s	1992		1987	1987
Article 22 (Individual Complaints)	+		+				+	+
Convention on the Rights of the Child	1991	1991	1991	1992	1992	1992	1991	1990

	Den	*Est*	*Fin*	*Ice*	*Lat*	*Lit*	*Nor*	*Swe*
Convention on the Rights of All Migrant Workers and Members of their Families*								
Convention relating to the Status of Refugees	1954		1968	1955			1954	1954
Protocol relating to the Status of Refugees	1968		1968	1968			1967	1967

B. COUNCIL OF EUROPE	*Den*	*Est*	*Fin*	*Ice*	*Lat*	*Lit*	*Nor*	*Swe*
Convention for the Protection of Human Rights and Fundamental Freedoms (European Convention on HR)	1953	s	1990	1953	s	1995	1953	1953
Protocol No. 1	1954	s	1990	1954		s	1954	1954
Protocol No. 4	1968	s	1990	1968		1995	1968	1968
Protocol No. 6 (Death Penalty)	1985	s	1990	1987			1988	1985
Protocol No. 7	1988	s	1990	1988		1995	1989	1988
Protocol No. 9	s	s	1994			s	1994	1995
Protocol No. 10*	s	s	1992				1992	1992
Protocol No. 11*	s	s	s	1995	s	1995	1995	1995
European Social Charter	1965		1991	1976			1965	1965
Additional Protocol			1992	s			1994	1992
Amending Protocol*			1994				1991	1992
Additional Protocol (Collective Complaints)**								
European Convention for the Prevention of Torture and Inhuman or Degrading Treatment or Punishment	1989		1990	1990			1989	1989
Protocol No. 1*	1994		1993	1995			1993	1994
Protocol No. 2*	1994		1993	1995			1993	1994
European Charter for Regional and Minority Languages*	s		1994				1993	
Framework Convention for the Protection of National Minorities*	s	s	s	s	s	s	s	s

s = Signature not (yet) followed by ratification
\+ = Separate declaration enabling individual complaints
* = The treaty has not entered into force internationally by 1 August 1995
** = The treaty will be opened for signatures on 9 November 1995

SUBJECT INDEX

(Please note that the page references relate to the text in the chapters only, i.e. not the annexes of various chapters)